WITHDRAWN

A Moment's Monument

A Moment's Monument

Revisionary Poetics and the
Nineteenth-Century English Sonnet

Jennifer Ann Wagner

Madison • Teaneck
Fairleigh Dickinson University Press
London: Associated University Presses

Associated University Presses
440 Forsgate Drive
Cranbury, N.J. 08512

Associated University Presses
25 Sicilian Avenue
London WC1A 2QH, England

Associated University Presses
P.O. Box 338, Port Credit
Mississauga, Ontario
Canada L5G 4L8

The paper used in this publication meets the requirements of the American National Standard for Permanence of Paper for Printed Library Materials Z39.48-1984

Library of Congress Cataloging-in-Publication Data

Wagner, Jennifer Ann, 1957–
    A moment's monument : revisionary poetics and the nineteenth
-century English sonnet / Jennifer Ann Wagner.
      p. cm.
    Includes bibliographical references and index.
    ISBN 0-8386-3630-6 (alk. paper)
    1. English poetry—19th century—History and criticism.
2. Sonnets, English—History and criticism. 3. Wordsworth, William,
1770—1850—Influence. 4. Space and time in literature. 5. Point of
view (Literature). 6. Romanticism—Great Britain. 7. Authority in
literature. 8. Poetics. 9. Sonnet. I. Title.
PR589.S7W34   1996
821'.0420908—dc20   95-21673
                                                    CIP

PRINTED IN THE UNITED STATES OF AMERICA

To the memory of my father,
Walter F. Wagner, Jr.
1926–1985

Contents

Acknowledgments

It gives me great pleasure to finally thank in print the two Yale faculty members who saw me through this project from the beginning. Paul Fry directed this study as a dissertation, and I have always known how fortunate I was to have such an attentive reader and advisor. John Hollander's enthusiasm for this project has been unwavering. Along the way, he has shared more than his literary knowledge; his wisdom helped me get through some difficult years a while back.

I was also fortunate to have several friends and colleagues read some or all of this manuscript at various stages. Their combination of expertise, criticism, and kindness was invaluable. Peter Manning, who visited the University of Memphis for the Spring 1993 semester, was a godsend, not only for his endless good cheer and continuing friendship but also for a more thorough and constructively critical reading of a draft of the entire manuscript than I could have dreamed of, much less hoped for. Stephen Behrendt, my reader for the Press, gave me an equally careful and generous reading, and his comments guided final revisions that were, at his urging, more than cosmetic. Parts of the manuscript were read by Charles Berger, who always provided encouragement when confidence faltered, and who saw a portion of the Keats chapter through to publication in *Western Humanities Review*. Harold Bloom and Sara Suleri read this manuscript in its dissertation form, and their comments initiated my revisions toward book publication. My former Memphis colleague Sharon Bryan commented on the first draft of the conclusion on Robert Frost. I am grateful to all for improving the manuscript immeasurably.

Though this project was begun at Yale, it was completed under the auspices of the University of Memphis, which has given me a Marcus W. Orr Center for the Humanities Fellowship, and three Faculty Research Grants for summer work. These awards provided the valuable time needed to begin molding a dissertation into a book and to begin other projects. I am particularly grateful to two former chairmen at the University of Memphis,

Professors William O'Donnell and Guy Bailey, and also to all those in both the English and philosophy departments who have become such great friends as well as colleagues. Memphis would be empty without them. Linda Austin at Oklahoma State has also given me valuable advice and support.

Other, older friends have contributed to this book, sometimes with professional advice, sometimes with encouragement, sometimes with commiseration, always with humor. To Margaretmary Daley, Charles Ford, Brigitte Szymanek, Kim Wallant, John Watkins, and Andrew Elfenbein, thanks. I am also grateful to the library staffs at Yale, Harvard, the Library of Congress, Boston University, and the University of Memphis for their help and expertise.

And to my mother, Margaret, Daniel, Jonathan, Betsy, Heather, Stephen, my godson Dylan, and Colin—thanks for being a great family.

I would like to acknowledge several journals for publishing earlier versions of book chapters. The Shelley chapter appeared first in *Southwest Review* 77, no. 1 (1992); a shorter version of the Keats chapter was in *Western Humanities Review* 45, no. 3 (1991); and an excerpt from the Rossetti chapter appeared in the *Journal of Pre-Raphaelite Studies*, n.s., 4 (1995). Portions of the Hopkins chapter appeared in a different form in *Nineteenth-Century Literature* 47, no. 1 (1992): 32–48, © 1992 by The Regents of the University of California.

A number of publishers granted me permission to quote primary source material:

Excerpts of Shelley from *the Complete Poetical Works of Percy Bysshe Shelley*, edited by Thomas Hutchinson (1929), and reprinted here by permission of Oxford University Press.

Keats material reprinted by permission of the publishers from *John Keats: Complete Poems*, edited by Jack Stillinger (Cambridge: The Belknap Press of Harvard University Press), © 1978, 1982 by the President and Fellows of Harvard College.

Excerpt from "The Celestial Omnibus," from *The Collected Tales of E. M. Forster* by E. M. Forster, published 1947 by Alfred A. Knopf, Inc. Reprinted with permission of Alfred A. Knopf, Inc.

Material from *The Poems of Gerard Manley Hopkins*, fourth edition, edited by W. H. Gardner and N. H. Mackenzie (copyrighted by The Society of Jesus 1967), is used by permission of Oxford University Press; in addition, passages from *The Correspondence of Gerard Manley Hopkins and Richard Watson Dixon*, edited by Claude Colleer Abbott (1935), appear by permission of Oxford University Press.

Material from *The Poetry of Robert Frost*, edited by Edward Connery Lathem. Copyright 1934, 1936, 1944, 1951, © 1962 by Robert Frost. Copyright 1964, 1970 by Lesley Frost Ballantine. Copyright 1916, 1923, 1928, 1930, 1939, 1944, 1949, © 1969 by Henry Holt and Co., Inc. Reprinted by permission of Henry Holt and Co., Inc. For quotation rights in the British Commonwealth, the author acknowledges the Estate of Robert Frost, editor E. C. Lathem, and British publisher Jonathan Cape.

Introduction

What is called its form may be simply that part of the poem that had directly to do with time: the time of the poem, the time in which it was written, and the sense of recurrence in which the unique moment of vision is set.

—W. S. Merwin

This book is a literary history that traces the second life, in the nineteenth century and into the twentieth, of the sonnet, a poetic form that had enjoyed its original heyday several hundred years earlier. It sets out to answer a number of questions: While the sonnet revival had been in force since about 1770, why did the sudden appearance of Wordsworth in 1802 among the sonnet writers so suddenly change the character of the form in English? What was it *about* his sonnets that made them so obviously different, even to contemporaries, from those that had come before? Why do so many major poets in the rest of the century, and why do so many in ours, take up as the model a particular mode of Wordsworth sonnet? What poetic problem does that mode of sonnet address, what strategy does it present for resolution—and why does it appear to be so important to grapple with that problem and that strategy?

The revival of the sonnet throughout the romantic and Victorian periods was certainly noted and written about both negatively and positively at the time. One anonymous detractor described the floods of new sonnets that were appearing as a "species of disorder" that he dubbed "sonnetto-mania." On the other hand, from the years 1814 through 1886 or so, a remarkable number of scholarly and popular accounts of the sonnet and its history appeared in the various literary magazines and intellectual journals. These essays were written in defense of the form against what appears to have been persistently bad public image. That bad image persisted despite its popularity, which is in evidence by flipping through the literary journals or through the many anthologies dedicated specifically to sonnets and sonnet sequences that appeared in the latter half of the century.

No doubt a large percentage of these sonnets are best left in obscurity, but while every self-fashioned poet hammered out his derivative and slight contribution, the best poets of the century were working sonnets out of a much finer metal. After the sonnet revival of the last century subsided, however, it was to receive—as a literary-historical phenomenon—something like an extended footnote's worth of treatment. This oversight has been somewhat corrected by the publication of Stuart Curran's *Poetic Form and British Romanticism* (1986) and, more narrowly, by studies considering the sonnet work of particular poets of the period, such as the final chapter of Alan Liu's impressive book, *Wordsworth: The Sense of History* (1989), and the fine essays on Keats's sonnets by William Fitzgerald. Nevertheless, a fuller account of the general nature, significance, and situation of the sonnet as a phenomenon specifically of nineteenth-century literary history has not appeared.

The purpose of this book is to argue that the history of the sonnet in the nineteenth century is more than a decorative strand in this century's textual history. By offering detailed rereadings of some of the major sonnets written during the romantic and Victorian periods, my purpose is to demonstrate that what became a general obsession with the form throughout the nineteenth century is the record of these poets' engagement with the problems of subjectivity, with the relationship of poetic form to temporality, and with the infiltration of aestheticist idealism into the literary ideology.

Furthermore, this study locates the rise and popularity of a particular *mode* of sonnet with the entry of Wordsworth into a sonnet-writing arena that already existed at the opening of the nineteenth century. The awareness of nineteenth-century writers that something new had happened in Wordsworth's sonnets created an unusually self-conscious attitude toward the form—both in the poems themselves, and in the essays about sonnets mentioned above. To a large extent, therefore, this book—even when it reaches the poetry of Robert Frost at its conclusion—is really about Wordsworth.

The sonnet revival was certainly already well underway by the time that poet took up the form suddenly and systematically in 1802. The strength of Stuart Curran's concise and informative outline of sonnet writing prior to Wordsworth is its focus upon the emergence of "the sonnet of sensibility," which finds its "underlying motive" in Thomas Gray's singular "Sonnet on the Death of Richard West" and its later success in William Lisle Bowles and Samuel Taylor Coleridge and in women poets like Charlotte Turner Smith and Anna Seward. These poets return to the Renaissance sonnet's function as—however fictively—the "voice of the poet"; only in Shakespeare's sonnets, it was then believed, could one hear the voice of the bard himself. Reemerging at a time when interest in the subjective and the emotional was burgeoning, the sonnet form became what Charlotte Smith defined as "no improper vehicle for a single sentiment."[1] The deluge of sonnets written in imitation of earlier poets attests to the sort of formal "validation" of sentiment, whether authentic or not, offered by the form, the brevity of which made it a formal metaphor for the very "melancholy moments" and "the sensations those moments brought."[2]

There is no doubt that Wordsworth learned from Bowles, Coleridge, and others about the association of memory with place, and, in a related generic development, about the way to fuse the sonnet with the loco-descriptive mode so popular throughout the eighteenth century. Indeed, a large percentage of Wordsworth's hundreds of sonnets obviously belong to this hybrid tradition. But while Curran demonstrates that much which seems "new" in the handling of the form can be attributed to Wordsworth's precursors, Curran's account simultaneously highlights, ever more so as it progresses, a suspicion of a kind of inauthenticity that undermines the strength of this movement. Bowles's own disclaimer against an apparent charge of insincerity in the preface to one edition of his poetry is symptomatic; he worries over criticism against melancholy poems composed "when possibly the heart of the writer had very little share in the distress he chose to describe."[3] And although the sonnet had already, by the turn into the nineteenth century, become a formal metaphor for the mind, for the "mental space" in which the work of cognition takes place, too often the sonnet's expression of that "lonely feeling" advanced little beyond a lament over sentimental self-division and over an impotence of will.

The popularity of this sentimental mode of sonnet—produced prolifically by not only Bowles but by other male and also, significantly, by many female poets—can be accounted for by the strength of the sentimental mode in English literature generally. While Wordsworth took much himself from the so-called Age of Sensibility, and while he openly admired the sonnets of Charlotte Smith and Anna Seward in particular, he offered no goods for the sonnet-writing market until he could find a strategy for revising the form for a purpose more suited to his own agenda. In doing so, he recuperated a form originally associated with the voice of a male poet from a "feminization" of the genre. Until 1802 he had regarded the form as "absurd" (his word) and trivial, but in a recollection that reveals a fascinating gendering of genre, Wordsworth describes a poetic conversion moment inspired by Milton, after which he returns to the form an authorizing and "manly" (his word again) voice that had seemed absent from it.

Wordsworth also took particular advantage of the sonnet's structure, not in order to thematize self-division, as his precursors and contemporaries had done, but to accomplish something entirely different. The general problematics of the sonnet's structure have long been a subject of scholarly as well as poetic meditation. Discussions of sonnet dynamics from a synchronic perspective have always emphasized its two-part structure: the "play" between octave and sestet, and indeed between quatrains and tercets—a play that opens the form to a variety of conceptual structures. Hans-Jürgen Schlütter suggests that we distinguish between two such structural models: the "dualistic" and the "dialectical," differing from each other primarily according to whether the poem breaks down into two or three sections. He might have added that this would distinguish the Petrarchan from the later so-called Shakespearean form, with its three-quatrains-plus-couplet structure.

But whether one views the sonnet form as essentially dualistic or as dialectical, what both models share is a *revisionary* motive, a characteristic movement of thought that leads from "then" to "now," from premise to conclusion. With Milton, as Wordsworth evidently recognized, there emerges a third possibility for a model of form—the "unitary" model. Schlütter mentions such a model, which he calls "die *monistiche*, bei der kein Gegensatz, keine Wendung vorliegt."[4] As has long been noted, the Miltonic sonnet, with its tendency toward enjambment and toward overrunning the sonnet's turn, offers the possibility of a unitary model that allows for an opposition or turn but subordinates that opposition to a final assertion of completeness. This assertion overrides any internal divisions not only formally but also—and this is the crucial matter—conceptually.

While late-eighteenth-century sonnets are often described as "Miltonic," this usually refers more to tone and diction than to conception. Wordsworth, in contrast, recognizes the significance in Milton's revision of the sonnet's conceptual structure, emphasizing the "spherical," as he described it, in the Miltonic form. His self-conscious handling of the formal, thematic and tropological implications of such a unitary conception of form sets the foundation for the overarching themes of this study: the shift from a compensatory to a revelatory function for the sonnet—its occasion not an expression of loss, necessarily, but a moment of heightened consciousness; the emergence of figures of space, light, and instrumentality that self-reflexively describe the form and its new mode; and the emphasis, through these figures, not so much on the brevity and constraint of the form as on its potential for expansiveness.

Through Wordsworth, the sonnet emerges as a form that, to borrow Coleridge's words, "miniaturiz[es] in order to manifest the Truth."[5] This new visionary mode of sonnet has a flexible bipartite structure that tends finally to subsume oppositions or turns through a revisionary strategy that the form itself tropes. And what Wordsworth gains primarily is what Geoffrey Hartman calls a "vision of voice"—now not just the private voice of the lonely speaker, as in the conventional sonnet, but also a public voice of a bard, a "man speaking to men."

It is on these grounds that Wordsworth stakes his claim, approaching the form not as a figure of constraint and unfulfillment but as a figure of potency, of potentiality, of expansive imaginative vision. In Wordsworth the sonnet is synecdochic: he stresses the way the infinite can be contained in the finite; the way large ambition can be contained in a small form; the way in which the constraints of this form force a poet to reflect on the nature of poetic form generally; and the way this "brief transcript of the heart" becomes a figuration of lyric itself. Kenneth Burke tells us that of the four major tropes, synecdoche is the one related to representation. In the context of poetry, that statement suggests a whole psychology of the imagination—a process by which an experience or series of thoughts (that must have occurred, temporally speaking, over many moments) is distilled into a single significant moment that is represented by the poem itself.

Wordsworth's attention to the form enters into an exploration of a new kind of space, a mental space that is quite literally its own "lyric plot." I mean this in two senses—for this line of sonnet is characterized by an underlying narrative of imaginative intuition and by an awareness of itself as a spatialization of a moment of self-conscious presence. This book's chapter on Wordsworth thus probes the self-reflexive interest of these sonnets in the metaphor of sonnet-as-space, for this poet a figuration not only for subjective "mental space" but also for the space of a lyric moment in which experience, partaking as it does of progressive temporality, can be made static. The sonnet for Wordsworth becomes an emblem of the moment—a "moment's monument" as Dante Gabriel Rossetti would put it in his famous 1880 sonnet on the sonnet.

But more subtly, the figurations of space just mentioned inevitably collapse: subjective space and lyric moment conflate in Wordsworth's attention to the mind's perception of reality, and to its re-vision of that perception within the poem itself. Out of this perception comes an extreme self-referentiality already mentioned as typical of Wordsworth's visionary sonnets; it results in a persistent formal reflection upon their own status as artificial constructs and as representations of experience as revision. Indeed Wordsworth introduces to the nineteenth-century sonnet a self-reflexivity that the form had not seen since Shakespeare; Wordsworth's keen awareness of the dialectics of constraint and freedom, of miniaturization and expansion, of resistance and potentiality, reinforces the structure of his poems with a thematization of those very dynamics. The conventionally oppressive formality of the sonnet is not taken by Wordsworth to be the trap of subjectivity that it is for previous sonnet writers (or, for that matter, for later ones, as I will show); instead, that self-reflexivity leads the poet into a consideration of his relation to poetic form itself and guides him to a conception of an "authority" that *uses* formal limitation to triumph over a resistance to formal "oppression."

These poems are clearly *about* their own formality and about the authority of the imagination over experience itself. The emergence into language of the intuition, of the "full" or "intense" moment, the ideal instant, the exquisite pause that lay at the center of nineteenth-century aestheticism, is characterized by an effort to make representation *presentation*—as if there were no temporal interval between vision and form. The ideal conclusion to the lyric plot is nothing less than the emergence of form itself from intuition. It is this that Wordsworth's sonnets, no matter what their subject, try to record. Beyond the negative function of the sonnet as a displaced process of experience, then, Wordsworth's engagement with the form achieves a more positive function, by which the poem itself reveals the poet's intuition of art's ability to structure, and thus to inform, experience. Revision and compensation—revision *as* compensation—spark the intuitive power that many of Wordsworth's immediate precursors lack. Wordsworth appeared to be paying close attention to that spark, that moment when experience and the revisionary imagination take form.

This poetic attention is at the center of this study, not simply for its own sake, but for the impact that it had upon the future poets who recognized the force of Wordsworth's formal intuition. My approach was initially guided by Jonathan Culler's suggestion that we look into "what the poem *itself* has to say about its own nature or the process of interpretation, granting special authority to the answer one discovers."[6] One of the primary intentions of this study is to discover what Wordsworth's sonnets are saying about themselves and to grant the answers that special authority, at least for some moments, in order to listen to the story that Wordsworth's sonnets tell about themselves and about the poet's strategies for handling experience. Not surprisingly, it is a forcefully persuasive story about imaginative authority, about the power of metaphor and about the compensatory claims of a revisionary poetic that can attribute a grandly self-authorizing significance to any experience existing still in the memory.

Forceful and persuasive as Wordsworth's claims are, however, the purpose of this book is not to swallow them hook, line, and sinker. Indeed, the formidable Shelley makes that impossible, as he in his own sonnets undermines the integrity of those very claims. Nor is he the only one to do so. For all their admiration of the great Lake poet, Shelley, Keats, and D. G.

Rossetti all reveal in their sonnet writing a need not only to explore the powerful metaphorics and the self-reflexivity of Wordsworthian sonnets but also to confront philosophical and imaginative dilemmas that Wordsworth himself either evaded or, what may be the same thing, simply did not perceive as problems. For this reason, out of the many possible writers of the nineteenth century I could have chosen, men and women, I have concentrated on the several just mentioned, as well as Gerard Manley Hopkins. Each concerns himself explicitly with a particular mode of Wordsworth sonnet and with the particular problems of formal self-consciousness, of temporality, and of vision and subjectivity that belong to that mode.

I would emphasize that this elaboration should be positioned alongside an alternate mode that is concurrently developing. Thus it is not oversight on my part that the post-Wordsworth authors I go on to consider do not include the well-known women sonnet writers of the later part of the century. For all that Christina Rossetti and Elizabeth Barrett Browning accomplish in their own handlings of this traditional form, neither one belongs in the subsequent chapters of this study. I take that to be Wordsworth's doing, suppressing as he does the private, sentimental and supposedly "feminine" mode in favor of that "manly" and characteristically self-aggrandizing deference to his own egotistical sublime.[7]

The story that Wordsworth tells in his most famous sonnets is one that subsequent poets would go far to deconstruct, however. Responding to the authority of Wordsworth's sonnets, Shelley, with his own revolutionary and apocalyptic politics, has the least trouble in accommodating his precursor's revision of the sonnet's function as a representation of a visionary moment. His political sonnets partake of the expansive Wordsworthian visionary poetics, their "access to power."[8] That momentum pushes Shelley's sonnets to the boundaries of their formality and toward an open-endedness, a resistance to closure, that was implicit in the visionary sonnet but generally not necessary to the self-authorizing strategy of Wordsworth. Indeed, Shelley and Keats alike pushed the sonnet toward a different form altogether: the ode. This shared impulse may have something to do with the fact that there is, paradoxically, something odelike in many of Wordsworth's sonnets— something he may have learned, in his turn, from Milton.

Shelley is typical of the post-Wordsworth sonnet writers studied here in his attention to the sonnet form's implicit notion of a visionary relation of individual and historical time. "Ozymandias," a reading of which will comprise a major part of the second chapter, opens a canny exploration of what becomes a crux for all these poets—the integrity of that visionary relation. Shelley's resistance to the constraints of the sonnet form can be read as more than mere impatience with poetic form generally, as it is often taken to be; there is also located in that resistance a confrontation with Wordsworth and the philosophical limitations of his visionary agenda.

Indeed, if Wordsworth's notion of the sonnet form depends most heavily upon a metaphor of spatialized time, which the first chapter will demonstrate, it is always possible to be betrayed by that same metaphor. Robert Frost tells us that there is a point at which any metaphor breaks down, and the spatial tropes of the sonnet do so before the problem of temporality. Wordsworth's sonnets do not resist his awareness that these poems are necessarily *re*presentations, that there can be no simultaneity of thought and form. But for Wordsworth that temporal interval is not loss but rather the gain of consciousness itself. The authority adhering to Wordsworth's sonnets emerges out of the poet's acceptance of that temporal gap as the space in which his *own* origins might lie, the kind of origination of imaginative self that Leslie Brisman and Edward Said explore.[9]

Keats's engagement with the sonnet is an even more intimate entanglement with the problem of literary history and originality. While Keats's sonnets are also profoundly Wordsworthian in their conception of a literal mental space as the represented "site" of vision, and thus are profoundly self-referential, they are strangely shadowed constructions. Their very structure is disrupted by the threat of formal closure, which for this poet is nothing short of a metaphoric death. Keats's resistance to formal closure in so many of his individual sonnets registers his resistance to the closure of literary history at any given moment—a resistance only successfully pulled off in a rare and overlooked blank-verse sonnet. Crucial to the development of the Wordsworth line of visionary sonnet is also Keats's initiation of a shift away from the Wordsworth-Shelley conflation of the public and private role of the poet and back toward a stance of withdrawal, toward the privileging of a postromantic aestheticist stance that one of the Victorian period's premier sonnet writers, Dante Gabriel Rossetti, will at once embrace and also deconstruct.

Dante Gabriel Rossetti's complicated figuration of the sonnet as a "moment's monument," followed by his haunted and haunting sequence called *The House of Life*, is nothing if not a dismantling of the sonnet tradition's own idealization of its objects, its subjects, and its very form and linguistic nature—not to mention its temporal nature. Rossetti's paradoxical formulation of the sonnet as a "moment's monument" betrays the metaphoric collapse that threatens in Wordsworth's poems: in order for anything to be a monument, the "actual presence" of the memorialized thing is denied; the presence of the moment has been swept away by time itself. Aestheticism's metaphysics of presence, of iconic moments, of enduring and "ideal" instants, is always at best a paradox, at worst a dilemma.

Thus Rossetti brings to light one deep evasion of the Wordsworth visionary sonnet: its connection with death. In his effort to immerse himself in the visionary moment, he is typically postromantic in suffering what Poulet calls an "incarceration in the instant" and in feeling that duration, *evoked* in his sonnets, is no longer the "genesis of life, but the genesis of death."[10] Rossetti is the poet in this study most invested in the idea of the iconic moment, a sort of pre-Bergsonian awareness of *durée* and of the representativeness of the "spot of time." But it is he who also is plagued most by the temporal contradictions. The effort in certain of his sonnets to fully present "the moment" turns inevitably into a confrontation with death. Rossetti was aware that while the materiality of language is a medium through which the reconstitution of the moment is possible, that inscription of the moment is also an encrypting of it. The sonnet for Rossetti becomes a space that, in attempting to represent the immediacy of a moment of experience, can do no more than record its absence. The implications of this disjunction between experience and vision are certainly visible in his mixed-media sonnet/paintings, the uncanniness of which are generated less by a sensation of life than by a vision of death.

The penultimate chapter of this book looks at the work of a poet who in several respects epitomizes the development of the sonnet over the entire century. While Gerard Manley Hopkins's notion of the sonnet is based predominantly upon the Petrarchan form, his instincts led him, toward the end of his life, to Milton, for the same reason as Wordsworth's instincts led him there: to find a form that could defeat the crisis of dialectics with vision. And like Wordsworth, with whom these sonnets resonate despite their Petrarchanism, Hopkins discovers in the sonnet's dialectics of formal constraint a figure for the poet's struggle toward lyric. If what Wordsworth and the later poets were doing was (to borrow an expression of Sharon Cameron) to pry into and "pry apart the walls" of the sonnet form's representation of the visionary moment, for Hopkins that prying also leads to the radical formal experimentalism for which he is best known. What is interesting about Hopkins is that his effort to reveal that discovered space has such divergent results; sometimes it produces sonnets that with Wordsworthian momentum transfigure the monumentality of the sonnet into a convincing image of eternity, and other times it produces sonnets that trope their own thematic mortification.[11]

This book's primary focus is to describe the generic modulation of the sonnet form in English since the emergence of the revisionary mode of Wordsworth's sonnet writing. The second, closely related task is to study the self-reflexivity of romantic and Victorian sonnets, to explore the way in which the allusiveness of the form to its own formal tradition has affected its development and function as form. The authors of nineteenth-century sonnets often meditate upon their awareness of the tradition in which they are working by developing various figures of form. These self-reflexive sonnets not only comment on their own formal history but on their own places in the form's development, even in the course of revising some conventional aspect of the form. This unusual self-referentiality makes the sonnet an exemplary site at which to raise questions concerning both synchronic and diachronic aspects of poetic form generally.[12]

As the title of this book suggests, this study is, on a more abstract level, about time. One after another, these poems betray what Sharon Cameron describes as "lyric curiosity about the moment, the vision of it as superimposed upon the long stream of moments that blur in the background to which the poem relegates them."[13] Wordsworth's "lyric curiosity" directs itself toward the visionary moment with a poetics of presence. His sonnets are fascinated by representing the lyric moment, in which "social and objective time, those strictures that drive hard lines between past, present, and future,"[14] are collapsed; implicitly, then, each sonnet is a synecdoche *for* that moment. The importance of Wordsworth's sonnets in nineteenth-century literature has much to do with the way they conceive of themselves not only as "moments" but as "momentous," powerful and significant in their representation of conscious and imaginative moments. Their importance also has to do with the way their thematics of synecdoche and self-reflexivity dovetail with the nineteenth century's general obsession with temporality, with the so-called significant moment, with the iconic present.

It can be argued that such a view of the form obscures the problem of progressive temporality: that an essentially ahistorical, so-called visionary moment pushes aside its historical nature. The brilliance of Alan Liu's analysis, in this context, is the way it recuperates the submerged history of Wordsworth's work and procedures. It is not my intention, in focusing upon formal matters, to in any way deny the presence of history in these poems, which would be difficult to do in any case, since some of them are so clearly *about* the problem of historical time. I do want to highlight the structure of this poetic form, because I take it to be the site of the poets' engagement with the world and with the metaphors that inform the textual representation of that world. Cameron reminds us that if

> a poem denies the centrality of beginning and ends, if it fails to concern itself with the accumulated sequence of a history, it must push its way into the dimensions of the moment, pry apart its walls and reveal the discovered

space there to be as complex as the long corridors of historical or narrated time. For the moment is to the lyric what sequence is to the story.[15]

It is the complexity of the sonnet's "discovered space"—its lyric plot—that this study will primarily explore. Romantic and Victorian interest in spatial form and in the relationship of form to the problem of temporality does focus the critical light upon the artistic object and upon the metaphor of poem as isolated mental space. But as W. J. T. Mitchell points out, a literary work that presents "a fixed, static space as part of its imaginative illusion" does not, in fact, necessarily exclude progressive temporality in its purview:

> The space of a literary work may be enveloped in temporality in the manner of the landscapes described in Wordsworth's "spots of time." . . . Spatial form . . . is our basis for making history and temporality intelligible; it abstracts us from reality only insofar as any explanation is necessarily abstracted from that which it explains.[16]

These are apt comments in the context of Wordsworth's sonnets, for each of the spatialized, static moments Wordsworth constructs in his sonnets is ultimately placed by him, sometimes years after their composition as isolated poems, into sequences—an interestingly retrospective acknowledgment of progressive temporality and historicity analyzed by Liu. Wordsworth's genius is that he can embrace both perspectives; the triumph of time for Wordsworth is the synecdochic nature of all moments with respect to the ultimate apocalyptic or visionary one.

The problematics of historical time and "sonnet time" are thus interconnected. My emphasis is on the latter, on the dynamics of the form in which historical time gets represented. While any moment does participate in an historical and temporal actuality, a certain detachment is also possible; indeed, it is, as Richard Jackson puts it, the "very detachment provided by self-consciousness, the chasm of separation," *by which* "the historical and temporal actuality is made known."[17] This suggests why so many of Wordsworth's sonnets, as well as those written by the poets who follow him, often thematize that detachment by highlighting their formality. Their reflexive interest in their own structure and formality is intimately tied to the dialectic of time, subjectivity, and the imagination.

This thematization is what I wish to study, looking at the self-reflexivity of, and the reflecting upon, the iconic moment that such sonnets attempt to achieve. But my interest in Wordsworth's use of this form is not to demonstrate an escape or annulment of history—a position in any case made impossible by the fact that so many of these poems are *about* historical movement and historic moments—but to demonstrate the way in which the sonnet becomes for him a site in which the historical and the static moment are fused, in furtherance of his effort to transform poetry into something that is at the same time public and private in its import. The kind of history this study talks about is one that is told through the perception of form, which I take to be not simply a "site" but rather a "situation," a time, a place, and a problem—a problem concerning the poet himself, and concerning that time and place—that is to be solved in the poem.

There is no doubt that the visionary sonnet, as described in the first chapter, is thus complicitous with romantic ideology of the prophet-poet, but it is precisely later poets' awareness of that complicity that I believe gives this kind of sonnet such complexity. The post-Wordsworth poets' resistance to his idealism comes to be the primary motivation for, and the very subject of, their sonnets. This book's simultaneous acceptance of and resistance to Wordsworth's version of the sonnet's function is therefore required by the analysis of the sonnet-writers that follow. The implications of Wordsworth's meditations upon poetic form and temporality, his poetics of presence, and his insights into the synecdochic nature of the form are profound; the readings that follow in the chapters on Shelley, Keats, Rossetti, Hopkins, and Robert Frost, an American heir to this particular tradition, attempt to reveal the depth of those poets' engagements in the problematics of temporality, and of the visionary mode of Wordsworth's sonnets.

For each of them, the story of the struggle against the formality of the sonnet and its antithetical dynamics is an allegory of form, an example *in parvo* of the struggle of imaginative vision toward representation. Even when the poet in question seems to be more interested in the Italian tradition than the Miltonic one in which Wordsworth was more engaged—and I am thinking particularly of Keats or Rossetti here—the impact of Wordsworth is crucial. That most Italianate of sonnet sequences, D. G. Rossetti's *House of Life*, whatever its affinities with Dante's *La Vita Nuova*, might not have been conceivable without Wordsworth's conception of the sonnet as a metaphor of "the moment" of heightened subjectivity and as a formal figure of subjective appropriation of everything outside the poet's own mind.

Those who wrote about the sonnet in the nineteenth century—and there were many, as the fourth chapter of this study will reveal—clearly perceived this small form to be a synecdoche for all lyric poetry. The sonnet became a kind of lens through which to focus the general problems of influence and of formal change, and even of poetry's relationship to culture. My reading of these essays will thus contextualize the manifest interest in the form among academics and literary journalists with broader cultural—especially aestheticist—concerns. What this peculiar body of critical work reveals is that the fascination with the sonnet is a consolidation of a certain political-poetical tradition; it reveals as well a related concern with form generally. This concern betrays a postromantic nostalgia for coherence—for "vision"—that contemporary history was not offering, and scarcely promising either. It is one avenue down which an aestheticist quest for the recovery of wholeness may move. For the sonnet writers of both the nineteenth and twentieth centuries, this is as much a problem of influence and of tradition as it is a problem of form—and my intent is to show how, for Wordsworth and writers after him, these two problems merge.

A Moment's Monument

1

Wordsworth's "Inquest" and the Visionary Sonnet

This chapter will explore the assertion that the distinction of Wordsworth's sonnets lies in the probing inquest of each of them, no matter what its subject or particular occasion, into its perception of its own form; it will explore as well the tropological implications of that perception. Wordsworth identified the sonnet form as a figurative procedure that is motivated by its own synecdochic nature: the way large ambition can be contained in small form; the way in which the form tropes one moment as all moments; the way in which the constraints of this form force one to reflect on the nature of poetic form generally; and the way this "brief transcript of the heart" becomes a figuration of lyric itself. The poet recognized that synecdochic procedure as related to the process of perception and composition, the "lyric plot" of representation itself; this recognition is evident in the emergence in so many of these sonnets of figures of form that emphasize the expansive potential of the sonnet form, not merely its "narrow room," as he called it.

My argument will be that Wordsworth's consistent exploitation of the form's dualistic structure leads him to a revisionary poetic that invests the form with a revelatory, rather than simply compensatory or consolatory, function. This set into play procedures and implications that would be engaged in the work of the nineteenth-century sonnet writers that followed and responded to him. Thus the particular line of Wordsworth sonnet that I am most interested in departs from the Petrarchan sonnet's poetics of conflict and absence, and from the poetics of sentiment represented not only by Bowles but also, significantly, by the many popular women poets of the day. Although Wordsworth expressly admired some of them, his own engagement with the sonnet form rejected that sentimental, "feminine" mode for the "manly" (his word) Miltonic mode.

Just as my selection of poets for this book depended upon their engagement, however problematic, with this particular poetic, so does my selection of poems in this chapter, which focuses upon those that display a formal self-consciousness. In the case of the discussion of temporality in the sonnet sequence, particularly, I pass over several important Wordsworth sequences from different times in his career in order to focus upon the late *River Duddon* sequence, with its overlay of a visionary poetic upon a more conventional "river tour" sequence. That overlay makes this sequence the most significant example within the parameters of this study, which concerns itself more with intrinsic formal matters, even as they engage extrinsic cultural ones.

I

Wordsworth was not the first to write a sonnet on the sonnet. Lope de Vega produced several in the sixteenth century, and Thomas Edwards (1699–1757) wrote "An English Travesty," a self-consciously playful metapoem that fills its fourteen lines by counting them down.[1] Of more immediate interest are those written by Anna Seward, a popular woman poet whose sonnet work preceded and was noted by Wordsworth. She composed three (sonnets 16, 64, and 100 in the third volume of her *Poetical Works*),[2] the most interesting of which constitutes her own literary history as well as her defense of the form:

> Prais'd be the Poet, who the Sonnet's claim,
>   Severest of the orders that belong
>   Distinct and separate to the Delphic song,
>   Shall venerate, nor its appropriate name
> Lawless assume. Peculiar is its frame,
>   From him derived, who shunn'd the city throng,
>   And warbled sweet thy rocks and streams among,
>   Lonely Valclusa!—and that heir of fame,
> Our greater MILTON, hath, by many a lay
>   Form'd on that arduous model, fully shown
>   That English verse may happily display
> Those strict energic measures, which alone
>   Deserve the name of Sonnet, and convey
>   A grandeur, grace and spirit, all their own.[3]
>   ("To Mr. Henry Cary, on the Publication of His Sonnets")

It is possible that Wordsworth had this poem and the "sonnet's claim" in the back of his mind when he composed "Scorn not the Sonnet" (1827). This poem is not only his own most complicated and inclusive defense of the sonnet form, but it is even more than that: the sequence of figures and authors offers not only a meditation in miniature on the sonnet form specifically and on poetic form generally, but is also a fascinatingly personal reading of the history of the form that will help us understand Wordsworth's revision of the sonnet more precisely:

> Scorn not the Sonnet; Critic, you have frowned,
> Mindless of its just honours; with this key
> Shakespeare unlocked his heart; the melody
> Of this small lute gave ease to Petrarch's wound;
> A thousand times this pipe did Tasso sound;
> With it Camoëns soothed an exile's grief;
> The Sonnet glittered a gay myrtle leaf
> Amid the cypress with which Dante crowned
> His visionary brow: a glow-worm lamp,
> It cheered mild Spenser, called from Faery-land
> To struggle through dark ways; and, when a damp
> Fell round the path of Milton, in his hand
> The Thing became a trumpet; whence he blew
> Soul-animating strains—alas, too few![4]

The self-reflection of the poem is apparent in the first line, particularly in the striking address to the "Critic." This is not the usual addressee of the sonnet; it is no personal friend, no political figure, no lover, none of the usual targets of the conventional sonnet's aim. It is rather a reader, who, Wordsworth suggests in the first line and a half, has misjudged the sonnet by taking the misuse of the form as a defect of the form itself.

Wordsworth asks that the reader think about the sonnet's function as a form, not only the nature of its format or structure. This dichotomy between function and format weaves its way through the argument that follows. The sonnet's attention revolves around figures for the form. At line 2 the sonnet is a "key" with which Shakespeare "unlocked his heart"—a device or instrument, held in the hand, perhaps like a pen, that opens the poet to emotion, that makes possible expression, that externalizes that which is inside. This is the poetic impulse itself, the impulse not simply to look into one's heart but also to *write* (to echo a poet who begins his sonnet sequence with an acute awareness of that rhetorical relief). Form, Wordsworth reminds us, makes expression possible, and that expression is a kind of consolation.[5]

The series continues, the sonnet now troped specifically as musical instrument, as in the Seward sonnet considered above: it is a "small lute" (4), a "pipe" (5), inspiration passing from the body not as song, not as the nightingale sings, but as "melody" created by a movement of strings or of breath through a pipe. Wordsworth is not simply troping the song of the lyric as such, but more strikingly, the instrumentality of the sonnet—its function—as that which makes melody possible. At line 7, the sonnet's center, the form is named again, for it is here that the metaphor of form changes from instrumentality to illumination or vision. "The Sonnet glittered a gay myrtle leaf" in Dante's crown; it is "a glow-worm lamp" for Spenser. These are images of light and radiance, rather than of instrumentality only.

Interestingly, Wordsworth has not troped form as a mold or vessel for emotion, but as a "Thing" (about which more in a moment) through which emotion passes into articulation. This notion of "passage" relates the first series of images to the second. This image of radiance has, however, interesting implications about the problem of form itself. A similar trope of radiance appears in the sonnet "To —— ['Happy the feeling . . .']," which became the dedication to the arrangement of poems published as "Miscellaneous Sonnets." Really another sonnet on the sonnet, this poem likens form to a stone from the sea beach, which, when polished, "discovers" veins "exquisite and rare"—as if the internal structure of the form itself radiated to the outside when its surface was worked. Its gleam is a recreation of the beauty, a reemergence of the "moist gleam" that was lost when the stone was gathered. The conflict of inner and outer structure emerges along with the characteristically Wordsworthian notion that this happiness is a consolation for the loss of an original gleam or beauty.[6]

Turning back to "Scorn not . . . ," then, the structure of the sonnet itself emphasizes the crucial pivot of the poem from instrumentality to vision. The octave, with its predominant figures of instrumentality, is overrun by the enjambment of line 8, emphasizing that the sonnet in its own way is capable of exceeding limits. In the sestet, the sonnet becomes an instrument of vision itself, illuminating dark ways. The gleam there is compensatory as well as revelatory; the form "gives ease," "soothes"; it glitters with life amid Dante's crown of death; it "cheers mild Spenser, called from Faery-land / To struggle through dark ways," possibly the chilling disapproval of his great poem by the politically powerful Burleigh. Whereas the function of the sonnet in the poem's first half is to "unlock" emotion and to "give ease," in the second half it is rather to "guide"; from line 7 on, the form becomes something that guides the poet's steps "through dark ways" or paths hidden by "damp," by virtue of a kind of illuminating radiance.

Thus does the sonnet become, in the poem's final figure, consolation to Wordsworth in his blindness. The poem's remarkable allusion to the Milton's blindness is signaled by that un-Wordsworthian word "damp" in line 11.

Indeed, the word is Milton's, and its most notable appearance is in *Paradise Lost*, where it describes Adam's recovery from depression upon learning from the Archangel Michael that he must leave Eden ("Adam by this from the cold sudden damp / Recovering, and his scatterd spirits returnd, / To Michael thus his humble words address'd" [*PL* 11.293]).[7] After these lines, Michael takes the fallen Adam to the "high Hill" where the angel "sets before him what shall happ'n till the Flood" ("The Argument"); Adam receives a new kind of vision, previously hidden from him.

In the Wordsworth sonnet, the word "damp" not only connotes emotional depression; it also compares the condition of Milton's blindness to a kind of veil of dew fallen around him. This metaphor recalls Milton's own description of his blindness as "So thick a drop serene [that] hath quencht thir Orbs, / Or dim suffusion veild" (*PL* 3.25–26)—the *gutta serena* which left his eyes looking clear (as his sonnet to Cyriack [sonnet 22] reminds us), while "Cloud in stead, and ever-during dark / Surrounds me . . ." (3.45–46). But here, Milton invokes Holy Light to

> Shine inward, and the mind through all her powers
> Irradiate, there plant eyes, all most from thence
> Purge and disperse, that I may see and tell
> Of things invisible to mortal sight.
>
> (Lines 52–55)

Milton regains "vision," asserting here and in the sonnet on his blindness that losing sight leaves one with another kind of vision far more powerful. The tropes of expanded vision and radiance implicit in Milton's attention to the visionary is crucial to the final movement of Wordsworth's sonnet on the sonnet. In the *Paradise Lost* scene, in the book 3 invocation, and in Milton's sonnet on his blindness, the discovery of the visionary, which both shines inward and radiates outward, is more than equal compensation for the loss of a previous condition of sight. Wordsworth's attention to this Miltonic moment underscores what is at stake in writing poems for Wordsworth. The consolation of composition is that it can recapture an original vision that has been lost. While for Milton that loss is quite literal, for Wordsworth the loss of vision in the figurative sense is ultimately the greater one. Wordsworth, from his early career, strives to regain the confidence of his precursor that the imaginative vision he feels he has lost *can* be replaced with something more powerful. The nature of this power, an obsession of Wordsworth's career, leads him over and over again to Milton, and not least in his sonnet writing.

In general, a large number of Wordsworth's sonnets concern themselves with moments of vision—of the imagination working upon literal scenes. Indeed, these glimpses constitute a compact version of Wordsworthian aesthetics, and I will return to a detailed exposition of this assertion later on.[8] That aesthetic is hinted at in "Scorn not the sonnet" in one of the larger movements of the poem. Looking once again at the series of figures there, one discerns a movement of expansion, an opening out from smallness to largeness. The theme of emotional imprisonment or constraint so present in many sonnets as to be almost characteristic of them is thematized in these images of the delicate and soft sound of Tasso easing his pain, of Petrarch soothing his wound. But by the end of the poem, this sound has become the blast of Milton's trumpet; the glittering of Dante's leaves becomes the glow-worm lamp of Spenser, radiating out. Sound and light curiously join when the form reaches the hands of Milton; instruments of sound and of radiance almost conflate in the soul-animating strains of his trumpet, as if that instrument itself illuminated the way for his country and audience of the fit few. The sonnets considered in this chapter are only a few of the many poems that have as their underlying procedure that expansion from the "real" or natural to the visionary.

What is finally striking about Wordsworth's vision of form here is that it is *im*personal; that is, while it is the vehicle for feeling, it is itself so much an instrument of that feeling, or of inspiration, that he calls it merely "The Thing," a most peculiar description. The word "thing" in Wordsworth is not frequent but always significant, as in "A slumber did my spirit seal." There the word refers to a materiality that presences the female figure in the poem by subsuming her to something much larger than herself, part of the "earth's diurnal course." So too here, where Wordsworth suggests that in Milton's hand this form, so small, delicate, and constrained, becomes something much greater, much fuller, and utterly complete. It is a form by which a visionary presence is evoked.

Furthermore, the nature of the poem's figures of form reveals something crucial about Wordsworth's conception of the form: in each case, the figure is of something small that opens up, or opens into, something much larger. What Wordsworth is pointing at, in his typically self-reflexive way, is the manner in which the synecdochic nature of the *image* (something small standing for something large), is analogous to (a figure for) the synecdochic nature of the procedure of the form itself, from articulation to vision. In his reading of this sonnet, J. Hillis Miller says that in each of the metaphors evoked in the poem, "the image is of something small and enclosed that is nevertheless articulated. Since it has a design, it can serve as the means by which inarticulate energies are at once controlled and released."[9] The usefulness of this remark is its reminder that *all* the figures of form in this poem are small, images of the synecdochic nature of the form itself.

The faceted brilliance of this sonnet does not fully shine without re-marking that it is also a miniature literary history, though a significantly idiosyncratic one. The scorn of this "critic" probably was directed at two main issues: the contemporary trendiness of sonnet writing, which produced for the most part mediocre and sentimental work, and the more serious charge that such a small and formally constrained form can only "accept" trivial contents. But the unhappy products of contemporary sonnet writers are of little concern to Wordsworth in this poem. Indeed, such a narrow view of the form is what Wordsworth urges the critic away from. In being "mindless" the critic is not supposed by Wordsworth to be "ignorant of" the just honors of the form but forgetful of them; this poem will recall for the critic its history.

But what an odd mapping of sonnet history this is. Consistent neither in nationality nor in chronology, the series foregrounds questions one does not ordinarily ask while producing a "straight" literary history. In such a history one wants to know simply: "What came next?" But when Petrarch follows Shakespeare, when Dante falls between Shakespeare and Milton, clearly another organizing principle is at work.[10] In a poem as self-referen-tial as this one, perhaps a clue is offered by the form itself, and sense can be made of the series if it is grouped by octave and sestet. In the octave, the literary lineage runs: Shakespeare-Tasso-Camoëns-Dante. This last poet (some of whose sonnets Wordsworth translated) hovers interestingly at the poem's center as a pivotal figure. In the sestet the series continues thus: (Dante)—Spenser—(and, finally) Milton. Wordsworth characterizes the sonnets of the first group of poets as private emotional expressions, brief records of large souls; in his 1815 "Essay, Supplementary to the Preface" to *Lyrical Ballads*, he observes of Shakespeare's sonnets that "there is not a part of the writings of this Poet where is found in an equal compass a greater number of exquisite feelings felicitously expressed."[11] Wordsworth recog-nizes Shakespeare's sonnets as the only place where one finds the "real voice" of the dramatist, who otherwise spoke only through the mouths of others.[12] Similarly, the remaining poets of the octave wrote sonnets char-acterized by the mode of the private voice. The second group of poets, however, is associated here not only with lyric, but also with epic. The movement from lyric to epic in the background of this sonnet is crucial and runs parallel to the movement of expansion discussed earlier.

This is a history concerned not with chronology but rather with mode, and the story's progress from the private mode to the public is tied in a complicated way to Milton. The achievement of Milton in this history, and the reason he is placed at its close, is the emergence in his poetry of the visionary from the private, the "vision of a voice."[13] Wordsworth's admiration of Milton's sonnets is won because of that poet's projection of voice far beyond the confines of conventional lyric; that is, the scope of address changes from self or close friend, to world-at-large, from an audience of one to an audience of a nation—from the lyric audience to the national audience of the epic. The imagined audience, furthermore, changes the very nature of the poem, or at least the figure of its form. In the early lines of the sonnet, the poem is called a "melody" (line 3), a delicate but slight sound from a lute, or a pipe. Milton's music, however, is a blast from a biblical trumpet that plays "soul-animating strains." Strain against form is what sonnet writing is about; that strain is not only soul-animating, but also form-animating.

This animation of form is the focus of Wordsworth's idiosyncratic vision of sonnet history. Milton's form is an inheritance, handed down by Shakespeare, Dante, Spenser—but it is also the instrument announcing a future vision of itself. That vision is clearly discerned by Wordsworth, if not by the Critic, and it accounts for his own reanimation of the form. The poem is finally a vision of its poet's future: that final trumpet is not just the instrument of prophecy but also, of course, the trumpet of fame. Like Dante, who crowned his own visionary brow with poetry, Wordsworth recaptures for himself a power—an authority—that originates not in that of a former literary age but in the poet's own visionary power. This self-crowning participates in the "myth of self-possession" and its "masculine metaphors of power" that Marlon B. Ross so ably outlines; it is a myth that this poet's sonnets, just as powerfully as his epics, would help to construct.[14]

II

The story behind Wordsworth's sudden "conversion" to the sonnet form is well known. The poet writes, "My admiration of some of the Sonnets of Milton first tempted me to write in that form. The fact is not mentioned from a notion that it will be deemed of any importance by the reader, but merely as a public acknowledgment of one of the innumerable obligations, which, as a Poet and a man, I am under to our great fellow-countryman."[15] But a more precise recollection of that moment gives us a more interesting view. According to the poet's report to Isabella Fenwick many years later, the conversion can be dated to the night of 21 May 1802:

In the cottage of Town-End, one afternoon in 1801 [1802], my sister read to
me the sonnets of Milton. I had long been well acquainted with them, but I
was particularly struck on that occasion with the dignified simplicity and
majestic harmony that runs through most of them—in character so totally
different from the Italian, and still more so from Shakespeare's fine sonnets.
I took fire, if I may be allowed to say so, and produced three sonnets the
same afternoon—the first I ever wrote, except an irregular one at school. Of
these three, the only one I distinctly remember is "I grieved for Buonaparté,"
&c. One was never written down; the third, which was I believe preserved, I
cannot particularise.[16]

This account of inspiration is a crucial and fascinating one. One wonders what, exactly, on that particular night, Wordsworth heard in Milton's
sonnets that he had not heard before, what he suddenly apprehended that
caused him to "take fire"—a complicated trope of literary influence indeed, suggesting both the passing on of poetic power and the usurpation of
it.[17] Unlike the most notable of his contemporaries—particularly Bowles
and Coleridge—Wordsworth had been nearly silent in the production of
and commentary upon this already-revived form. He would remember that
before this night in 1802 he had regarded the sonnet form as "egregiously
absurd, though the greatest poets since the revival of literature have written
in it."[18]

Wordsworth never pinpoints what that absurdity was—though one possibility will be explored shortly. Nor does he ever mention which particular
Milton sonnet caught his imagination. Perhaps there was only what he would
call a "pervading sense"—but that, at least, can be speculated about. The
most detailed description we have from Wordsworth on the Miltonic sonnet form, as well as his most complete statement on sonnet form generally,
comes in a letter to Alexander Dyce that was probably written in the spring
of 1833. In response to Dyce's solicitation for "specimens of the best sonnet writers in our language" for a new anthology, Wordsworth suggests the
following:

Do you mean to have a short preface upon the Construction of the Sonnet?
Though I have written so many, I have scarcely made up my own mind upon
the subject. It should seem that the Sonnet, like every other legitimate composition, ought to have a beginning, a middle, and an end—in other words,
to consist of three parts, like the three propositions of a syllogism, if such an
illustration may be used. But the frame of metre adopted by the Italians does
not accord with this view, and, as adhered to by them, it seems to be, if not
arbitrary, best fitted to a division of the sense into two parts, of eight and six
lines each. Milton, however, has not submitted to this. In the better half of

his sonnets the sense does not close with the rhyme at the eighth line, but overflows into the second portion of the metre. Now it has struck me, that this is not done merely to gratify the ear by variety and freedom of sound, but also to aid in giving that pervading sense of intense Unity in which the excellence of the Sonnet has always seemed to me to consist. Instead of looking at this composition as a piece of architecture, making a whole out of three parts, I have been much in the habit of preferring the image of an orbicular body,—a sphere—or a dew-drop. All this will appear to you a little fanciful; and I am well aware that a Sonnet will often be found excellent, where the beginning, the middle, and the end are distinctly marked, and also where it is distinctly separated into *two* parts, to which as I before observed the strict Italian model, as they write it, is favorable. Of this last construction of Sonnet, Russell's upon Philoctetes is a fine specimen; the first eight lines give the hardship of the case, the six last the consolation, or the *per-contra*.[19]

Although Wordsworth certainly highlights the dualistic, *per-contra* structure of the sonnet form, he is particularly interested here in the way that that dualism could be overcome in favor of "that pervading sense of intense Unity." The notion of "intensity" here, with its suggestion of inwardness, of concentration, and power, captures the paradox of the Miltonic sonnet form's tendency to find expansive imaginative power by turning inward. (As we will see later on, "intensity" is the term that Victorian critics and scholars of the sonnet use to describe Wordsworth's sonnet and the power of the romantic sonnet generally.) That intensity inheres not only formally, but also tropologically. Wordsworth's sonnet on the sonnet, "Scorn not the sonnet," suggests that what Milton gave Wordsworth was a principle of troping form *as* voice. Wordsworth perceives the originality in Milton's use of form not simply to express the constraint and impotence of some "lonely feeling" or passion but to create a voice originating *out of* (in the sense of "because of" as well as "outward from") the constraints of the form itself.

In addition, through Milton's troping form as voice, through his ability to fill the form, through his presentation of the private thought in the public role, the earlier poet gives the sonnet a kind of heroic "gigantism." But such a notion has long been entertained with respect to Milton's sonnets. Johnson alludes to it negatively in his well-known remark about carving a Colossus upon a cherry stone; a turn-of-the-century critic, Sir Walter Alexander Raleigh, admires Milton's "economy," the way in which the poet "packs meaning into the fewest possible words, and studies economy in every trifle."[20] F. T. Prince looks at it in a slightly different light, seeing Milton's sonnets as a contraction of something larger: "The sonnets are therefore essays, on a small scale in the 'magnificent' style."[21] Prince is also first to remark that the development of this sonnet style may have been a rehearsal for the heroic verse with which Milton would blaze forth his epic poems—a notion that Wordsworth himself at least hints at in his comment that Milton's sonnets have "an energetic and varied flow of sound crowding into narrow room more of the combined effect of rhyme and blank verse than can be done by any other kind of verse I know."[22]

The importance of this matter of "narrow room" is reflected by the reappearance of this expression in Wordsworth's first sonnet on the sonnet, "Nuns fret not" (date unknown; published 1807). This poem reminds us once again that synecdoche is a radical trope for and in his sonnet writing—though this time the spatial metaphor is more dominant:

> Nuns fret not at their convent's narrow room;
> And hermits are contented with their cells;
> And students with their pensive citadels;
> Maids at the wheel, the weaver at his loom,
> Sit blithe and happy; bees that soar for bloom,
> High as the highest Peak of Furness-fells,
> Will murmur by the hour in foxglove bells:
> In truth the prison, unto which we doom
> Ourselves, no prison is: and hence for me,
> In sundry moods, 'twas pastime to be bound
> Within the Sonnet's scanty plot of ground;
> Pleased if some Souls (for such there needs must be)
> Who have felt the weight of too much liberty,
> Should find brief solace there, as I have found.

The constraint of the sonnet form itself, as a spatial trope for the self-bounded mental space of the poet, is countered by the trope of instrumentality that underlies the poem. This "scanty plot of ground" is where the imaginative work of poetry takes place, on the one hand;[23] on the other, that space becomes the expression of thought exploding the poet's emotional constraint and silence. Figures of form in the octave stress constriction of space and range, while the sestet reminds us that only through work within some set of boundaries is poetry even possible.

For Wordsworth as for Milton, the matter of poetic form in the sonnet is intimately tied to the notion of "freedom," in every possible sense of the word—political, imaginative, and formal. And so for Wordsworth as for Milton, sonnet writing was a refuge from another major life work, namely, the epic. Perhaps not so strangely, for both poets sonnet and epic would ultimately come to be tropologically connected. Indeed, this connection is crucial. In his scattered remarks, Wordsworth seems to have apprehended the way Milton used the sonnet as a synecdoche of his epics. Milton deepened the import of those small poems, creating a site where the great public hero becomes, also, "representative man," and where private feeling becomes available and useful for public hearing. Thus does Wordsworth rediscover a "dignity" for the short Italian form that counteracts the "absurdity" (as he had put it) of its contemporary use. Like Milton, he recasts both the role of the poet and the function of the form.

Before leaving the Milton-Wordsworth connection, I would like to outline another possible reason for Wordsworth's conversion excitement, one that lies unacknowledged by the poet himself but that is implied clearly enough. Recent scholarly work by Margaret Homans and Marlon Ross, among others, has highlighted the gendering of genre in the nineteenth century—and certainly the sonnet is not excepted from that. Epic was still unequivocally man's literary territory—but the sonnet had been "permitted" as a lyric venue for women poets, associated as it was with the sentimental (the "transcript of the heart"), with the domestic, with "small subjects" worth a very short poem (but no more). It was a genre taken up with great success, commercial as well as aesthetic, by women. Despite Bowles and Coleridge, it is Seward and Smith who were best known as sonnet writers in 1802.

In this light I would reconsider Wordsworth's "conversion narrative." For after all, it is not strictly true that Wordsworth had *never* written sonnets before 1802; he had written at least three, one of which was his first published poem. And that poem, "Sonnet on Seeing Helen Maria Williams Weep at a Tale of Distress," published in 1787 and never again by Wordsworth, is itself in the sentimental and by then generically feminized mode of sonnet writing that may have been the real "absurdity" that Wordsworth shied away from. This may also help to explain Wordsworth's characterization of Milton's sonnets as "*manly* and dignified compositions" (emphasis mine). In associating himself with this strain of sonnet writing, and thus with the shift from the private to the public/visionary mode described above, Wordsworth can justify the employment of the form as an instrument of public and "manly" speech as he could not before. With the language of feeling subordinated to the "language of men," the impersonality noted above in Wordsworth's figuration of the sonnet may seem less odd.

While John Hollander asserts that "It was Milton alone whom Wordsworth's sonnet writing was, in a peculiar formal sense, about," Wordsworth's sonnet writing was also, in an equally peculiar way, precisely *not* about the popular female poets whose work Wordsworth knew, nor about the feminine, non-"manly" mode of sonnet that he rejected.[24] In this context, the figure of the *nun* that opens "Nuns fret not" is particularly significant, a liminal figure in being at once female and engaged in an activity supremely "of the heart," and yet subject to a (masculine) institutional discipline. She is thus an instance of the private/public conflation that Wordsworth seeks in the discipline of form—both in the name of a cause greater than the self.[25]

III

It is not surprising that Wordsworth's attitude toward his own sonnet writing was ambivalent: in a letter to Walter Savage Landor in 1822, for example, he disparages his sonnet writing habit: "since that time [of his first sonnet compositions], from want of resolution to take up anything of length, I have filled up many a moment in writing Sonnets, which, if I had never fallen into the practice, might easily have been better employed"[26]— a comment which offhandedly but nevertheless importantly conflates spatial and temporal images. Jared Curtis and Miller after him suggest looking at Wordsworth's sonnet writing as a mark of "poetic impotence" with respect to his more ambitious poetic projects; that is, they follow Coleridge in suggesting that the proliferation of sonnets was an evasion of the more burdensome task of writing *The Recluse*.[27]

But I am proposing quite a different role for the sonnets in Wordsworth's career. In my discussion of Milton earlier, I mentioned an argument put forward by Prince that Milton's sonnets were a sort of alternate or small version of the heroic style that would blaze forth in his epics. In his 1807 "Advertisement," and in both sonnets on the sonnet, Wordsworth implies a similar synecdochic relation between the sonnet and epic genres. It is the largeness of ambition, the "weightiness" of his epic work, that he finds constricting. But as with Milton, the sonnet's "brief solace" from epic writing does not preclude a similarity of subject matter. If his intention in *The Prelude*, for example, is to trace the development of the Poet's mind, the analysis of that mind is no less the intention of his sonnet writing as a whole.

Wordsworth's sonnet writing would itself take on a sort of epic proportion,[28] the lyric plot of the individual sonnet developing into the narrative plotting of the *Miscellaneous Sonnets*. Wordsworth's rearrangement of his early sonnets into a long sequence in later years would make of his short poems only a different *kind* of autobiographical long poem. Those "moments" that he wasted by "filling" them with sonnets became moments that would open out into a larger conception of his own life history. The "smallness" of the sonnets was transformed, as these poems, reorganized under larger, abstract categories, took on an overarching narrative dimension. Wordsworth had not originally planned this; the poet's rearrangements contextualized the "miscellaneous" sonnets as their author saw common themes emerge over the years.[29]

The judgment that Wordsworth's sonnets reflect a poetic impotence is too accepting of Wordsworth's, and especially Coleridge's, occasional denigration of his work in small forms. For indeed, what his sonnets, whether categorized as "miscellaneous" or as "dedicated to Liberty," are typically *about* is poetic power, poetry's ability to celebrate a moment of heightened perception and consciousness, and the "shock" of discovering meaning in that moment. However trifling these sonnets individually appear, what Wordsworth actually found himself up to could not be of greater importance, and remarks from the poet reveal that he was absolutely aware of it.

In a well-known 1807 letter to Lady Beaumont, Wordsworth responds to her evident worry about several negative reviews of his just-published *Poems in Two Volumes* by pointing out to her that "It is impossible that any expectations can be lower than mine concerning the immediate effect of this little work upon what is called the Public." Citing not just envy and malevolence but also, and primarily, the "pure absolute honest ignorance" of such readers of the "thoughts, feelings, and images, on which the life of my Poems depend," Wordsworth blames the city life of this reading public for their insensitivity:

> The things which I have taken, whether from within or without,—what have they to do with routs, dinners, morning calls, hurry from door to door, from street to street, on foot or in Carriage; with Mr. Pitt or Mr. Fox, Mr. Paul or Sir Francis Burdett, the Westminster Election or the Borough of Honiton; in a word, for I cannot stop to make my way through the hurry of images that present themselves to me, what have they to do with endless talking about things nobody cares anything for except as far as their own vanity is concerned, and this with persons they care nothing for but as their vanity or *selfishness* is concerned; what have they to do (to say all at once) with a life without love? . . . It is an awful truth, that there neither is, nor can be, any genuine enjoyment of Poetry among nineteen out of twenty of those persons who live, or wish to live, in the broad light of the world. . . . This is a truth, and an awful one, because to be incapable of a feeling of Poetry in my sense of the word is to be without love of human nature and reverence for God.[30]

This passage contains a great deal that is characteristically Wordsworthian: the obvious distaste for the city and its effect on human affections and on the imagination; the justification of a poet's consequent disdain of "Society"; the distancing of himself from society's entertainments and politics

alike, in order to preserve from their dulling vanities his own love for poetry and for humanity.

But having thus written off the majority of his readership as uncongenial, if not outright unfit, Wordsworth goes on to explain why his poems, these "Moods of my own Mind," are *necessary* even though "the majority of those poems would appear [insignificant] to very respectable persons." He centers his argument in the conviction that these very "thoughts, feelings and images" that make up his poems of the private self have *public* significance:

> . . . I would say boldly at once, that these Sonnets, while they each fix the attention upon some important sentiment separately considered, do at the same time collectively make up a Poem on the subject of civil Liberty and national independence, which, either for simplicity of style or grandeur of moral sentiment, is, alas! likely to have few parallels in the Poetry of the present day.[31]

The ultimate importance of these artifacts of the imagination is, as Wordsworth's letter to Lady Beaumont clearly expresses, that they spark in his benighted readership the same freeing imaginative processes. Wordsworth would awaken a public in whom, as he puts it, "imagination has slept" and he anticipates that in the future, the "destiny" of these lyrics will be "to console the afflicted, to add sunshine to daylight by making the happy happier, to teach the young and gracious of every age, to see, to think and feel, and therefore to become more actively and securely virtuous; this is their office. . . ." He is "well aware" how grandiose these claims will sound— "how far it would seem to many I overrate my own exertions when I speak this way."[32] But Wordsworth elaborates by returning to the "Moods of my own Mind" and offers what is essentially his own *ars poetica*:

> There is scarcely a poem here of above thirty Lines, and very trifling these poems will appear to many; but, omitting to speak of them individually, do they not, taken collectively, fix the attention upon a subject eminently poetical, viz., the interest which objects in nature derive from the predominance of certain affections more or less permanent, more or less capable of salutary renewal in the mind of the being contemplating these objects? . . . This is poetic, and essentially poetic, and why? because it is creative.[33]

According to this passage we could choose any of the sonnets to demonstrate that each is a miniature study of "a subject eminently poetical" and creative; each poem, he implies, is a different "take" on a mundane moment that opens out, through the operations of the imagination, from a

mere perception of an instance in nature into some more permanent significance. Wordsworth goes on to describe the poetic moment as a procedure
that is essentially synecdochic, that is, with one significant detail or thought
or sentiment singled out for attention:

> [Who] is there that has not felt that the mind can have no rest among a mul-
> titude of objects, of which it either cannot make one whole, or from which it
> cannot single out one individual, whereupon may be concentrated the atten-
> tion divided among or distracted by a multitude? After a certain time we
> must either select one image or object, which must put out of view the rest
> wholly, or must subordinate them to itself while it stands forth as a Head:

> > Now glowed the firmament
> > With living sapphires! Hesperus, that *led*
> > The starry host, rode brightest; till the Moon,
> > Rising in clouded majesty, at length,
> > Apparent *Queen*, unveiled *her peerless* light,
> > And o'er the dark her silver mantle threw.
> > [*Paradise Lost* 4.604–9; emphasis his]

> Having laid this down as a general principle, take the case before us.[34]

The synecdochic procedure is evident here, with this passage's language of
part and whole, of "concentration" of a multitude of images by attention to
a single one. The image or object of any poem is figured as a "Head" or
landmark for the poetic quester in what is transformed by the imagination
from a literal to a poetic landscape.

The poet illustrates this more precisely with reference to his own sonnet, "With ships the sea was sprinkled far and nigh"; in the "case before us"
the central image is a single ship, which

> may . . . be said to come upon a mission of the poetic Spirit, because in its
> own appearance and attributes it is barely sufficiently distinguish[ed] to rouse
> the creative faculty of the human mind to exertions at all times welcome, but
> doubly so when they come upon us when in a state of remissness. The mind
> being once fixed and rouzed, all the rest comes from itself; it is merely a
> lordly Ship, nothing more.[35]

Characteristically, Wordsworth borrows the Miltonic image of Hesperus
from the quoted *Paradise Lost* lines ("Hesperus, that *led* The starry host")
as an image of his own mind's visionary power. The "preeminence" Hesperus
holds "of his own Nature" in the heavens simultaneously incites ("calls
forth") the poetic faculty. This linkage between the Miltonic star and his

own poetic vision is akin to the figuration discussed previously of "taking fire" from Milton's sonnets; it is a linkage Wordsworth will use recurrently, and its significance will not be missed by Shelley, Keats, Hopkins, and Frost.

Furthermore, Wordsworth, in explicitly erotic imagery, describes how his mind "wantons with grateful joy in the exercise of its own powers" and in the creation to which the Ship—and synecdochically the poem that emerges from this scene—"[gives] body and life." In a fascinating move, Wordsworth both follows and transforms the figuration of the Miltonic passage quoted in his letter. There, the brightness of Hesperus suddenly is dimmed by the appearance of the Moon, who, "Apparent Queen, unveiled *her peerless* light, / And o'er the dark her silver mantle threw." Wordsworth aligns the poem's image of the ship, feminized as "her" whom "I pursued . . . with a lover's look," with the Moon, "making her [the ship] a sovereign or a regent, and thus giving body and life to all the rest." But Hesperus/ Wordsworth, far from being dimmed, becomes even more powerful, and the feminized object of his mind's praise, the ship, is "nought to me, nor I to her." What survives as important and preeminent is not the Moon/ship (as in the Milton passage)—but Hesperus/Wordsworth, and the egotistically sublime power that creates significance. The letter thus also remarkably confirms the gender metaphorics that trope the Wordsworthian appropriations of external reality—and the *re*-appropriation of the sonnet form from its feminized mode of sensibility for a masculinist strategy.[36] The mere *fact* of the poet's attention, or more precisely, the poet's awareness that that attention is being given, makes the moment a charged experience.

In a similar procedure to the one just described, each sonnet becomes a "spot of time" in Wordsworth's poetic autobiography; each engages in some way the problematics of the moment of vision in a poet's experience. This important letter to Lady Beaumont marks his clear explanation of the function of the short lyric, both as a genre and as a synecdochic emblem of his general poetic and formal procedures. It also exemplifies Wordsworth's general myth of self-possession: "Solipsistically magical," says Ross, "the [romantic poet's] 'self' can transform any external object into an aspect of itself while pretending to deny the externality of that object; it can envision and contain the infinite world by peering with the finite self, appearing to liberate the self from its own borders, appearing to capture the world for itself, appearing to father the world."[37]

I suggested in the introduction that Kenneth Burke's connection of synecdoche as a master trope with representation implies a whole psychology of the imagination; Wordsworth's poetic procedure, described so explicitly in the letter quoted above clarifies that connection. While the perception of power, a Miltonic conflation of private and public modes in poetry, attracts Wordsworth to this form, the power and peculiarity of Wordsworth's sonnets lie in their recording of what Hartman calls "a new attitude toward consciousness—a radical consciousness of consciousness"[38]—a fact that is most evident in the letter to Beaumont. Leigh Hunt, in an 1835 essay, asserted that "Wordsworth has proved himself the greatest contemplative poet this country has produced,"[39] going on to remark upon the way the poet can "express, at will, those innumerable shades of feeling which most other writers . . . either dismiss at once as inexpressible, or find so difficult of embodiment, as to content with shaping them forth but seldom. . . ." Nearly a century and half later, Hartman, calling Wordsworth "truly a subjective thinker," would identify this as the source of the poet's originality, noting "the way [his ideas] emerge from the depth of felt experience." Hartman adds that what he means by "subjectivity" is the following:

> Subjectivity means that the starting point for authentic reflection is placed in the individual consciousness. Not, necessarily, the empirical starting point, but the ontological, or what might also be called the Archimedean point. . . . If this Archimedean point is genuinely within the personal consciousness, dualism is overcome, for the source of inspiration (the empirical starting point) can be anything and anywhere.[40]

I would argue that the Wordsworthian sonnet is an emblem of the poet's effort to overcome this dualism. Each of the sonnets is a synecdoche of the much larger and more powerful visionary world that his imagination can create out of such moments; each poem can enclose a single moment or thought and hold it forth as a monument to that moment of heightened consciousness or fancy:

> Verily I think,
> Such place to me is sometimes like a dream
> Or map of the whole world: thoughts, link by link,
> Enter through ears and eyesight, with such gleam
> Of all things, that at last in fear I shrink,
> And leap at once from the delicious stream.
>   ("How sweet it is, when mother Fancy rocks")
>   (Lines 9–14)

This "place" is just the kind of ontological starting point I think Hartman means, an "anyplace" that opens up, out of itself, a whole dream or visionary world to explore. Note once again the synecdochic figuration of "this place" as "a map of the whole world," the literal place of nature containing whole worlds inside it. The sonnet's lyric plot is both the space of the poem and also the narrative of its "mapping" and exploration.

This troping of form as moments of thought or vision appears in one more sonnet that could also be classified as a sonnet on the sonnet, "'There is a pleasure in poetic pains.'" The octave describes the difficulties of the poet's work as wearing the Muses' "lightest chains" of rhyme (like Keats's fetters), particularly at the moment when that perfect rhyme eludes him. The sestet, however, names the compensation for those pains with figures of form that are already familiar to us:

> Yet he repines not, if his thought stand clear,
> At last, of hindrance and obscurity,
> Fresh as the star that crowns the brow of morn;
> Bright, speckless, as a softly-moulded tear
> The moment it has left the virgin's eye,
> Or rain-drop lingering on the pointed thorn.
>
> (Lines 9–14)

The star, the tear, the raindrop: all are figures of the "orbicular body" Wordsworth sees in the sonnet, miniature versions of that visionary gleam, left behind at that moment of clarity.

IV

Wordsworth's ability to create poetical emblems of significant moments, whether imaginative or political, developed even before 1802; as mentioned above, although Wordsworth's conversion moment initiated his programmatic sonnet writing, he had in fact written a handful of such poems. Some were mere exercises, but some few pointed already to Wordsworth's originality in this form—and thus further complicate our reception of his 1802 conversion narrative. "When slow from pensive twilight's latest gleams," probably composed between late 1788 and the end of 1791 and never included in any later collection, anticipates Wordsworth's handling of imaginative vision, temporality and poetic form, which becomes the crux of so many of his later sonnets:

> When slow from pensive twilight's latest gleams
> "O'er the dark mountain top descends the ray"

That stains with crimson tinge the water grey
And still, I listen while the dells and streams
And vanished woods a lulling murmur make;
As Vesper first begins to twinkle bright
And on the dark hillside the cottage light,
With long reflexion streams across the lake.
The lonely grey-duck darkling on his way
Quacks clamorous; deep the measured strokes rebound
Of unseen oar parting with hollow sound
While the slow curfew shuts the eye of day
Soothed by the stilly scene with many a sigh,
Heaves the full heart nor knows for whom, or why.[41]

With the echoes of Milton, Gray, and Goldsmith permeating the entire work, the sonnet is clearly an early effort to position oneself in relation to a tradition; the text here becomes—in a manner not dissimilar to Keats's work later on—an echo chamber of previous poems. Beyond the literariness of its language, however, the sonnet is also an early struggling with the psychology of imagination, with the relationship of poet, nature, and imagination also coming to the fore. The poem has an almost double movement; there is a peculiar way in which imagery simultaneously fades and emerges. Since the "latest gleams" of twilight are said to "descend," one imagines darkness, conversely, to "rise." And, indeed, images do rise up in the subsequent lines, *from* the fading of light: the color of sunset "stains with crimson tinge the water grey / And still"; the "vanished woods," dells, and streams become sources of "a lulling murmur."

This process of emergence from darkness is figured once again in the image of the star, Vesper, whose very form is only *possible* in the fading or absence of all other visible forms and all other light (again, opposite to the Miltonic overshadowing of Hesperus by the moon). The dominant figure of the sonnet, in fact, is that star, an emblem of natural form there. And yet at line 7, Wordsworth crucially connects that starlight with the twinkling of a distant cottage light on the dark hillside. In a move so characteristic of Wordsworth, heaven and earth are intimately joined in the image of a "gleam" or light, the long reflection of the cottage light no doubt joining the reflection of the sky and of Vesper in the lake.[42] They are separate forms transformed into one by the reflecting mind of the poet.

The sestet is marked by a gradual blacking-out of nature as the "eye of day" closes. Geoffrey Hartman has remarked that Wordsworth tends to emphasize sound over sight;[43] the movement of this sonnet is an early instance of what will become that characteristic preference for the aural. As the sestet begins, it is unclear whether or not the grey-duck, himself devoid of color and (Miltonically) "darkling on his way" like the twilight itself, is visible at all; it is his "quacks clamorous" that are registered. The poem continues in a sort of "descent" into sound; the deep strokes of the "unseen oar" are called "hollow sound."

The vision of emptiness is resisted, however, by the presence of the poet. The only direct reference to the poet is as a listener, as visual images fade. But the dialectics of the seen and unseen, presence and absence, are recontained by the "full heart" of the poet, which itself is a metonymy for his perceiving mind and the emotional and intellectual reflections upon the fading scene. Ultimately, the "full heart" that expresses itself in sighs is a figure for the poem itself, a small, contained form that remembers the fullness of the scene as it passes away into time. Thus from the standpoint of temporality the poem is also complex: although it records a moment filled with sights and sounds, this record emphasizes the mutability of that moment; the stillness of the scene is countered at each point by the progress of time. The moment is continuously passing out of itself, and the signs of its presence fade away. The poem comes to be *about* the fading of the original moment, and the way the full heart and the poem can preserve it. Out of the fading of the scene emerges the star that is reflected in the lake; out of absence emerges the poem.

Formally, too, the sonnet is early evidence of Wordsworth's originality as a sonnet writer. The division of the octave into quatrains, though preserved by rhyme (albeit an unconventional scheme, *abbacddc*), is violated by the enjambment at line 4, where the poet's perceptions of dells, streams, and woods overflow the sonnet's quatrain structure. Although the octave ends where it should, the sestet does not bring an expected "turn" in the poem, unless it is a turning inward—not so much a *volta* as an involution.[44] The rhyme scheme supports such a notion, since the sestet opens with a *b*-rhyme, linking the second part of the sonnet closely to the first. Verbal repetitions of "slow" (lines 1 and 12) and "still" (4 and 13) further draw the poem's structure back around on itself.

This early poem is less mature than later ones, but is nevertheless remarkable for its paradigmatic handling of the form. Wordsworth had already discovered for himself the "orbicular" or "dew-drop" structure that he defined many years later, and that had produced the unity he would so admire in Milton. The poem is, like so many of the later sonnets, an inquest into the imaginative process that *creates* poetry, an anatomy of imagination that revolves around the formal impulse. The poet explores here, as he would in so many later sonnets, the dialectic of presence and absence, of the moment and the passing away of that moment, and the emergence of form out of the memory's renewal or reflection of images. Thus does this sonnet become more than that echo chamber of previously written poems, for all its literariness; Wordsworth has already discovered the process by which his own individual experience will contain everything outside, or previous to, himself.

The mature version of the early sonnet is undoubtedly the sonnet "Composed by the Side of Grasmere Lake," probably written in 1807 and first published in 1819:

> Clouds, lingering yet, extend in solid bars
> Through the grey west; and lo! these waters, steeled
> By breezeless air to smoothest polish, yield
> A vivid repetition of the stars;
> Jove, Venus, and the ruddy crest of Mars
> Amid his fellows beauteously revealed
> At happy distance from earth's groaning field,
> Where ruthless mortals wage incessant wars.
> Is it a mirror?—or the nether Sphere
> Opening to view the abyss in which she feeds
> Her own calm fires?—But list! a voice is near;
> Great Pan himself low-whispering through the reeds,
> "Be thankful, thou; for, if unholy deeds
> Ravage the world, tranquillity is here!"

The disjunction of the earlier poem is once again explored through Wordsworth's utilization of the binary structure of the sonnet. But the obvious and striking trope of this poem is reflection, and the sonnet form's octave/sestet structure is used not only in its conventional argumentative or analytical mode but also as a trope for mental renewal or reflection. This is true in many Wordsworth sonnets, but perhaps nowhere more so than in this one. De Man reads the trope of reflection in the poem as a figure for

the kind of double vision that allows him to see landscapes as objects, as well as entrance gates to a world lying beyond visible nature. "Tranquillity," it seems, is the right balance between the literal and symbolic vision, a balance reflected in a harmonious proportion between mimetic and symbolic language in the diction of the poem.[45]

A formal reading of this poem would certainly support this conclusion. Wordsworth uses the play of quatrains and tercets, octave and sestet, to its fullest, balancing the two quatrains between descriptions of direct and imagined vision, and opening wide the disjunctive relationship of these two kinds of vision just at the point where the sonnet itself, its octave complete, mirrors itself formally in the sestet.

The *volta* is an important point in any sonnet, but crucial for this poem. The surprising question that opens the sestet—"Is it a mirror?"—must be answered equivocally from a *formal* standpoint. The octave *is* "mirrored" by the sestet—but of course it is different by being spatially "under" and temporally "after" it. Wordsworth plays with these additional tropes of "above" and "below" by describing a vision that is not direct but mediated by imagination and thought.[46] While agreeing that the poem is a symbol of the "complex act of pure vision," I would add that the poem is a symbol of the complex act of *re*vision; thus would I highlight the fact that these two kinds of vision are not simultaneous; one follows, and follows from, the other.

De Man notes that at the end of this sonnet, the eye is drawn inward, "from an open to an enclosed space,"[47] with the conflated heights and depths of the scene's description delimited by the "solid bars" that open the poem. I have discussed the significance of self-enclosure in Wordsworth's sonnets, and here, as in "Nuns fret not" or "Scorn not the Sonnet," that enclosure is emblematic of Wordsworth's attention to the subjective, the self-enclosed reflections of the poet's own mind opening out into a kind of vision wider than mere perception. And like so many of his sonnets, this one also includes a figure of form itself: the reeds through which Pan whispers. The visionary thoughts, while having their starting point in the visual, are expressed, finally, through instrumental form.

The Grasmere Lake sonnet has an added dimension absent from the juvenile sonnet, "When slow from pensive twilight's latest gleams": an awareness of historical presences—those incessant wars that underlie the scenery and the mythology of the poem's language. But that awareness is itself delimited by Wordsworth's tendency to absorb the historical into the subjective, a conflation that achieved for Wordsworth the Miltonic sonnet stance we looked at earlier. Imagination is the source of "power" in Wordsworth, and even in poems that concern themselves with political power, this poet returns frequently to the matter of imaginative power. Stuart Curran is thus correct when he observes that Wordsworth's political sonnets are as "psychological in their orientation" as those apparently devoid of political content.

A particularly striking example of this general pattern is the set of sonnets "Composed While the Author Was Engaged in Writing a Tract, Occasioned by the Convention of Cintra" (1808; published 1815). The octave of the first sonnet resonates with Miltonic imagery and diction:

Not 'mid the World's vain objects that enslave
The free-born Soul—that World whose vaunted skill
In selfish interest perverts the will,
Whose factions lead astray the wise and brave—
Not there; but in dark wood and rocky cave,
And hollow vale which foaming torrents fill
With omnipresent murmur as they rave
Down their steep beds, that never shall be still:

(Lines 1–8)

As in Milton's Piedmont Massacre sonnet, which must be intertextually behind this one, Nature herself echoes with the injustices of human operations. But Milton's sestet never took this kind of evasive turn:

Here, mighty Nature! in this school sublime
I weigh the hopes and fears of suffering Spain;
For her consult the auguries of time,
And through the human heart explore my way;
And look and listen—gathering, whence I may,
Triumph, and thoughts no bondage can restrain.

(Lines 9–14)

The apocalyptic opening out of this sonnet's close is typical of the Miltonic sonnet mode, but this sestet's turn to nature and to the private heart and mind plays out in a more fully Wordsworthian mode Milton's own conflation of the public and the private man, by which the poet's own examinations of Nature can lead to moral truths with universal implications. The momentum of this sonnet's close is brought about by the power of Wordsworth's vision of "the human heart"; indeed that momentum is so strong that it pushes Wordsworth beyond the limits of this single poem and compels him to add, as if spontaneously, a second, more remarkable sonnet, "Composed at the Same Time and on the Same Occasion":

I dropped my pen; and listened to the Wind
That sang of trees up-torn and vessels tost—
A midnight harmony; and wholly lost
To the general sense of men by chains confined
Of business, care, or pleasure; or resigned
To timely sleep. Thought I, the impassioned strain,
Which, without aid of numbers, I sustain,
Like acceptation from the World will find.
Yet some with apprehensive ear shall drink

> A dirge devoutly breathed o'er sorrows past;
> And to the attendant promise will give heed—
> The prophecy,—like that of this wild blast,
> Which, while it makes the heart with sadness shrink,
> Tells also of bright calms that shall succeed.

The surprising opening of this poem marks the immediacy of the poet's apprehension of the implications of his thought. Wordsworth's vision of his own private freedom in the first poem is so apocalyptic in its public implication, that the poet drops his pen as if stunned by the momentum of the thought itself.[48] The poem's connection of the blast of historical violence, the blast of the wind outside, and the blast that is the utterance of the poet himself is a remarkable conflation that reveals the source of "power" or "momentum" in Wordsworth's sonnets: his consciousness of his own subjectivity at the moment.[49] The voicing of that moment of self-awareness becomes the very occasion of the sonnet.

V

Thus far this discussion of Wordsworth's sonnets has stressed their visionary nature, but it is important to note that Wordsworth's characteristic inquest toward that visionary stance involves once again a revisionary strategy. Theresa M. Kelley has described a "revisionary aesthetic" as characteristic of Wordsworth generally, and her book develops a number of fine readings that connect that aesthetic and its procedures to Wordsworth's handling of political themes. Particularly relevant to my study is her discussion of Wordsworth's *Ecclesiastical Sonnets* and of the 1822 *Memorials of a Tour of the Continent*, a series that includes several sonnets. Kelley's interests are not formal. But her conclusions regarding the speaker's association of liberty and resistance, and her attention to the juncture of the mind and sensations of the sublime in these political verses, dovetail with my argument's focus on the revisionary impulse that is visible, and is indeed formally troped, in nearly all of Wordsworth's sonnets.[50] Indeed, despite Wordsworth's emphasis, in his comments on the sonnet and in his own work, on a unitary model of the sonnet, Wordsworth *does* characteristically employ the Italian octave-sestet division in order to trope formally the disjunctions of the poetic process.[51] One example is the well-known "The world is too much with us" (published 1807), which, like Hopkins's "The Sea and Skylark" (a poem that may allude to Wordsworth's), laments the gap between what one sees and what one *can* see in the mind's eye:

> The world is too much with us; late and soon,
> Getting and spending, we lay waste our powers:
> Little we see in Nature that is ours;
> We have given our hearts away, a sordid boon!
> This sea that bares her bosom to the moon;
> The winds that will be howling at all hours,
> And are up-gathered now like sleeping flowers;
> For this, for everything, we are out of tune;
> It moves us not.—Great God ! I'd rather be
> A Pagan suckled in a creed outworn;
> So might I, standing on this pleasant lea,
> Have glimpses that would make me less forlorn;
> Have sight of Proteus rising from the sea;
> Or hear old Triton blow his wreathèd horn.

The octave sets up the distance between nature and humanity, the polarities of "too much" and "little," "late and soon," "getting and spending" underlying a paradoxical trope of "possession": while we lay waste "our powers," we are unable to see that Nature, in which we see little that is "ours," is the source of those powers. The power we waste is very simply being able to *see* Nature through the imagination, as it is that power that reveals our connection to Nature. The highly figured description of the sea, giving back to the moon the light it reflects from its bosom, contrasts with the man who has given his heart away to the trivialities of a life without vision, without harmony with nature: "For this, for everything, we are out of tune."

The sestet's revision of this "forlorn" view, signaled by the "surprised" exclamation "Great God," is controlled by a crucial allusion to Spenser that I have seen acknowledged but not explicated, and that underscores the poem's obvious turn away from "the world" and toward a visionary world in which man's relation to nature is much more intimate. "Colin Clout Comes Home Again" shares several themes with this sonnet, including the proper place of a poet in the world of power and the relationship between the private and the public modes of the poet. William Oram describes Spenser's poem as a myth that "presents us with a world in which it is necessary to choose between competing values, and in which self-transcendence may be gained only with the loss of one's old self, and with it one's worldly name."[52] And at the moment in the poem to which Wordsworth alludes, the poem is precisely about the inability to "see" imaginatively. Colin Clout, Spenser's poet-figure, is describing to a group of shepherds and shepherdesses his sea trip from Ireland to the land of the "great shepheardesse, that *Cynthia* hight" (234), and has brought them as far as the headlands of the English coast, "An high headland thrust far into the sea, / Like to an horne, whereof the name it has, / Yet seemed to be a goodly pleasant lea" (lines 281–83). Cuddy interrupts to ask what land it is he means, "And is there other, then whereon we stand?" (line 290).

> Ah *Cuddy* (then quoth *Colin*) thous a fon,
> That has not seen least part of natures worke:
> Much more there is unkend, then thou doest kon,
> And much more that does from mens knowledge lurke.
>
> (Lines 292–95)

He goes on to describe a place where "learned arts do florish in great honor, / And poet's wits are had in peerlesse price" (lines 320–21). In Spenser's poem the land is one in which "God his gifts there plenteously bestowes, / But gracelesse men them greatly do abuse" (lines 326–27); so too in Wordsworth's poem, which picks up the trope of giving and transforms it into the more commercial "giving and taking." In the context of those Spenserian lines, line 4 of Wordsworth's poem ("We have given our hearts away, a sordid boon!") also suggests that in being unable to see anything in Nature that is "ours," we are giving away what was given to us gratis. We too (like the corrupt members of the court that Colin describes later in the poem) are deadened by the "selfe-regard of private good or ill" (line 682).

The sestet of Wordsworth's sonnet asks the reader to revise "the world" by reseeing it as through a poet's eye; the poem leads us not to a vision of any real specificity but to vision per se, or even more generally, to creative perception. The poet would "have glimpses," "have sight," "hear." The perception and the *awareness* of the perception are the power that opens out this poem's ending; as Carl Woodring has said, "[Wordsworth] does not speak of personal experience, but of poetic appearance of experience."[53] As a place of "perspective," Wordsworth's "pleasant lea" is an interesting transformation of the Spenserian one: Colin never actually *stands* on that lea, as he is coming toward it from the ocean; it is the mark of the new land's boundaries. But here, the poet is "standing" on that threshold itself, facing toward the sea, looking and listening. The poem's final image of the wreathed horn is a figure for the poem itself, an instrument that blasts a vision of the world forth to those "that [have] not seen least part of natures worke." It shepherds men in to that vision as Spenser's Proteus shepherds the "flocks" of the sea.[54]

A much more difficult example of just this process of a visionary reseeing is in Wordsworth's "Composed Upon Westminster Bridge, September 3, 1802":

Earth has not anything to show more fair:
Dull would he be of soul who could pass by
A sight so touching in its majesty:
This City now doth, like a garment, wear
The beauty of the morning; silent, bare,
Ships, towers, domes, theatres, and temples lie
Open unto the fields, and to the sky;
All bright and glittering in the smokeless air.
Never did the sun more beautifully steep
In his first splendour, valley, rock, or hill;
Ne'er saw I, never felt, a calm so deep!
The river glideth at his own sweet will:
Dear God! the very houses seem asleep;
And all that mighty heart is lying still!

Like the previous poem looked at, this one is about a reseeing: never before had the poet seen this scene in this way. The reseeing, however, is as a scene of poetry; that is, it is no longer the phenomenal reality that is being described but the poet's experience of it. This same process is visible in "It is a beauteous evening," where, as the sight of nature fades with the twilight, the poem emerges with its highly figured picture of the scene as a worshipping nun. In that poem, as in this one, there is a curious relationship between conscious and unconscious things: there the two "awakened" creatures are the "mighty Being" and the poet himself; here, by contrast, "that mighty heart" seems asleep, and only the poet awake. Typically, the poem's attention finally revolves around the figure of the poet himself.

Recent readings[55] of this sonnet have highlighted its profoundly problematic relationship to referentiality, signaled by figuration so elaborate that Wordsworth had to explain in a letter in 1836 that an apparent contradiction of trope in the poem existed "in the words only."[56] This figuration includes the catalog of "sights" that disperses the scene not simply into "plural generality"[57] but into a picture of things that the poet could not possibly see at all; his imagination expands far beyond the frame of this picture into "the fields" and "the sky," and gathers all the figures of the octave into the "All" of line 8. At the end of the octave the poet is essentially standing on "this pleasant lea," opening the immediate scene into a wider one of field and sky; the vision of the city is described in terms *so* general that the octave's final figure is simply a light that illuminates everything. As Liu points out, these sights are unmappable; the poem's plot or narrative is its breaking out of formal barriers, expanding into the visionary.

The intensity of the octave is mirrored in the sestet; the poem's first line, "Earth has not anything to show more fair," is reiterated by the assertion that "*Never* did the sun more beautifully steep / In his first splendour," lines 9–10). It is as if this particular sunrise were the first one, and the poet the first man to see it—or else as if it were the *last*. The sestet's claim of "never before" engages the sonnet form's temporal intensity, gathering all previous moments into this single revelatory one; the shift from "Never did sun" to "Ne'er saw I" is crucial, as it marks finally the radical specificity of the poem lying in the "I" himself. Hartman reminds us that this "I" is distinctly not the physical "eye"; this descriptive poem is typical of Wordsworth in its "movement into vacancy, this dying of nature to the mind. . . ."[58] The bridge from the eye to the "I" is crossed just here, the city lying between field and sky, nature and the supernatural—and somewhere between the actual and the figurative, the poet's mediate perspective locating him between two shores. Liu is thus profoundly correct when he compares the poet in this scene of "imaginative imperialism" to the Keatsian poet-figure of the Cortez-I in "On First Looking into Chapman's Homer," each of whom "exclaims, and *claims*, '*I* see it!'"[59] The limits of the mental space that the sonnet form tropes are challenged by the all-encompassing expansiveness of poetic vision.

The poet's perspective in this poem is as much a threshold position as "this pleasant lea" in the last—though here the perspective has more finally to do with the paradox of temporality in the imaginative moment. The intensity of this moment and Wordsworth's characteristic celebration of its insight invest the scene with a static quality and contribute to a kind of monumentalism;[60] although it is not a sonnet on a painting, Wordsworth's Westminster Bridge sonnet almost has the feel of one, as it describes a calm and a deathlike quietness. But that same monumentalism signals this poem's disturbing uncanniness. While the poet has affixed this place and moment with a certain visionary significance, by the end of the octave Wordsworth's "consciousness of consciousness," as Hartman called it, is so radical that even that vision is revised.

The figuration of the disturbing factor highlights the presence of another "will"—that is, the river's. Although the river partakes of the calm, it is a figural disturbance associated *not* with the poem's general movement upward (particularly in the sestet's first couplet) toward the brightness of the air and sky, but with a new movement in the sestet both inward and downward, into the "depth" of calm and of the river itself. This involution includes a recognition of the somatic aspect of the poet's imaginative engagement with the scene. Line 11's shift of senses from vision to "feeling"—"Ne'er saw I, never felt, a calm so deep!"—is a shift from eye to heart, essentially, that signals a momentary blanking out of what phenomenal vision there is in the octave.

The collapse into radical subjectivity is arrested by the intrusion of the river, with its paradoxical reminder of eternality, on the one hand, and ephemerality on the other. This recall of temporality reminds the poet of his own somatic existence, which, while highlighting the correspondence between inner and outer feeling, also highlights the monumental aspect of this visionary moment. The poem's second climax records what Miller calls a proleptic awareness of Wordsworth's own death.[61] The stilled heart of the city becomes analogous to an anticipation of his own stilled heart, whether that heart emblematizes the death of the poet, as Miller suggests, or more immediately the death of the revelatory moment as the sonnet is composed.

While the poem itself memorializes either one and both, Wordsworth's notion of the sonnet as a "transcript of the heart" suggests one last dimension: that this sonnet's final image of the heart, disembodied as it is in the poem, could also relate to a figuration of the poem itself, of the poem's own somatic aspect. The poem's inquest into the momentary "calm" or tranquility, which always signals in Wordsworth the recognition of imagination's insight, is accompanied by the poem's awareness of its own materiality as a transcript that will outlast both the poet himself and the moment the poem records. Indeed, this poem's figure of itself hovers between the heart and the river, since the poem is a monument to that heartfelt, mind-created moment of calm and revelation—and to its own eternality as a poem, preserving a visionary moment that is long past.

VI

This monumentalism brings me to one final matter to consider before leaving Wordsworth: his handling of temporality in the sonnet. That matter has been implicit in much of the previous discussion, for what I have been calling "momentum" in the Wordsworthian sonnet springs from the "moment"-ness of the occasion itself. The emergence of form that so often constitutes the sonnets themselves is a presencing for which the poem becomes a self-reflective emblem or icon. This framing of the moment leads Wordsworth to write sonnets not only about the subjective experience of particular moments but also about the framing itself. Wordsworth reinvigorates a subgenre of sonnet, the sonnet on paintings. While the implications of these so-called ekphrastic sonnets will be fully explored by poet-painter Dante Gabriel Rossetti, Wordsworth's own sonnets on pictures set the terms. A poem like "Upon the Sight of a Beautiful Picture [Painted by Sir G. H. Beaumont, Bart.]" (1811; published 1815) is itself a sonnet on the sonnet, meditating not only on the occasion of the painting but also on its own occasion:

> Praised be the Art whose subtle power could stay
> Yon cloud, and fix it in that glorious shape;
> Nor would permit the thin smoke to escape,
> Nor those bright sunbeams to forsake the day;
> Which stopped that band of travellers on their way,
> Ere they were lost within the shady wood;
> And showed the Bark upon the glassy flood
> For ever anchored in her sheltering bay.
> Soul-soothing Art! whom Morning, Noontide, Even,
> Do serve with all their changeful pageantry;
> Thou, with ambition modest yet sublime,
> Here, for the sight of mortal man, hast given
> To one brief moment caught from fleeting time
> The appropriate calm of blest eternity.[62]

The attention to the painting itself is concerned less with actual description than with the ability of painting to freeze time. The octave emphasizes the way the poem "stays" or "fixes" the moment, neither smoke nor sun nor travelers are allowed to pass out of the perspective of the frame. In a letter to Beaumont to which this sonnet was appended, Wordsworth noted that while "the images of the smoke and the travellers are taken from your Picture[,] the rest were added, in order to place the thought in a clear point of view, and for the sake of variety."[63] The primary image Wordsworth added is the ship, anchored "for ever" in the motionless and glassy bay, an emblematic figure of the stillness of the moment.

The sestet moves from description of the painting itself to general statement: the progressive temporality implicit in the narrative that underlies the painting—the escaping of smoke, the wandering of the travelers—is countered by Art's ability to catch "one brief moment" from "fleeting time." Wordsworth so privileges these memorialized moments that he suggests that the pageantry of time, with its constant changing of forms and light, "serves" Art by providing it an infinite number of such "brief moments." Fixed and framed in this painting or in this brief poem,[64] each of these moments can be taken as a synecdoche for all time; the whole of mutable time is absorbed into the "calm eternity" of the moment.

Although the poem's final line works to expand the moment into an eternity, there is still an undertone of the paradox that would so trouble Rossetti in his own sonnets later in the century: Even while rendering the moment immovable in the painting or in the poem, the artist has paradoxically deadened it. The profound question is whether art in fixed forms like painting, sculpture, or poetry *can* really resist the death of the moment, when in a subtle way the work of art actually tropes that death.[65] Wordsworth's sonnets on paintings are efforts to probe this connection of the moment not to experience and life, but to death.

Wordsworth's contextualization of such moments in sequences—framing of a different sort—is one way in which he handles this paradox. If the sonnet is a spatialization and emblem of a moment, the river, which underlies his tour sequences,[66] the *River Duddon* sequence, and even the *Ecclesiastical Sonnets*, is clearly a figure of "time's changeful pageant." For this reason Dublin archbishop Richard Chenevix Trench, also a sometime literary commentator with a great interest in the sonnet, identified Wordsworth as

> the first who conceived a poem made up of a succession of Sonnets, each complete in itself, but each at the same time constituting, so to speak, a stanza of that larger poem whereof it formed a part; just as in a bracelet made up of a string of cameos, or mosaics, each may be a perfect little picture in itself, while at the same time contributing to the beauty and perfection of a larger whole.[67]

While I agree with James Chandler, who sees the sequence form and the river as analogues of each other, emblematizing time "from a point of view which is traditionalist, in that it sees time as always passing on and never passing away,"[68] I also see these sequences and contextualizations more as a stay against the discontinuity of the moment. That which the single sonnet, with its contracted intensities and tensions, can only imply is explored more fully in the sequence, and in this the *River Duddon* sequence excels. If Wordsworth's single sonnet is a visionary inquest into the fullness of the poet's apperception of the moment, his sequence is a "radiant progress," as the *Duddon* sequence names itself in sonnet 32, that attempts to trace the hidden origins of the river. These two projects clearly coincide at *Duddon*'s "Conclusion" (sonnet 33), when Wordsworth turns from the river to "thy Poet":

> And may thy Poet, cloud-born Stream! be free—
> The sweets of earth contentedly resigned,
> And each tumultuous working left behind
> At seemly distance—to advance like Thee;
> Prepared, in peace of heart, in calm of mind
> And soul, to mingle with Eternity!

(Lines 9–14)

The poet's "calm of mind and soul" expands out of itself just as the river itself does in sonnet 32: "in radiant progress toward the Deep / Where mightiest rivers into powerless sleep / Sink, and forget their nature—*now* expands / Majestic Duddon, over smooth flat sands / Gliding in silence with unfettered sweep!" (lines 4–8). Wordsworth had said that in the sonnet series there was a "restriction" of his development of subject, since "the frame of the Sonnet imposed upon me, narrowing unavoidably the range of thought, and precluding, tho[ugh] not without its advantages, many graces to which a freer movement of verse would naturally have led."[69] Nevertheless, the final poem widens the narrow room of the single poems that make up this mental journey by casting itself, and all the previous poems in the series, in a retrospective light. Retrospection is not simply memory, however, but a reseeing that reveals something new. The final poem, "After-Thought" (sonnet 34), opens the sequence *out* of the moments that the individual sonnets have captured, and in an expansive sweep gathers all those moments into a single final one in which past, present and future are collapsed:[70]

> I thought of Thee, my partner and my guide,
> As being past away.—Vain sympathies!
> For, backward, Duddon! as I cast my eyes,
> I see what was, and is, and will abide;
> Still glides the Stream, and shall for ever glide;
> The Form remains, the Function never dies;
> While we, the brave, the mighty, and the wise,
> We Men, who in our morn of youth defied
> The elements, must vanish;—be it so!
> Enough, if something from our hands have power
> To live, and act, and serve the future hour;
> And if, as toward the silent tomb we go,
> Through love, through hope, and faith's transcendent dower,
> We feel that we are greater than we know.

The sequence becomes, as the introductory poem to his brother describes it, a series of "Moments, to cast a look behind, / And profit by those kindly rays / That through the clouds do sometimes steal, / And all the far-off past reveal" ("To Rev. Dr. Wordsworth," lines 69–72). The sequentiality of the sonnets defies the transience of the moment ("I thought of Thee . . . As being past away") by reilluminating all that came before with an assertion of being "greater than we know," an assertion of duration even as the language of death, the body "mingling with Eternity," creeps in.

Wordsworth's pattern was similar in his other sequences. "Author's Voyage down the Rhine (Thirty Years Ago)," which concludes his *Tour on the Continent, 1820* sequence, also brings together tropes of sequentiality and of passing time with the "calm eternity" of a moment of meditation:

> The confidence of Youth our only Art,
> And Hope gay Pilot of the bold design,
> We saw the living Landscapes of the Rhine,
> Reach after reach, salute us and depart;
> Slow sink the Spires,—and up again they start!
> But who shall count the Towers as they recline
> O'er the dark steeps, or on the horizon line
> Striding, with shattered crests, the eye athwart?
> More touching still, more perfect was the pleasure,
> When hurrying forward till the slackening stream
> Spread like a spacious Mere, we there could measure
> A smooth free course along the watery gleam,
> Think calmly on the past, and mark at leisure
> Features which else had vanished like a dream.

From the most general perspective, what these sequences highlight is a movement characteristic of nearly all his sonnets, whether the single sonnet or a sonnet series: Wordsworth attempts to shift the function of the sonnet from the merely consolatory or compensatory to the revelatory. The figures of light so characteristic in his sonnets do not cast shadows—that is, the light is not simply a negative image of absence—but a radiant light that symbolizes nothing less than godlike vision, with its all-encompassing perspective upon temporality itself. So, too, at the conclusion of the *Ecclesiastical Sonnets in Series* (1821; published 1822), where the river image, the origin of which he sought "upon the heights of Time" ("Introduction," line 9) is troped as the biblical "living waters":

> Why sleeps the future, as a snake enrolled,
> Coil within coil, at noon-tide? For the WORD
> Yields, if with unpresumptuous faith explored,
> Power at whose touch the sluggard shall unfold
> His drowsy rings. Look forth!—that Stream behold,
> THAT STREAM upon whose bosom we have passed
> Floating at ease while nations have effaced
> Nations, and Death has gathered to his fold
> Long lines of mighty Kings—look forth, my Soul!
> (Nor in this vision be thou slow to trust)
> The living Waters, less and less by guilt
> Stained and polluted, brighten as they roll,

> Till they have reached the eternal City—built
> For the perfected Spirits of the just!

(Sonnet 47)

This final sonnet is typical of Wordsworth in its final experiencing of eternity in a moment or the revelation of the eternal in the ephemeral or passing.[71] As in his single sonnets, so in his sequences: Wordsworth's revisions of form stem from what Abrams would call a "re-creative way of seeing"[72] that includes a visionary resolution of the dialectics of temporality. The separateness of moments and of sonnet stanzas takes on a resonance in the sequence's ultimate revision of itself as a luminous, revelatory moment.[73]

VII

The title of this chapter, "Wordsworth's 'Inquest' and the Visionary Sonnet," was suggested to me by the last of this poet's sonnets that I wish to consider, "It is no Spirit who from heaven hath flown" (composed around 1803; published 1807).[74] This tailed sonnet, with three lines added beyond the conventional fourteen-line scheme, brings together the visionary and spatial tropes introduced in this chapter:

> It is no Spirit who from heaven hath flown,
> And is descending on his embassy;
> Nor Traveller gone from earth the heavens to espy!
> 'Tis Hesperus—there he stands with glittering crown,
> First admonition that the sun is down!
> For yet it is broad day-light: clouds pass by;
> A few are near him still—and now the sky,
> He hath it to himself—'tis all his own.
> O most ambitious Star! an inquest wrought
> Within me when I recognized thy light;
> A moment I was startled at the sight:
> And, while I gazed, there came to me a thought
> That I might step beyond my natural race
> As thou seem'st now to do; might one day trace
> Some ground not mine; and, strong her strength above,
> My Soul, an Apparition in the place,
> Tread there with steps that no one shall reprove!

The poem is itself an inquest wrought into the limits of phenomenal vision and into the power of the poet's imagination to trace an area beyond that.

Lying between the boundaries of heaven and earth, the star—that recurrent Miltonic image of imagination's preeminence for Wordsworth—belongs to neither realm, but to the transitional twilight, not a "place" at all but a time or a "state." The octave ends in a moment of repletion in which the star, far from being diminished by the vastness of the surrounding sky, dominates it. "Crowned" with its own glittering light, the star radiates outward and "takes possession" of the heavens: "and now the sky, / He hath it to himself—'tis all his own." Neither a messenger from some supernatural realm nor a pilgrim from the natural one, Hesperus is almost an agent of the transition from one realm to the other, and stands not only as a signal or emblem but as a forerunner of that transition.

The sonnet's *volta,* however, drastically shifts the perspective of the poem. The octave locates the poet below, watching clouds pass by and the star emerge in the darkening sky. But the meditations that accompany these observations are broken at the *volta* by the poet's shock of recognition—a recognition of an image of *himself* in the star. Whereas the poet began this sonnet located at a fixed point, by the sonnet's end the perspective has radiated outward into what Hopkins, at the other end of this study, would call a "belonging field of the self." That identity is strengthened by the intrusion of the apostrophe at line 9, introducing an I-Thou relationship absent in the octave.

Thus does this poem too become an anatomy of Wordsworth's imaginative process, and like the poems considered previously it succeeds in describing not just the impulse that led to the poem but also the composition of the poem itself[75]—the lyric plot of the sonnet, the "myth of self-possession" (Ross). The "inquest wrought / Within me" at this recognition scene is not simply a mental journey inward. It is an "inquest *wrought*" (emphasis mine), or fashioned; it is an inquest into the gleam of form. The poet realizes that in order to describe the imaginative expansiveness that this moment brought to him, the poem's form must, like the star itself, be "ambitious,"[76] ready to "step beyond" its own form as the star "seem[s] now to do." The boundaries defined at the poem's opening are redrawn; the poet traces with a visionary finger wider boundaries, "some ground not mine" that the poet can come to possess.

That imaginative expansiveness is troped by the very form of the poem, as just there, at the poet's announcement of his *own* ambition, the sonnet breaks beyond its own "natural race," with the word "trace" at the end of the fourteenth, enjambed line leading into new sonnet "ground." Through this breaking of new formal ground, the poet clearly affiliates himself with the star: "and, strong her strength above, / My Soul, an Apparition in the place, / Tread there with steps that no one shall reprove!" The implicit challenge in the last line underscores the forcefulness of Wordsworth's *own* possession of the star-as-trope; with its light he decks himself (like the Dante of "Scorn not" perhaps) with his own glittering crown. With characteristic bravura, Wordsworth's caudate sonnet powerfully reanimates the star as an ambitious trope for the poet, who has in effect not only taken Milton's fire but has defined a poetic that powerfully appropriates that precursor, and locates that fire within Wordsworth himself. But the sonnet also shows how poetic form itself is co-opted into Wordsworth's myth.

Despite the lateness of his arrival as a sonnet writer, Wordsworth's impact on the history of the genre is difficult to overestimate. It essentially forced a diversion from the sentimental, "lonely feeling" strain that had predominated contemporaneously (and would continue to flourish), but that, Wordsworth implies in his critical comments, he considered undignified and sentimental—"unmanly." For each of the poets whom I will go on to discuss, the impact of the reconception of the sonnet was different, though always palpable and profound. While one would find there formal strategies for handling his own poetic burden, another would highlight implicit paradoxes—particularly regarding temporality—from which it is difficult to escape. In the latter category falls Percy Bysshe Shelley, who clearly detected Wordsworth's success in transforming the sonnet into a formal metaphor for a powerful consciousness and for a "heroic" or public voice, but who also detected in that procedure the weakness of his precursor's position regarding the engagement of subjectivity and history.

2

A Figure of Resistance:
The Conspiring Reader in Shelley's
Sonnets and "West Wind" Ode

Percy Bysshe Shelley is not a "sonneteer"; he never wrote sonnets system-atically, as did Bowles, Coleridge, Wordsworth, Keats, or Hunt, and we have no critical comments on the form from him. And yet he has a place in this account, for he is an eminent sonnet writer. The few sonnets he did write display a mastery and comprehension of the form and its power. Although R. D. Havens remarks that none of them "show[s] any influence from Wordsworth,"[1] my argument here is that the Wordsworthian "author-ity," gained in the sonnet form and through Wordsworth's revisionary poetics there, informs Shelley's employment of the sonnet. Shelley's engagement in the form preserves the Wordsworthian dialectic of radiance and contain-ment, of progressive and static temporality; these poems clearly partake of the connection that Wordsworth makes between private and public voice, or between personal and social history.

This is not to say, however, that Shelley accepts that authority uncrit-ically; indeed this poet's critique of Wordsworth's monolithic stance is matched by a pressuring of the tyranny of a poetic form. The construction of Shelley's sonnets suggests that the poet recognized *closure* as form's most tyrannical element, closing off the poem from any possibility of change or development—for these sonnets are characterized by an open-endedness that resists closure. The implications of that are hardly incidental. The open-endedness of the sonnet space, which Wordsworth so clearly associated with "mental space," leads toward a revised view of subjectivity that better serves Shelley's revolutionary politics. Ronald Tetreault has argued that Shelley's notion of authorial subjectivity is "decentred" in his public poems by his awareness of *the reader*. The participation of the reader "generates a process by which meanings come to be shared, but this process is a dialogi-cal one in which the 'otherness' of readers' intentions is acknowledged."[2]

That acknowledgment of the reader certainly informs the sonnets, and underlies an effort to destabilize the authority of the speaker in favor of the reader. The poems' open-endedness is a refusal to monumentalize a single vision—as that results only in the kind of tyrannical leaders and habits of thinking that Shelley loathes—by deferring finally to the interpretation of the reader herself. By this means, the sonnet remains the radiant figure as Wordsworth envisions it, its tropological momentum directed outward—but its agency is directed now toward the future, not toward the conflation of past and present that we see in Wordsworth's visionary sonnets. Shelley's notion of the temporality of the sonnet is also apocalyptic, but it is essentially anticipatory rather than retrospective.

Shelley is usually described as finding the sonnet an inimical form,[3] one with which he grew quickly impatient and therefore quickly abandoned. Walter Mönch suggests that the power of Shelley's own restless and radical thoughts explode the form from inside, or disable it, as it were:

aber die Form wird vom Gedanken zerbrocken, oder aber der Gedanke zerbricht an der Form selbst und bleibt Torso;—aber gerade das Torsohafte des Gedankens ist dem Sonett wesenfremd. Shelley vermag seine Kraft und Genialität nicht wie Lope oder Shakespeare im Sonett zu bändigen; sie reissen ihn fort. . . .[4]

Mönch does except "Ode to the West Wind," admiring its "unerhörte metrische Bewegheit," though implying that there is a lack of real control. Impatient Shelley may have been, but even his earliest sonnet efforts are extremely skillful. His later sonnets are not only masterful in their form and in their awareness of the form's history, but also formally original in their near-dissolution of generic boundaries.

The significant early poems include "Sonnet: To a Balloon laden with Knowledge" and "Sonnet: On launching some Bottles filled with Knowledge into the Bristol Channel," both composed in August 1812. Of these sonnets I would assert what Mönch says of Shelley's sonnets in general: "Was er an Sonetten hinausschludert, sind geballte Ideen, packend, aufruttelnd, erregend. . . ."[5] Mönch's evocation of Shelley flinging out sonnets as clenched or clustered "Ideen" is an apt one, for that really is the image of both sonnets, each a vessel, whether airborne or water-borne, for knowledge. In both poems this knowledge is figured as a radiance that, when the balloon itself is burst or the bottle opened, will project itself beyond those vessels to become, in the first sonnet, "A watch-light," "A beacon in the darkness of the Earth," "A Sun which, o'er the renovated scene, / Shall dart like Truth where Falsehood yet has been."[6] In the second sonnet

("On launching some Bottles . . ."), knowledge is a radiance that will gleam "from pole to pole, / And tyrant-hearts with powerless envy burst / To see their night of ignorance dispersed" (lines 12–14). If we may for a moment take these images of vessels as images of poetic form as well, what Shelley is trying to imagine is a way in which the contents are liberated from the form itself. Form is troped not simply as containment but as an active "vehicle" of the dispersement of power—and thus as open-ended.

These crucial early sonnets already suggest a role for poetic form in Shelley's revolutionary and apocalyptic vision of the world, about which so much has already been written. With their central trope of radiance and their concern with revolutionary change and the imaginative vision that must accompany or even prepare that change, these sonnets align Shelley with the revolutionary and revelatory sonnet writing of Milton and Wordsworth before him—a lineage Shelley clearly recognizes. The figure of radiance we have already seen in the sonnets of Wordsworth was passed from Milton to Wordsworth, and now it passes to Shelley.

That recognition is accompanied, however, by a sense of irony, disappointed as Shelley was by what he saw as Wordsworth's political apostasy; the authority of Wordsworth's Miltonic stance is undermined by what the younger poet regarded as misuse of that authority. It is, interestingly, around an image of radiance, a star—the figure of poetic originality identified in the last chapter—that this irony plays itself out in an early sonnet, "To Wordsworth." The star image appears in Wordsworth's well-known sonnet "London, 1802," which is addressed to Milton; it is a metaphoric link Wordsworth had made as early as 1794, when in a revised version of *An Evening Walk*, Wordsworth recalls the earlier poet at work on *Paradise Lost*, in hiding from vengeful Royalists:

> So Virtue, fallen on times to gloom consigned,
> Makes round her path the light she cannot find,
> And by her own internal lamp fulfills
> And asks no other star what Virtue wills . . .
> In dangerous night so Milton worked alone
> Cheared by a secret lustre all his own
> That with the deepening darkness clearer shone.
> (A398/9, de Selincourt, *Poetical Works,* 1.35)

According to Nicholas Roe, these lines should be linked to Wordsworth's awareness of the arrest and imprisonment of Britain's leading reformers in May, 1794—just when *An Evening Walk* was undergoing a reworking.[7] Exhibiting the same heroic stance and style as in Milton's heroic sonnets,

Wordsworth asks in "London, 1802" that Milton "return to us again" to "raise us up." "Thy soul was like a Star," he continues at the opening of the sestet, "and dwelt apart: / Thou hadst a voice whose sound was like the sea" (lines 9–10): the paratactic lines align "star" and "voice," both figures here of guidance and of freedom. It is not incidental, then, that the star should also be associated in another Wordsworth sonnet with the poet's country, England:

> Fair Star of evening, Splendour of the west,
> Star of my Country!—on the horizon's brink
> Thou hangest, stooping, as might seem, to sink
> On England's bosom; yet well pleased to rest,
> Meanwhile, and be to her a glorious crest
> Conspicuous to the Nations. Thou, I think,
> Shouldst be my Country's emblem; and shouldst wink,
> Bright Star! with laughter on her banners, drest
> In thy fresh beauty. There! that dusky spot
> Beneath thee, that is England; there she lies.
> Blessings be on you both! one hope, one lot,
> One life, one glory!—I, with many a fear
> For my dear Country, many heartfelt sighs,
> Among men who do not love her, linger here.

The poem's central anxiety is about the poet's separation from England. Composed (the title tells us) "by the Sea-Side, near Calais, August, in 1802," (and published in 1807), it is structured around a "there-here" opposition. The dash in line 12 registers that separation, situated as it is between the "one glory" that is England, and the forlorn "I." The emblematization of the star becomes an imaginative solution to that, bringing there here. But even more extraordinarily, the star and the poet become identified with each other in the poem, as both linger, the one physically, the other imaginatively, over England.

The integrity of this linkage (Milton-star/England-Wordsworth) is another matter, however. Nowhere is it more seriously questioned than in Shelley's "To Wordsworth" (1814 or 1815), where he too picks up the star image:

> Poet of Nature, thou hast wept to know
> That things depart which never may return:
> Childhood and youth, friendship and love's first glow,
> Have fled like sweet dreams, leaving thee to mourn.
> These common woes I feel. One loss is mine

Which thou too feel'st, yet I alone deplore.
Thou wert as a lone star, whose light did shine
On some frail bark in winter's midnight roar:
Thou hast like to a rock-built refuge stood
Above the blind and battling multitude:
In honoured poverty thy voice did weave
Songs consecrate to truth and liberty,—
Deserting these, thou leavest me to grieve,
Thus having been, that thou shouldst cease to be.

Published in 1816 along with *Alastor* and "Mutability," this sonnet is part of a pointed critique of Wordsworth's myth of loss and consolation, as well as his Miltonic posturing—the very "authority" that the last chapter located in his sonnets. Haunting this sonnet are several allusions to Wordsworth's poetry; Shelley's first quatrain, for example, echoes "Tintern Abbey" and the "Intimations Ode" in the tears marking the poet's knowledge "that things depart which never may return" (lines 1–2) and in the "common woes I feel" (line 4). In these echoes we hear the Wordsworthian imaginative agenda, though Shelley here elides the process of consolation in the loss.

As the sonnet moves, in its second quatrain, from what is gained by and from Wordsworth to what is lost, Shelley employs these allusions with increasing irony. The star that becomes for Wordsworth a figure of guidance emerges in Shelley's sonnet as a figure for a failed visionary. Yet another allusion may be to Wordsworth's invocation to the "prophetic Spirit" in "The Recluse" fragment of the preface to the 1814 edition of *The Excursion*: "upon me bestow / A gift of genuine insight; that my Song / With star-like virtue in its place may shine" (lines 87–89). But this quatrain emphasizes what "I," Shelley, feel as loss—and there is no consolation for it.

That gift of genuine insight is what Wordsworth thought he gained from Milton, an insight that would, to borrow Milton's words from his Sonnet 22, "lead me through the world's vain mask." Shelley too had hoped for no better guide than the example of a Wordsworth in his role as poet-prophet. But the star of "London, 1802," the elegiac emblem of the soul of Milton that dwelt apart, becomes in Shelley's sonnet "a lone star, whose light did shine / On some frail bark in winter's midnight roar" —but whose light has faded. Shelley recognizes the Miltonic nature of Wordsworth's project but also recognizes in it what he sees as Wordsworth's imaginative failure, an increasingly wide disjunction between poetical and political issues.[8]

It is worth noting that this sonnet is clearly modeled after a sonnet by Guido Cavalcanti to Dante ("Io vengo il giorno a te infinite volte") that Shelley translated in 1814 or 1815:[9]

Returning from its daily quest, my Spirit
Changed thoughts and vile in thee doth weep to find:
It grieves me that thy mild and gentle mind
Those ample virtues which it did inherit
Has lost. Once thou didst loathe the multitude
Of blind and madding men: I then loved thee—
I loved thy lofty songs and that sweet mood
When thou wert faithful to thyself and me.
I dare not now, through thy degraded state,
Own the delight thy strains inspire—in vain
I seek what once thou wert—we cannot meet
As we were wont. Again and yet again
Ponder my words: so the false Spirit shall fly
And leave to thee thy true integrity.

Shelley's translation differs from the original[10] in softening the intimate tone of personal loss of Cavalcanti's poem, and highlighting the feeling of *artistic* loss. The contact between the two poets in Shelley's version is more intellectual, a younger poet finding himself disappointed, even betrayed, by the diminution of the other's spiritual and artistic integrity.

"To Wordsworth" follows just this structure and tone. Shelley's elegy for Wordsworth can be nothing *but* ironic here, since, of course, the poet still lives, now in a sort of poetic death-in-life. The poem's final allusion, for example, once again uses Wordsworth's own lines against himself. The sonnet's conclusion—"Deserting these, thou leavest me to grieve, / Thus having been, that thou shouldst cease to be"—may revise in a more personal context another sonnet of Wordsworth's, "On the Extinction of the Venetian Republic" (1802; published 1807):

And what if she had seen those glories fade,
Those titles vanish, and that strength decay;
Yet shall some tribute of regret be paid
When her long life hath reached its final day:
Men we are, and must grieve when even the Shade
Of that which once was great, is passed away.

(Lines 9–14)

Like Venice, Wordsworth lives as a shade of his former self, both former defenders of freedom ("safeguard of the west"), both surviving but perhaps not recovered from imaginative failure.

The very form of the sonnet underscores this survival. Initially this sonnet is one of Shelley's more formally conventional ones. The first two quatrains are clearly distinguished (*ababcdcd*), marking a shift in perspective from Wordsworth to the poet himself. But the apparently conventional rhyme scheme breaks down at line 9, the usual turning point, with the presence of a double rhyme or couplet, followed by a final quatrain, *fgfg*. The presence of this closural device in the middle of the poem may parallel Shelley's perception of the imaginative life of his precursor; that is, the closural device, appearing prematurely, may formally mirror Wordsworth's premature imaginative death. The poem should have ended with these couplet lines—"Thou hast like a rock-built refuge stood / Above the blind and battling multitude"—the locking of rhymes there supporting the image of Wordsworth as guide, as refuge, as rocklike in his uprightness and fixity. The final four lines are therefore necessarily a "falling-off," a quatrain that survives beyond its place, describing a voice, once powerful, that no longer, as Shelley says of the "star"-like soul of the idealized poet-figure, Adonais, "Beacons from the abode where the Eternal are." Like Gray's elegiac sonnet to Richard West, this sonnet's ironic employment of the memorializing function of the conventional sonnet turns this one into a poetic tomb.

But this play with the ending points to a characteristic move in Shelley's sonnets: a move toward open-endedness that formally signals a resistance to just that entombment or "enslavement," as he and Mary deemed it, by society itself. The irony that permeates the movement of "To Wordsworth" is in keeping with Shelley's tendency to use the sonnet form as a figure not merely of "power" but of "potentiality," by which I mean a form of power that is always looking forward, beyond the structures of power that presently exist. Thus while Shelley's two early sonnets on the balloon and bottle as vehicles of knowledge are devoid of that irony, their employment of the Wordsworthian figure of radiance already partakes of *anticipation* rather than retrospection and points toward a Shelleyan preference for prophecy rather than for memory.

It is this resistance to closure that also marks Shelley's most famous sonnet, "Ozymandias" (1817), in which the poet's resistance to the monumentality of the visionary moment in the Wordsworth sonnet is registered by the poem's complex narrative structure:

> I met a traveller from an antique land
> Who said: Two vast and trunkless legs of stone
> Stand in the desert . . . Near them, on the sand,
> Half sunk, a shattered visage lies, whose frown,
> And wrinkled lip, and sneer of cold command,
> Tell that its sculptor well those passions read
> Which yet survive, stamped on these lifeless things,

The hand that mocked them, and the heart that fed:
And on the pedestal these words appear:
"My name is Ozymandias, king of kings.
Look on my works, ye Mighty, and despair!"
Nothing beside remains. Round the decay
Of that colossal wreck, boundless and bare,
The lone and level sands stretch far away.

What one notices first about the sonnet structurally is its unique "Chinese-box structure," as critics have come to call it:[11] the consciousness of the reader on the outside; the voice of the speaker; the voice of the traveler; the sculptor; the inscription of Ozymandias; and at the center of the poem not a voice but an image, the broken colossus. This structure breaks down the typical sonnet structure of quatrain and sestet; instead the poem is unified by its organization of several consciousnesses around the central, but variously-interpreted, image. What is so immediately striking about the "I" of this poem is how little it appears to "say," that task being almost immediately handed to the anonymous traveler.

Within the traveler's discourse there is a similar decentering of consciousness, from "Ozymandias" to the anonymous sculptor, who has "well those passions read" that gave this king his power, and who has well represented or "mocked" them. As Paul Fry has pointed out, the sculptor is himself shown to be secondary, in that he is presented in the poem as merely a "reader," rather than a creator, a "mocker" in the conventional sense—an imitator whose "art" is derived "from that which precedes him and conditions his response."[12] Fry goes on to argue that the "poem's dispersive structure (the formal equivalent of their mutual disdain)" in fact aligns these various figures of consciousness, such that the notion of lyric subjectivity in this poem is questioned. What finally results is a "chain of interpreters that ends with ourselves,"[13] each interpreter shown to be superseded by a later reader. The sonnet is not a "single lonely thought," as sonnets have conventionally been, but a series of them, separated from each other by a later subject, whose consciousness "frames" the previous one.

The implied seriality of this sonnet's structure stresses the importance of the reader at the outer edge or outside frame, and highlights the way in which each limited viewpoint within the poem is overcome. But the argument of the poem suggests that the only thing that distinguishes the reader from the previous subjects is his place in time—that is, he is only the latest of interpreters in that chain. The poem's exposure of history as a series of interpretations, mirrored formally by the "Chinese-box framing" of the sonnet, is a fascinating revision of the conventional sonnet's relation to time. While the "fiction" of the typical sonnet is generally that it is a record of a moment—a "moment's monument," to anticipate Rossetti—Shelley's sonnet undermines the momentousness and the monumentality of the sonnet (indeed, of art itself) by reminding the reader that all interpretations will be revised in time; *in time*, in history, neither kingdoms, nor ideologies, nor poems remain unchanged. A single "frame" may always have to be replaced or recontained in a larger one. The closed completeness of the Wordsworth sonnet and its visionary poetics is essentially deconstructed.

The power of "Ozymandias" rests in the deferral of its final irony; only at the end of the poem is that irony discernible, and it becomes a shadow that history itself has cast over the memory of tyrant-king. The ironic judgment of fame is only made when fame has forgotten the ruler; the judgment must be made by the reader. This sort of open-endedness has a curious effect, resisting altogether the typical closure of the conventional sonnet. The resistance to closure tropes subjectivity in such a way that it becomes impossible to identify a central consciousness or "I," reinterpreted as each subject is by later figures. Such an operation could not be more different than what we found in Wordsworth's sonnets, where the integrity of the sonnet space is so clearly identified with the integrity of the poetic self, and with the figuration of his lyric voice.

As the role of the poet's self is destabilized, as well as the status of his "voice," so too is the role of the work of art—both the sculpture and the poem "Ozymandias"—itself. Anne Janowitz has argued that Shelley's use of the sonnet form is based upon its conventionally memorializing function: "The yoking together of an image of a reliquary with that of the sonnet is felicitous, for the sonnet has traditionally served as a monument to the endurance of poetic figuration over the ephemerality of human life."[14] The poem's central concern is with art's own memorializing function and the vulnerability of art to the ravages of time that it had claimed to escape. The central image of the broken colossus reminds us that when time has broken the forms of art, those forms may not lose meaning but come to mean something else, something that will comprehend the old meaning, if only ironically.

Although Janowitz recognizes and unravels lucidly the ironic structure of the poem, seeing in it a play with conventions in its monumentalizing of "this de-monumentalizing project,"[15] she does not state the final irony quite so clearly. She concludes that the poem's open-endedness "leaves a path open for the sonnet to then turn round on itself—i.e., turn upon its espoused theme of proving how the mighty fall—and reveal how art again makes permanent the passing of power." This conclusion, while highlighting the self-reflexive aspect that characterizes the sonnet genre, fights against a finer point earlier in her argument—that the poem "makes a central concern out of the problem of how one *can* moralize."[16] I would stress instead that the open-endedness of the poem refocuses our attention back on the imagination itself and on the reader's own perception of those "beautiful idealisms" that Shelley describes in his *Defence* as the prize of a free individual.

The poem, then, points to another kind of power—the imagination's own ability to break apart such monumentalizations. The importance of "Ozymandias" as a poem, as form, as writing, is diminished by the poet's will that it mean something, just as the tyrant's image of himself is diminished by time's reduction of that image into sand. What is perhaps more important is the meeting of the poem's "I" with the "traveller from an antique land," a faceless figure I tend to associate, probably because of his origin in some "antique land," with the time of Ozymandias himself. Though clearly this is impossible, the timelessness of that traveler figure suggests something about the temporal setup of the poem: that by the end of the poem, we are asked to remember this poem *only so that we may look forward*, rather than back at the institutions of the past that have controlled human society. The traveler is a timeless figure because the poem wants to break out of its own temporal and structural conventions. The past is put in its place, precisely in the past. The poem moves beyond fame, which tends to memorialize ideologies of one sort or another; it advocates creative imagination, rather than simply memory, as that which will break the fossilized institutions that enslave men. Similarly, Shelley's sonnet form wants to break out of the formal development conventionally ascribed to it. In "Ozymandias," Shelley revises his view of the sonnet function, seeing it not so much as that which memorializes but more importantly as that which forces one to look forward, since the poem teaches us that history—the progression of time forward—will not allow one to monumentalize any single stance, and indeed will itself mock the mouth or the hand that thinks so.

The open-endedness of this solution is a crucial marker to Shelley's later use of the sonnet form or even, for that matter, to Shelley's broader view of the role of art. The poem accomplishes what Shelley sets out for the artist in his preface accompanying *Prometheus Unbound*:

> Didactic poetry is my abhorrence. . . . My purpose has hitherto been simply to familiarize the highly refined imagination of the more select classes of poetical readers with beautiful idealisms of moral excellence; aware that until the mind can love, and admire, and trust, and hope, and endure, rea-

soned principles of moral conduct are seeds cast upon the highway of life which the unconscious passenger tramples into dust, although they would bear the harvest of his happiness.[17]

The image of the seed in this passage recalls the two early sonnets discussed above, whose balloon and bottle may remain aloft or buried in sand until someone perceives them. Shelley's aims were finally much wider and more abstract than attacking a particular regime or manifestation of injustice, though he did both often. He had become more forward-looking, his view of time not so much historical as apocalyptic. The very aims of art, under this view, change; art and poetry lose their function as "memorializers" and become something else, not just barometers nor even forecasters of change but *visions* of it (note in the quotation above that Shelley says simply, vaguely, "*until* the mind can love . . ."). This poem is political, of course— but it also hints at the crucial issue for Shelley: how art may not simply expose political wrongs but correct them. Like Wordsworth, Shelley saw in Milton a fusion of private (or artistic) and public modes:

> We owe the great writers of the golden age of our literature to that fervid awakening of the public mind which shook to dust the oldest and most oppressive form of the Christian Religion. We owe Milton to the progress and development of the same spirit; the sacred Milton was, let it ever be remembered, a Republican, and a bold enquirer into morals and religion. The great writers of our own age are, we have reason to suppose, the companions and forerunners of some unimagined change in our social condition or the opinions which cement it.[18]

The sonnet "Ozymandias" too is not simply a memorial to the passing of power, and certainly not a memorial to political power, but it may memorialize and celebrate the power of art merely to make aware to a "highly refined imagination" *its own* access to moral truths, itself a far greater power for Shelley than any merely political one. The sonnet becomes a myth not of memory, or even of power, but of a kind of foresight or Prometheanism.[19] "England in 1819" repeats Shelley's employment of irony and power in the sonnet form, revealing a continuing concern with the dialectic of form and content and the potential for breaking the resistance of conventionalized forms:

> An old, mad, blind, despised, and dying king,—
> Princes, the dregs of their dull race, who flow
> Through public scorn,—mud from a muddy spring,—

> Rulers who neither see, nor feel, nor know,
> But leech-like to their fainting country cling,
> Till they drop, blind in blood, without a blow,—
> A people starved and stabbed in th' untilled field,—
> An army, which liberticide and prey
> Makes as a two-edged sword to all who wield,—
> Golden and sanguine laws which tempt and slay;
> Religion Christless, Godless—a book sealed;
> A Senate, Time's worst statute, unrepealed,—
> Are graves, from which a glorious Phantom may
> Burst, to illumine our tempestuous day.

The encumbrance of the individual by fossilized social institutions is art-fully mirrored by the poem's rhythm and devices: the lines are impossibly muscle-bound, the phrases short, yet overburdened by alliteration that slows the reading down. Even in the first line, one wants to stress each of those adjectives, but the line will not scan properly unless one readjusts. Perhaps not insignificantly, it is the word "mad" that causes the metrical stumbling. The catalog-like structure of the poem contributes further to this halting progress, each phrase holding the reader back.

As in "Ozymandias," and even in the earlier sonnets, the force of the sonnet is weighted toward the end and points to an open-endedness that fights the sonnet's conventional drive toward closure. This resistance is cru-cial, as it points at an insistence of the possibility of further interpretation. This is important to Shelley as a *political* gesture; Curran speaks of the "syntactic potentiality" in the positioning of line 13's "may" as a formal analogy of "the revolutionary explosion that will invert the anti-forms re-pressing contemporary society. The form symbolically consumes itself, as surely as does the society it catalogs."[20]

As others have noted, this poem owes its rhetoric to the public mode of Milton's and Wordsworth's sonnets. However, while Wordsworth celebrates the "narrow room" of the sonnet form, Shelley's resistance to it represents an oppositional attitude toward a "tyranny" of poetic form that is analo-gous to his resistance to social authority. What is missing in this sonnet, however, is the precise agent by which this removal from degradation and constraint, this bursting forth *into* revelation, is going to take place. The vision is there, but the instrument of its accomplishment is unclear. In Shelley's "Ode to the West Wind," the poet returns to the problem of the poetic self and its voice, and revaluates what role it plays in the politics of revolution (or revelation).

The implications of Shelley's poetics of potentiality in the sonnet form emerge in the West Wind ode, a sonnet sequence of sorts that recuperates from the irony of his individual sonnets the strength of the Miltonic-Wordsworthian mode of the form. This ode is often regarded as Shelley's most perfectly executed lyric; from my perspective, it is a recognition of the full implications of the Wordsworth sonnet mode from which Shelley learned not only technical aspects of the sonnet but also simultaneously an attitude, the assertion of a public voice in lyric. The dialectic of private and public voice is the radical one in the poem, and the structure of the poem revolves around that problem.

The ode is generally recognized to be a structural amalgamation of a sonnet sequence and the terza rima rhyme scheme, and a number of discussions of this innovation exist. The general critical assertion has been that the ode is an "interplay" of a poetic form, with its conventional rhetorical structure and rhyme schemes, and the *conflicting* metrical and rhyme schemes of terza rima.[21] Shelley employs terza rima to escape the constraints of the conventional sonnet form; it lends to these sonnet stanzas an inherently oppositional attitude, as it were, toward themselves. Richard Cronin writes that the ode is "a poem that attempts to hold together the contradictory notions of explosive energy and containment, a paradox that Shelley achieves in the pun on 'Vaulted,' in a phrase like 'congregated might', but also in the poem's simultaneous use of two apparently antithetical verse forms, terza rima and the sonnet."[22] Several critics go on to note that the effect of this interplay "increases the tension in the poem: the sonnet restrains the speed of the terza rima; terza rima, in turn, loosens the sometimes ponderous sonnet, giving it flexibility and speed."[23]

Other commentators have focused upon the relationship of this interplay with both the lyric and epic modes. Terza rima is of course the verse form of Dante's epic; thus, the argument goes, Shelley is alluding formally to that poem, which casts its shadow upon Shelley's own.[24] According to Ben L. Collins, who seems to have initiated this journal discussion, the poet's use of Dante's verse form suggests that the ode, like *The Divine Comedy*, has in it something of "the *epic*, the '*religious*,' and of a push toward reform structures." After this tantalizing suggestion, Collins concludes that this combination of epic verse form and sonnet stanza

> shifts the poem from epic to lyric structure: from [quoting Joyce's *A Portrait of the Artist as a Young Man*] "the image in mediate relation to the self and to others" to "the image in immediate relation to the self." In doing so, Shelley in no way detracts from the *general* import of his poem, but he adds the *personal* touch which makes concrete the universal implications and which allows him to communicate as artist and for art.[25]

My own reading of the poem would place these axes, if one may call them so, the other way around: that is, the shift is from lyric to epic, and whatever Collins means by the "general import" of the poem is only achieved by Shelley's opening out from the personal (or perhaps, better, "private") realm to the public audience.

One effect of the interplay of modes and schemes is that the conventional dualism of the sonnet stanza, the octave and sestet division, is overrun in this ode in a way altogether different from Milton's and Wordsworth's sonnets. The ode's first three stanzas, like the Shelley sonnets looked at earlier, are weighted entirely to the end of the stanza, as if running a breathless footrace to the couplet and particularly to that final "hear, O hear." The disjunction marking the typical octave/sestet division, which Wordsworth consciously thematizes even as he overruns it, is deferred until the very last line of the stanza—and leaves speaker and reader hanging over the white space between stanzas. Every impulse of Shelley's sonnet stanza in the ode is directed toward the larger matter of bridging the abyss between the speaker-poet and the wind. The idea of formal play in the ode inheres in Paul Fry's observation that "[t]he form of Shelley's stanza, then, corresponds with the poles of dialectic in the ode: prophetic afflatus, rising out of the natural cycle with Dante, and terminal defeat, falling out of the natural cycle into nothingness with the Shakespeare of the sonnet."[26] At this point in the poem, that disjunction is too close to absolute, and the poem can only continue by the speaker asking that his voice merely be acknowledged. The momentum of each of the first three stanzas is a desire for agency or instrumentality, the general trope I take to be at the center of the poem.

In a curious way the first thirteen lines of the first three stanzas have the effect of an inhalation of breath, released by the exhalation of the imperative "hear, O hear." This is perhaps a fanciful comment, yet to say this of the individual stanzas may anticipate the real curiosity of the ode: the metaleptic transformation of all images in the poem, including those from nature and that of the speaker himself, into the figure of the wind. Furthermore, the poem, in a breathtaking rhetorical tour de force, ends by transforming all these figures, including that of the wind, into a figuration of *the poet's* voice and, simultaneously, of an apocalyptic vision.[27]

The shift[28] from passivity to agency is evident in the poem's final trope of instrumentality: the poet is no longer "*thy* lyre," but rather a "trumpet of prophecy" that will blow the wind itself through his ("my") lips. The wind is now the breath of the poet that blows words that will animate the dying world. Recalling that Wordsworth's vision of the sonnet moves from figures of sound to figures of light, we can see in Shelley's ode a similar movement toward the visionary and the apocalyptic, where sound and light, both important figures in the poem, become the same figure, where imagery is no longer compensatory but *revelatory* or incantatory.[29] By the poem's characteristically transumptive logic, the poet's own voice comes to stand for that trumpet of prophecy, itself the same "clarion" of line 10 that will awaken "the dreaming earth." The wild west wind, which once moved everywhere, has become a synecdoche for the poet's own active and inspiring voice by some imaginative revision of the poet's own status from passive instrument to active agent, like the wind itself. The transumptive structure of the poem permits voice to override form, in the sense that the poem as form becomes *nothing but* voice, or something like what Valéry calls "voice in action."[30] Agent and instrument have been made identical.

It is not paradoxical to speak of this sequence of sonnets as an ode, for it is Shelley's recognition of the odelike status of Milton's and Wordsworth's sonnets that may have prompted him to this strategy. And thus in this ode, a form that is essentially and always concerned with voice, Shelley's use of the sonnet form returns again to tropes of instrumentality. Shelley highlights the crucial matter of voice in the sonnet by turning the sonnet into that form whose essential "vocality" is part of its conventional mythology. This returns us to the matter of address. In its odic mode this poem is nothing but address, and to whom? Some have argued that the poem's final question implies the "presence" of a reader or audience, not only of the original addressee, the west wind; "the voice of the poet moves from the solitude of creative subjectivity to a social discourse that finds its *telos* in its audience."[31] However, a principal addressee of the poem may actually be the voice of the poet himself, both the agent and instrument by which his thoughts, as poems, as renovating influences of the imagination itself, will be carried "in order to bring about the Promethean renovation of the world in words,"[32] as Angela Leighton has phrased it. In terms of John Hollander's "deep grammar" of such moments, the ode represents not just "prayer"[33] but also conspiracy, a "breathing-together" that plots out a revolutionary future.

The fiction of the momentariness of the sonnet reaches a sublime conclusion here; Shelley wishes to contain, in this small vessel, not just a moment of imaginative revelation, as we have seen in Wordsworth, but a final moment in which all are contained.[34] Unlike Wordsworth, however, Shelley emphasizes a vision of the future; the momentum in Shelley's sonnets is once again anticipatory rather than retrospective. Critics often find themselves talking about Prometheanism in Shelley, and my general argument in this chapter brings me to the same point. Shelley's use of the sonnet form involves not only an accommodation of Wordsworth's new vision of the sonnet but also a deployment of his own imaginative "foresight." That anticipatory motive in Shelley displays itself in the structure of his sonnets and in the recurrent motif of the anticipated reader—that reader who picks up the bottle on the shore, or who sees the airborne balloon as it bursts its radiant message upon the earth. Those early sonnets were troped as "vessels" that would bring figures of light, and Shelley hoped for an imaginative enlightenment that would lead to a universal political and ethical enlightenment as well.

The effect of Shelley's anticipatory motive, registered formally by the open-endedness that marks nearly all of Shelley's sonnets, is to markedly distinguish Shelley's political sonnets from their Wordsworthian model. One of the most obvious differences is that nowhere in Shelley's sonnets do we find the tendency toward pictorialism and monumentality that we saw in Wordsworth; indeed, Shelley's open-ended form is designed to resist that in favor of what are sometimes no more than anticipatory intimations of vision, assertions of the *possibility* of vision for him who resists tyranny. This is certainly the message of his "Sonnet: To the Republic of Benevento," also known as "Political Greatness." Its sestet makes explicit the connection between enslavement in social convention and in poetical convention:

> —What are the numbers knit
> By force or custom? Man who man would be,
> Must rule the empire of himself; in it
> Must be supreme, establishing his throne
> On vanquished will,—quelling the anarchy
> Of hopes and fears,—being himself alone.—

Punctuated by dashes, commas, semicolons, and question marks, the poem resists the tyranny of conventional closure as virulently as he who refuses to become one of "those herds whom Tyranny makes tame" (line 3); the man who refuses tyrannical convention in the social sphere will refuse it in the poetical one as well. There is, as Curran argues, a "counterurge" to the Wordsworthian sonnet's "apocalyptic thrust," and so Wordsworth's "retreat to solid ground"[35] is not repeated by Shelley. His insistence is on that integrity of self, "—being himself alone.—" and "the King / Over himself" (*Prometheus Unbound* 3.4.196) that his Wordsworth, who should have been a "lone star," retreated from. And unlike Wordsworth, Shelley's motivation in his sonnets is "conspiratorial" in its engagement of the reader as coagent of change. While Wordsworth's sonnets explore obsessively the mind's revelation of imaginative vision, their comfortable acceptance of their own formality betrays, Shelley intimates, an imaginative failure. The impatience of Shelley's sonnets and the motivation behind his shift into the ode are fueled by Shelley's insistence on taking on that form's conventional association with a self-reflexive "moment" of poetic subjectivity and opening it up to the possibility of an ever-shifting field of interpretation that takes place in the reader himself. Wordsworth's revisionary procedure is used to a different purpose as the apocalyptic mode shifts into the prophetic. The self-authorization so characteristic of Wordsworth is also clearly available for Shelley. But through the proleptic structure so visible in these poems, Shelley also empowers *the reader* to envision an imaginative procedure by which both poetical and political vision can remain unbounded.

3

"Jealous of Dead Leaves":
Keats's Sonnets and Literary History

E. M. Forster never published a sonnet in his life. But he did write about one once, Keats's "To Homer," in a short story called "The Celestial Omnibus." The story's hero, a small boy from Surbiton, is attracted by a sign across the street from his home; it points down a dead-end alley and reads "To Heaven." His parents claim it to be only a joke; their more erudite friend, Mr. Bons, adds that it was the undergraduate prank of Percy Bysshe Shelley. But the boy, unsatisfied, pursues the matter and discovers the alley to be the depot for a "celestial omnibus" that leaves at sunrise and sunset. One morning he visits the spot at dawn; he does indeed find the omnibus, and is launched into the heavens in it. His driver, Sir Thomas Browne, takes him to a land with mists and lightning, with rainbows that are "like dreams," with precipices and cliffs illuminated by sunshine, with pools of water inhabited by maidens that sing "Truth in the depth, truth on the height." The boy returns from his trip, and is rewarded for his report of it by the strokes of a cane. His father, having thus grimly dismissed the fantastic story, orders him to recite poetry before the slightly more sympathetic Mr. Bons (proud owner of seven different volumes of Shelley), who notes that "It is odd how, in quite illiterate minds, you will find glimmers of Artistic Truth." The boy begins:

> "'. . . Standing aloof in giant ignorance.'"
> His father laughed again—roared. "One for you, my son! 'Standing aloof in giant ignorance!' I never knew these poets talked sense. Just describes you." . . . [The boy's father leaves the room for some whiskey, leaving Bons to endure the recitation.]
> "'Standing aloof in giant ignorance, of thee I dream and of the Cyclades, as one who sits ashore and longs perchance to visit——'"
> "Quite right. To visit what?"
> "'To visit dolphin coral in deep seas,'" said the boy, and burst into tears.

"Come, come! why do you cry?"

"Because—because all these words that only rhymed before, now that I've come back they're me."

Mr. Bons laid the Keats down. The case was more interesting than he had expected. *"You?"* he exclaimed. "This sonnet, *you?"*

"Yes—and look further on: 'Aye, on the shores of darkness there is light, and precipices show untrodden green.' It *is* so, sir. All these things are true. . . . There *is* light upon the shores of darkness. I have seen it coming. Light and a wind."

[Mr Bons, though still intrigued, declares all this "nonsense," to which the boy mournfully responds:] "It has all happened as the people up there warned me, and Mr. Bons has disbelieved me like every one else. I have been caned. I shall never see that mountain again."[1]

The story (which does, it turns out, transport the boy and Bons into the visionary heavens) is certainly an allegory of the belated status of romantic poetry even in Forster's world—but it is also an allegory of something more radical: the nostalgic nature of romantic poetry itself. "I shall never see that mountain again" is a lament that echoes a considerable amount of (particularly Wordsworthian) romantic poetry. Forster creates a child-version of the Keatsian poet figure, "standing aloof in giant ignorance," stationed at the edge of a visionary realm that he seems unable to return to. More narrowly, then, the story is a version of the "To Homer" sonnet itself, an allegory of belatedness and anticipation, hope and skepticism, insight and blindness, potentiality and limitation, power and impotence. It is around these axes that most of Keats's sonnets revolve, for in those short lyrics, especially, Keats tries to station himself *as* a visionary poet, and explores through them—like Shelley—both the potentialities and the limitations of that stance.

For Keats the sonnets of Wordsworth must have seemed to have sprung out of Wordsworth's head fully armed, as Minerva from Jove. This overshadowing literary presence, in addition to that of Shakespeare, makes the sonnet story in Keats more complex than it was for Shelley. Because Shelley's stance with respect to Wordsworth is so self-consciously confrontational, the "predicament" or "alien entanglements" (as Frost called them) in his sonnets are more overt than in Keats's. Like Shelley, Keats finds in the sonnet form itself ways of resisting the "trap" that literary history lays before young poets, but Keats's sense of irony is not, in his sonnets at least, his usual mode. Though clearly his struggle against his literary past is at least as fierce as Shelley's, Keats long saw his own poetic powers as always something to come.[2] While for Wordsworth the sonnet is a successful emblem of the self-authorized power of imagination and subjectivity, and for Shelley of potentiality and a revolutionary decentering of subjectivity, for Keats the sonnet is an emblem of poetical *potentia* that defies his own attitude of literary belatedness and impotence. Such a defiance leads the poet to see in the sonnet form not closure and repetition, but a principle of continuity by which difference from tradition, rather than sameness, is possible.

While Keats clearly learned about sonnets from Shakespeare and Wordsworth,[3] what is new in Keats's sonnets is the liminal nature of the stance taken there, a characteristic Forster clearly observed and explored in his story. That liminal stance is one that previous critics have called "prospective" or "anticipatory";[4] it is an unstable one insofar as the poet desires always to move beyond it. What is most interesting from a formal standpoint in Keats's sonnets is that the poems themselves register that liminality, and they do so—again like Shelley—primarily by the way they end.

Barbara Herrnstein Smith describes the sonnet form as one that "represents a statement or speech of some kind: an argument, perhaps, or a declaration or lament. It concludes, therefore . . . with the completion of that utterance."[5] Wordsworth's sonnets rest in their completeness of utterance; it is not closure but the dialectic of octave and sestet that that poet problematizes. In so many of Keats's sonnets, as in Shelley's, there is a *resistance* to formal closure. Keats's early verse letter "To Charles Cowden Clarke" characterizes the sonnet as "swelling loudly / Up to its climax and then dying proudly" (line 61)—a characterization that itself suggests a defiance of that death. For Keats, closure is a kind of death, because it effects silence. It is no surprise that in his most well-known statement about sonnet form, the letter passage that precedes his sonnet on the sonnet, it should be the "pouncing rhymes"—line endings—and the closing couplet that most concern him.

A proleptic awareness of closure haunts Keats's sonnets, and the heightened sense of temporality that must accompany that awareness casts the elegiac shade that darkens so many of them. The technical result of Keats's hypersensitivity to formal closure is a characteristic resistance that takes several forms: the introduction of images in the sestet (of threshold figures, of expanding vistas—or sometimes both at once) that counteract the metrical closure; the lapse into catalogic syntax in the sestet; and an experimentation with rhyme that pries open the epigrammatic close of the Shakespearean form he came to favor. All three strategies lead to an open-endedness or, ultimately, to a *suspension* of closure that becomes characteristic of Keats's sonnets.

The question I am asking of Keats's sonnets is the same I have asked of Wordsworth's and Shelley's: What did these poems—what did this poetic form—*do* for Keats? Why did he choose it so often that it is him that we think of as the sonnet-writer of the English romantic period, even before Wordsworth, who wrote so many more? And while Walter Jackson Bate has explained how Keats transformed the sonnet into an ode stanza, he has not explained exactly why Keats lingered with that form to the point where it became the basis for a new one.

I

Keats's first published poem was a sonnet called "On Solitude" (1815), a poem less about solitude per se than about writing poetry, less about absence from society than about the presence of the materials of poetry, nature, thought and words, which he calls, in line 11 of this early poem, the "images of thought refin'd." Of particular interest from my perspective is that the poem actually alludes to Wordsworth's 1802 sonnet on the sonnet, "Nuns fret not":

> O Solitude! if I must with thee dwell,
>   Let it not be among the jumbled heap
>   Of murky buildings; climb with me the steep,—
> Nature's observatory—whence the dell,
> Its flowery slopes, its river's crystal swell,
>   May seem a span; let me thy vigils keep
>   'Mongst boughs pavillion'd, where the deer's swift leap
> Startles the wild bee from the fox-glove bell.
>
> (Lines 1–8)

"On Solitude" suggests that Keats's initial sonnet writing recognizes the sonnet's association with limitation and compactness, and already investigates poetic form as a synecdochic figure for the spaces of the imagination. I have previously mentioned the tropes of form as space and as instrumentality in Wordsworth's employment of the "fox-glove bell" image; one recalls also Hollander's argument that the Wordsworth poem considers "the work of art" (taking "work" also in the active sense of "labor"), the poem itself, a troped locus of that work. Keats's octave describes a scene akin to those solitary Wordsworthian scenes of labor; the sonnet space is a solitary mental space where the work of poetry takes place. The figure of limitation is a densely woven refuge of "boughs pavillion'd,"[6] a naturalized scene of labor. Those lines, the threads of the loom that form the material of Wordsworth's figure of form, are transformed into natural lines that form themselves.[7]

The poem is an answer to Wordsworth's description of poetic necessities—poetic form and the solitude of the intellectual work necessary to create that form. The solitude of the poet in nature gives a vantage point, a perspective from which vision opens out, "May seem a span." Already Keats has intuited the expansive vision typical of sonnets looked at in previous chapters; he has also intuited the self-reflexivity—the power of the subjective—of Wordsworthian sonnets. He does, as Curran puts it, "partake" of Wordsworth's intensity in that he understands from Wordsworth that the sonnet is a self-reflexive transcript—not so much of the heart, as Wordsworth says, but of the poet's mind seeing, thinking, composing.[8]

Those aesthetic intuitions lie behind several of the best of the other sixteen sonnets that were included in Keats's first volume of poetry (1817); these sonnets are among the few poems there that early critics admired. Keats's friend John Hamilton Reynolds writes in a contemporary review (9 March 1817) that "with the exception of Milton's and Wordsworth's, we think them the most powerful ones in the whole range of English poetry." Josiah Conder, himself a minor poet, remarks in the *Eclectic Review* of September 1817 that "the sonnets are perhaps the best thing in the volume," and, more interestingly, that most of these poems are "*all about* poetry." Conder did not mean this as a compliment, for he described this kind of writing as a youthful indulgence, "the first efflorescence of the unpruned fancy, which must pass away before any thing like genuine excellence can be produced."[9] Nevertheless, the reflexivity of Keats's work is evident, and nowhere more so than in those sonnets that address the problem of being a poet.[10]

Wordsworth sometimes, Coleridge always, considered sonnets a diversion or formal truancy from what they saw as the poet's proper employment: writing epic. Keats inherited the notion that the greatest poets must write epics ("Did our great Poets ever write short Pieces?"), and his decision to write sonnets partakes of this tradition of sonnets-in-lieu-of-epic as a sort of career move. The feeling of unreadiness is thematized in Keats's 1817 selection of sonnets, many of which are not just "all about" poetry but more specifically about the ability to write it in the face of such precursors as Milton, Wordsworth and (it seemed to him then) Leigh Hunt.[11] Several sonnets handle this problem simply by emulation: "Written on the Day that Mr. Leigh Hunt left Prison," "Addressed to Haydon," "To Kosciusko," and "Happy is England! I could be content"—each has a distinctly Wordsworthian cast. So does the second sonnet addressed to Haydon ("Great spirits now on earth are sojourning"; 1816, published 1817), the first line of which is a revision of Wordsworth's own "Great men have been among us" (1802; published 1807). But while Wordsworth's sonnet is a tribute to political and poetical celebrities of the past (Sidney, Marvell, Harrington,

Vane, and Milton) Keats's sonnet is an up-to-date tribute to his own literary heroes and friends, as well as an announcement—indeed, glorification—of his own literary ambition:

> And other spirits there are standing apart
>   Upon the forehead of the age to come;
> These, these will give the world another heart,
>   And other pulses. Hear ye not the hum
> Of mighty workings?——
>   Listen awhile ye nations, and be dumb.
>
> (Lines 9–14)

Contemporary reviewers correctly presumed that Keats imagined himself standing first among those standing apart. But the sestet's figure of anticipation is without voice—indeed, Keats rather startlingly (upon a suggestion from Haydon) curtails the thirteenth line.[12] Those skeptical reviewers who claimed to listen to that blank and hear only silence cannot be altogether blamed, even with their predisposition to dislike Keats for his association with Hunt and the so-called Cockney school; the last line of the poem itself suggests that the voice is faint, and Keats might have agreed that the world had to wait a while longer to really hear it. Nevertheless, the resistance to closure in literary history is clearly registered in that sestet, which challenges the reader to listen not to a complete utterance but, very pointedly, to one that has barely begun. The space in line 13 is itself a sort of chamber or ear to catch that sound.

The sestet's figure of anticipation at the edge of literary history, with a voice *animating* "mighty workings" but not yet articulate, is a figure characteristic of several of Keats's best sonnets in this first collection. The poet's earliness is the subject of "On Leaving Some Friends at an Early Hour," in which Keats heaps up images of poems and the writing of poems, images of radiance and of music whose divinely inspired harmonies come to a "delicious ending" (line 10) and become the harmoniously rhymed lines of poetry. But the sonnet's final two lines remind us that this is a vision and admit to unreadiness for standing apart: "For what a height my spirit is contending! / 'Tis not content so soon to be alone."

The problems of finding voice and of finding an opening in literary history are handled more complexly in the best two sonnets in the volume, "How many bards gild the lapses of time" (probably 1816; published 1817) and "On first looking into Chapman's Homer" (October 1816; published 1816). The first of these is overtly about the occasion of writing:

How many bards gild the lapses of time!
   A few of them have ever been the food
   Of my delighted fancy,—I could brood
Over their beauties, earthly, or sublime:
And often, when I sit me down to rhyme,
      These will in throngs before my mind intrude:
      But no confusion, no disturbance rude
Do they occasion; 'tis a pleasing chime.
So the unnumber'd sounds that evening store;
      The songs of birds—the whisp'ring of the leaves—
      The voice of waters—the great bell that heaves
With solemn sound,—and thousand others more,
      That distance of recognizance bereaves,
Make pleasing music, and not wild uproar.

One imagines the poet sitting down to rhyme under his "boughs pavillion'd"; the setting of this poem as well is the mental space of the poet's work. Stuart Sperry describes the poem as "more than anything else" about "the creative process itself. It concerns the way in which the sensations first of art, then of nature, are accumulated, then combined or distanced in imagination so as to achieve a unity and harmony of effect."[13] So too Claude Lee Finney:

> In this sonnet he analyzed the two methods by which he was composing his poems—the method of *imitation*, which he had learned from Thomson, Gray, and other poets of the eighteenth century, and the method of originality, which he was learning from Hunt and Wordsworth. He explained the harmony with which poetic reminiscences and natural impressions fused in his mind in the process of composition.[14]

Both critics, however, neglect to discuss the poem's peculiar repression of influence, although Sperry acknowledges that "the sonnet does not succeed in characterizing the nature of the 'chime' or the greater 'music' it distills, nor is there any real effort to do so."[15] This apparent lack of effort is worth considering, for it shows up a crucial evasion. While poetic memory returns to him "in throngs," indeed "intrudes" upon his mind, he claims there is "no confusion, no disturbance rude . . . 'tis a pleasing chime." The turn of the poem contrasts those "number'd sounds" with "the unnumber'd sounds" of nature, but the contrast is transformed by simile (the "So" that opens the sestet) into likeness rather than difference. The sounds of nature, each figured as voice or utterance ("songs," "whisp'ring," "voice," "heavings" of bells) join the sounds of past bards' voices to blend into one harmonious noise that "distance of recognizance bereaves."

If my theory about Keats's strategy of closure as a momentary stay against absorption into tradition is correct, then that strategy should be operating in full force here, and indeed it does. The first strategy is the catalogic style of the sestet, whose movement is not the "logical" movement toward a close but a heightening of hearing, as sensations are overlaid. In his discussion of the Elgin Marbles sonnet, Curran marks this mannerism as one way Keats "collapses the distinctions he confronts."[16] This is surely the motivation of the sestet here. But the complexity of this move goes beyond that general description, for it is not the distinction between literary and natural sounds that the poet is trying to collapse.

The peculiar syntax of the penultimate line, which almost forces the reader to look and work it out, points to the real issue here: how to forget those voices. If the sestet begins by muffling those voices into echoic sounds of nature, line 13 transforms them by silencing them with a kind of death. In the word "bereave," which can simply mean "to take away," we cannot help but recall its figurative meaning, particularly with the "solemn sound" of a funereal bell still tolling in our ears from lines 11–12. Of what is the poet bereft? Of "recognizance"—of memory's ability to identify the *original* sounds. However, this dispossession of memory makes possible the ascendancy of his own voice. This is the willful forgetting de Man finds in Keats's poetry generally, which "thrives on dreams of pure potentiality [instead of on memory, the enemy of poetic language for Keats]."[17]

This dispossession of the original is more remarkably highlighted in the final two words of the poem, "wild uproar," a quotation from Satan's description of the Creation in *Paradise Lost* 3.708: "I saw when at his Word the formless Mass, / This world's material mould, came to a heap: / Confusion heard his voice, and wild uproar / Stood rul'd, stood vast infinitude confin'd."[18] Keats's allusion to this Miltonic moment (itself an allusion to Spenser), in which "vast infinitude" is "confin'd," must remind us of the trope of Wordsworthian intensity or miniaturization of the apocalyptic that I have been tracing. Robert Gleckner has probed this allusion, and concludes that

> as the "Word" creates order out of this confusion, so Keats's (the Poet's) imagination creates out of "throngs" of remembered poetry "a pleasing chime," and out of "unnumber'd sounds" "pleasing music." What better way to elevate to its proper sublimity the matter of greatest moment in Keats's mind, not merely the rivaling but even the hope of surpassing those great "bards [who] gild the lapses of time"—as well as analogizing the disorder of

the sensitively receptive mind and memory in terms of the chaos of the sea [the 'wild uproar' of *Paradise Lost* 2.539–41] and angelic war.[19]

My only objection to this reading is that it overlooks Keats's sublimation of his own aggressive move against the past; while the allusion does initiate the analogy that Gleckner describes above, Keats is claiming these voices of the past are *not* "wild uproar." Fitzgerald calls this move a "de-fusing," and sees the move as a successful one:

> By concentrating the bard-studded lapses of time into a natural cycle whose scale is commensurate with the temporality of the individual poet, and then fusing the processes of nature and of composition, Keats is able to defuse the threat of his forbears without aggression, allowing them to make their own music while at the same time giving his composition a role in the realization of that music.[20]

By perceptively locating Keats's "suspension" of the wild uproar, Fitzgerald still allows the poet the final victory. Nevertheless the aggression is there, and its shadow is in the trope of death that darkens the sestet.

In "How many bards," Keats introduces a figure of the poet as creator of a new world, a figure who is analogous to the poet figure in another contemporaneous sonnet, the Chapman's Homer sonnet. In this poem, the occasion for sonnet writing becomes the poet's awareness of literary belatedness and inadequacy, and Keats reconsiders the problem somewhat more precisely than he had before:

> Much have I travell'd in the realms of gold,
>   And many goodly states and kingdoms seen;
>   Round many western islands have I been
> Which bards in fealty to Apollo hold.
> Oft of one wide expanse had I been told
>   That deep-brow'd Homer ruled as his demesne;
>   Yet did I never breathe its pure serene
> Till I heard Chapman speak out loud and bold:
> Then felt I like some watcher of the skies
>   When a new planet swims into his ken;
> Or like stout Cortez when with eagle eyes
>   He star'd at the Pacific—and all his men
> Look'd at each other with a wild surmise—
>   Silent, upon a peak in Darien.

Leigh Hunt would recall the impression Keats's early poetry made upon him, and singled out the Chapman's Homer sonnet, "which terminates with so energetic a calmness, and which completely announced the new poet taking possession."[21] Even this early evaluation of the poem, with its oxymoronic formulation of "energetic calmness," recognizes the dialectical action of its Petrarchan form and of the vision of fullness and blankness, of "wild surmise" and silence. Hunt recognizes in that announcement of "the new poet taking possession" the appearance of the sublime, which *is* a kind of possession, in several senses of the word.[22]

Curran describes this sonnet as the first of many "to record, or enact, an artistic experience," and to transform the sonnet form into "a revelation of the psychology of aesthetic experience."[23] The general point glides over crucial complexities. The psychology of the imagination apparent in the Wordsworthian visionary sonnet does deepen into the psychology of the aesthetic in Keats, as Curran suggests. But while Wordsworth's poems record the aesthetic shock in the confrontation of mind and nature, Keats's sonnets more often record the aesthetic shock of the confrontation between mind and *art*, as if for Keats art takes nature's place in the Wordsworthian scheme. Keats's concerns in these early sonnets at least are more narrowly literary than Wordsworth's, and therefore the severest complication for Keats becomes once again his relation to his literary past.

Even from the beginning, the uncomfortable relation of Keats to Wordsworth emerges through his stance in the sonnets, and his resistance is partly registered in his turn to the same figure that Shelley turns to: the reader. The self-reflexivity of these poetic occasions is highlighted by Keats's frequent return to tropes of reading. Literary voice, in these and later sonnets, is figured as "echo"—as if what Keats is hearing is no longer original but only a version of it. But it is also frequently troped as *writing*. In these poems, reading and interpretation become a process of hearing writing; Cynthia Chase notes this process in other poetry of Keats's, particularly the odes. During this process, she says, the poet engenders "the figure of the reader."[24] Keats blurs the issue of poetic impotence by thematizing *himself* as reader; reading and interpretation are the only means by which he hears those voices at all.

Unlike the Wordsworthian subjectivity, which emerges from the mind's interaction and self-conscious separation from nature, Keatsian subjectivity is tied more specifically to the literary. In imagining it so, however, Keats constructs for himself a prison-house, as it were, of tradition, of memory, of form. The symptomatic claustrophobia of many of his sonnets, a quality that only increases with time, is countered by the sonnets' efforts, so often, to announce Keats as a poet—but paradoxically, that announcement is threatened by silence, as in that blank half-line of "Great spirits now on earth are sojourning."

The Chapman's Homer sonnet is one of several in the 1817 volume that highlight the figure of the poet just having read or seen a great work of art. In later sonnets as well, such as the *Lear* sonnet or the one "To Homer," the act of reading will be tied to the problem of secondariness. As if to underscore the point here, it is not actually Homer that the poet reads but a *translation* that has become so strong that it is itself primary rather than secondary.[25] The competitive reading underlying the poem animates its dominant tropes, the most crucial of which is spatial. Earlier critics have already mapped out the landscape of the poem, sublimed in the sestet to a kind of heavenly geography. The dialectic at the poem's end operates through the simultaneous evocation of the boundlessness of the sea and the mountain peak, the site of visions in classical and biblical poetry. In Wordsworth and Shelley alike, the miniaturization of large or apocalyptic contents into this tiny form is troped as power or potency (more specifically as light, or as prophetic utterance); so too in this sonnet, where, as Fry points out, "the new poet surrounds all the others, dwarfs them . . . this poet's world encompasses the entire cosmos."[26] I would go even a step further, and say that the "poet's world" is troped finally in the poem as *another globe*, the globe of the poet-Cortez figure's *eye*.

This conflation highlights the second dominant trope of the sonnet, which appears in the sestet of the poem: vision and revelation. Behind the eagle eyes of Cortez and the looks of his men are the blind eyes of the epic poets. Keats's "pure serene" must recall Milton's description of the *gutta serena*, his "Homeric handicap."[27] Furthermore, the logic of the imagery suggests that this watching and seeing is associated with reading and interpretation. The Cortez figure seems to look merely at the vastness of the sea, a kind of blank landscape. But, of course, that very blankness is itself a kind of sublimity, a figure for incompleteness and desire in that it leads his eye to the horizon and to imaginings of what lies beyond.[28]

Because nearly every trope in the poem is finally condensed into the eye-orb of the Cortez figure, the sonnet becomes a perspective, a launching pad from which vision is made possible. As in "How many bards," this is a significant conflation that tropes the poem's own dialectics of intensification and expansion toward a vision of a new world at the poem's close. The mountain-top of the final line underscores the reader's apprehension of some vision about to happen. William Fitzgerald adds a fine interpretation of this point:

> [The] travel metaphor is now transmuted so that the resolution of the poet's wandering becomes an invitation to further discovery, and the space that had been narrowed down is now opened again. . . . What we arrive at in the final lines is . . . an intensified repetition of an opening. . . .[29]

The success of this sonnet resides in its victory over closure and over a repetition of sameness or imitation. The resistance to closure here, in other words, offers a principle of continuity that rests not simply in this vision of anticipated revelation but also in the figure of voice. Whereas Chapman is said to "speak out loud and bold," a formulation that Fry associates with Milton, the figure of Cortez at the close of the Chapman's Homer sonnet is resoundingly and sublimely *silent*.

There is more being said in that silence than anywhere else in the poem, as if all his energy—and what he might actually *say*—were summoned to his eye instead. Certainly this silence is more articulate than the blank half-line in the sonnet considered earlier, "Great spirits now on earth." Harding comments that Cortez's silence is a "refusal to re-utter or reinterpret the tradition, [and] conveys the tradition's oppressiveness and inaccessibility"; he calls the poem itself a "projection" of an "ideal speech that is translucent, immediate, and primary."[30] In other words, the poem itself is a strategy for taking power, for literally fulfilling the potentiality of the tropes of the poem in order to *avoid* literary repetition and secondariness.

Thus does Keats figuratively resist closure and silence, and by such resistance the poem achieves articulation. The occasion of impotence becomes the occasion of composition, and endings become beginnings.[31] The close of the sonnet, then, has once again opened the poem *out*, its imagery resisting the final balance or resolution that one expects. Perhaps the best gloss of the poem I have found is from an explication by Anthony Hecht of another poem (one of his own called "Meditation"). He describes the ending of this poem as an

> articulate silence; that is, from a perilous oscillation between order and chaos to an intuition of an unapprehended order, a posited one, like the music of the spheres. And there is oscillation also between a real world and an imagined one; or, rather, not oscillation but interpenetration. The imagined world is art, whether as music or painting. But it is a world into which we enter, and even seem to inhabit, however briefly.[32]

If he were not talking about his own work I could imagine Hecht saying this with a copy of the Chapman's Homer sonnet before him.

Taken together, the poems of the 1817 volume are anticipations of Keats's own coming-into-being, or perhaps more specifically, coming-into-vision, as a poet. Literary history is a story whose ending is always right at the point where the new poet stands, but Keats revises that history as an anticipation of himself. As in Wordsworth's sonnets, it is the moment of surprise or "surmise" (aesthetic shock, as Curran calls it) that creates the occasion for Keats's verse.[33] However, it is also important to note that it is the *private* voice of Wordsworth, rather than the public voice of Milton, that Keats tends toward. The movement of withdrawal in his early sonnets is matched by an obsessive self-reflexivity that betrays the lack, as of yet, of the empowering myth of authority that Wordsworth already enjoyed from the 1802 sonnets on. Keats's shifting from the Wordsworthian procedure toward a *tradition*-authorized procedure—what James Kissane calls the shift from *logos* to *lexis*—also widens the aesthetic distancing of these poems. Wordsworth's stated aims, for all his egotistical appropriation of reality, were directed outward; the inward focus of Keats's sonnets is ironically strengthened by his effort to locate poetic authority within the literary.

By composing poems whose conclusions are projections of potency, of a literary beginning, the temporal and imaginative structures of Keats's sonnets become anticipatory, even proleptic, while being, thanks to the poet's near-constant sense of inadequacy, strangely elegiac at the same time. Incompleteness becomes a characteristic trope of Keats's sonnets, their psychological motive, because it is the incompleteness of literary history that Keats needs. The poems' sonnet form and their figurations become, as Barbara Herrnstein Smith puts it, "mutually metaphoric."[34] The open-endedness of Keats's sonnets creates a sense of expectation, an "atmosphere," as Valéry put it, "a special state [in which] a new order, a *world* would be announced, and your attention would be organized to receive it."[35] This announcement was made in the 1817 sonnets; its import is very successfully handled again in "On The Sea" (1817; published 1817):

> It keeps eternal whisperings around
>   Desolate shores, and with its mighty swell
>   Gluts twice ten thousand caverns; till the spell
> Of Hecate leaves them their old shadowy sound.
> Often 'tis in such gentle temper found
>   That scarcely will the very smallest shell
>   Be moved for days from whence it sometime fell,
> When last the winds of heaven were unbound.
>
>   (Lines 1–8)

The poem, written during Keats's self-imposed solitude at the Isle of Wight in order to compose *Endymion*, is born of a literary haunting—Lear's "Do you not hear the sea?" The entire octave is dominated by tropes of sound and space: the barely audible "whisperings" and "old shadowy sound" come from caverns that alternate between emptiness and fullness with the "spell" of the tides, a movement nicely mirrored by the swelling and breaking of the Petrarchan rhyme scheme.

The figures of form in the octave retain a sound even in emptiness, but in that very emptiness a new and articulate fullness will be found:

> O ye who have your eyeballs vext and tir'd,
>> Feast them upon the wideness of the sea;
>> O ye whose ears are dinned with uproar rude,
> Or fed too much with cloying melody—
>> Sit ye near some old cavern's mouth and brood
> Until ye start, as if the sea nymphs quired.
>
> (Lines 9–14)

The cavern in line 13 is now a "mouth," which Sperry rightly calls an image of "infinite receptiveness but also [of] the power of articulation."[36] The image of wind or breath being unbound at the close of the octave supports that reading: the empty cavern is full at the same time. Figures of form that merely echo in the octave speak out loud and bold in the sestet; an original source, absent in first half of the poem, emerges in the imagery of the second.

Anthony Hecht once again provides an appropriate gloss, when he speaks (again, of his own poem) of an "archive of departed sound that reaches infinitely back into the past, and at the same time reverberates indefinitely into the future."[37] That indefinite reverberation, the quiring of sea-nymphs that "starts" the speaker, is akin to the "surmise" of the Chapman's Homer sonnet, a glimpse into an unexplored realm that is figured in both sonnets as the "wideness of the sea." The "surprise ending" of these poems allows the poet to look ahead. Keats has, once again, troped the very spaces where the poetic echoes haunt him into spaces that become instruments of original voice.[38]

II

When Keats composed his *own* sonnet on the sonnet, "If By Dull Rhymes" (1819; published 1836), it was "endings"—line endings, couplets, enforced formal closure—that led Keats to his late experimentation with the sonnet, and to his most complex statement about the form and what he wanted it to do for him. The introductory passage in Keats's letter clearly expresses impatience with the form:

I have been endeavoring to discover a better sonnet stanza than we have. The legitimate [the Italian or Petrarchan] does not suit the language over-well from the pouncing rhymes—the other kind [the English or Shakespearean] appears too elegi[a]c—and the couplet at the end of it has seldom a pleasing effect—I do not pretend to have succeeded—it will explain itself—

> If by dull rhymes our english must be chaind
>   And, like Andromeda, the Sonnet sweet,
>   Fetterd in spite of pained Loveliness;
> Let us find out, if we must be constrain'd,
>   Sandals more interwoven & complete
> To fit the naked foot of Poesy;
>   Let us inspect the Lyre & weigh the stress
> Of every chord & see what may be gained
>   By ear industrious & attention meet,
>   Misers of sound & syllable no less,
> Than Midas of his coinage, let us be
>   Jealous of dead leaves in the bay wreath Crown;
> So if we may not let the Muse be free,
>   She will be bound with Garlands of her own.[39]

This sonnet on the sonnet "takes as its theme the pattern-making faculty that gives a poem form," as Aileen Ward put it first.[40] What many readings of the poem downplay is the issue of sonnet history and the influence upon the poet's vision of the form. Hollander does touch on it, noting that the word "jealous" in line 12 "is used in the OED senses 5 and 6—'apprehensive, vigilant, mistrustful,' and the whole line implies something of Keats's expressed desire to 'load every rift with ore,' to replace metrical and imaginative filler."[41] One could add OED sense 3, "zealous or solicitous for the preservation or well-being of something possessed or esteemed; vigilant or careful in guarding. . . ." Wordsworth's jealousy of dead leaves prompts his second metasonnet, "Scorn not the sonnet"; Keats's betrays a consciousness of intertextuality that underlies his entire sonnet-writing project.

The "poetic necessity" of form, as Valéry put it,[42] is accepted; the "must" of the opening line acknowledges the limitations of a specific fixed form—and perhaps of poetic form in general—even as the poem itself searches for ways to push beyond the limitations. But poetic necessity *includes* the limits of tradition, and this poem remembers that, even if it does not handle the issue as overtly and confidently as Wordsworth's does. Recognizing an inherent conservatism in the nature of the sonnet form, indeed perhaps of any fixed form that must already remember its own history, he acknowledges the *value* of that conservatism. Chains may become garlands, as

Hollander points out, those garlands being "the evolved poems themselves."[43] Nevertheless, I have been unable to rid the word "bound" in line 10 of the sense of remaining tied, even by the garlands themselves, as if that rock, to which the Muse figure is bound in the poem, were tradition itself. A form that brings, with each repetition, the burden of its past[44] will memorialize itself before the poet, bound by its own conventional formality, and will close off a literary future unless some principle of originality is discovered.

"If by Dull Rhymes" points to a problem one step beyond Wordsworth's presentation in his metasonnets—the problem of "modernity," no matter when a poet actually writes, the dialectical confrontation of convention and innovation, of repetition and originality. A conventional form *wants* to be repeated, is confirmed "existentially," as it were, by repetition and by the reader's recognition of that form. But of course the flip side of this coin, as Burke explains, is that conventional form "becomes an obstacle if it remains as categorical expectancy at a time when different effects are aimed at."[45] This is when formal innovation is born.

In an important article on the ode form, Cyrus Hamlin writes that "the tradition of form is sustained within such a consciousness as an aspect of intertextuality.[46] But the obstacle for Keats in the sonnet form was twofold: its formal association with self-consciousness and its formal awareness of its own historicity, which was troped in Keats's sonnets as a struggle with formal closure. In "If by Dull Rhymes," the primary innovation is the *suspension* of closure by introducing at the end a new quatrain, a new beginning. This is the motivation of Keats's sonnets from the beginning. Yet this promise of a beginning in the close itself was not satisfactorily met by Keats in his sonnets at all, as his final sonnets show. The egotism conventionally associated with this form—the "single thought," the poetic analyses of perception, thought, and vision—had an opposite effect in Keats from the one it had in Wordsworth and Shelley, for whom the constraints of the form tempered perception into vision and into a sense of the power of originality. For Keats, the constraint of the form only mirrors the constraint of imagination that is associated with being tied to a tradition dominated by figures that the new poet could only try proleptically to overpower.

If Keats struggles against the sonnet form and its traditions, it is because doing so fights on a miniaturized battlefield the problem of belatedness that preoccupies him in so much of his poetic enterprise. His recognition of the traditional nature of the form—of the form's own internal memory—brings him to those entanglements with his own literary historicity. His apparent dissatisfaction with the form, and his efforts to revise it, center on those very preoccupations with belatedness and repetition. For Keats the sonnet is a self-consciously literary space in which battles of poetic impotence, very clearly caused by anxieties of influence, are waged. That anxiety reflects itself in his tentativeness regarding the form and in his awareness that the sonnet form "remembers" its own literary history. And the sonnet's anticipation of its own ending is what Keats therefore is compelled to resist. Keats's sonnets, then, enact his attitude of prospectivity (to borrow from Burke), an assimilation of the past into the present, thus opening up a space for himself in a literary future. The entanglement Keats's sonnets record is with his literary past and his own modernity.

III

The relation of poetic vision and subjectivity to reading and repetition continues to be an explicit concern in Keats's Shakespearean sonnets. According to Bate, Keats had been reading Shakespeare's sonnets in the autumn of 1817 and had "the structure, cadence and rhetorical devices . . . in his mind," including Shakespeare's characteristic parallelism, alliteration, and antithetical balance. The switch to the Shakespearean pattern, he argues, is a turn away from Hunt's mannerisms and from his own habits of writing; the Shakespearean form was also, Bate reminds us, "temptingly unpopular." Although Bate views these sonnets as "frankly in imitation" and "little more than exercises," more recent critics sense something else going on in the move from the Petrarchan to Shakespearean form,[47] particularly in the well-known "On Sitting Down to Read *King Lear* Once Again" (1818; published 1838):

> O golden-tongued Romance, with serene lute!
>> Fair plumed syren, queen of far-away!
>> Leave melodizing on this wintry day,
> Shut up thine olden pages, and be mute.
> Adieu! for, once again, the fierce dispute
>> Betwixt damnation and impassion'd clay
>> Must I burn through; once more humbly assay
> The bitter-sweet of this Shaksperean fruit.
> Chief Poet! and ye clouds of Albion,
>> Begetters of our deep eternal theme!
> When through the old oak forest I am gone,
>> Let me not wander in a barren dream:
> But, when I am consumed in the fire,
> Give me new phoenix wings to fly at my desire.

The poem is generally described as a rededication, as an expression of the poet's intent to redirect himself. Fitzgerald correctly notes that the willfulness of this announcement is registered formally in the "syllabic overload"[48] of the final line: "Give me new phoenix wings to fly at my desire." Unlike previous sonnets, in which reading is an activity always just completed and a mark of the reader's necessary belatedness, the Lear sonnet describes a poet *about* to start rereading. The repetition is conceived as one that preserves the poet's identity as it creates a new one. The phoenix that closes the poem supplies an image by which the process of repetitive reading, again a sort of competitive reading, promises a rebirth out of the ashes of tradition, as if indeed the poet-reader would engender himself or herself with the rereading of the play. The death and resurrection of the poet figure suggest an emergence of a new subjectivity that is formed by, but now free of, the influences of the past. Death brings not silence but voice, and a visionary stance. Interestingly, the Miltonic/Wordsworthian image of the fire or gleam as a figure for "tradition" continues in this poem, the flamelike rising of the phoenix from the fire yet another passing-on of that Promethean spark.

Based, however, on the sonnets that follow, this vision of rebirth was only a vision, the turn a belated one. The *Lear* sonnet notwithstanding, Keats's identification of himself with his own literariness only deepens with the very first full Shakespearean sonnet he writes, "When I have fears" (1818; published 1848). Here he figures himself as *writer*, rather than as just a reader, something he rarely did in the sonnets after the immature "On Leaving Some Friends At An Early Hour." The poem approaches anew his (and Shakespeare's) concerns with poetic ambition and intertextuality:

> When I have fears that I may cease to be
>   Before my pen has glean'd my teeming brain,
> Before high piled books, in charactry,
>   Hold like rich garners the full ripen'd grain;
> When I behold, upon the night's starr'd face,
>   Huge cloudy symbols of a high romance,
> And think that I may never live to trace
>   Their shadows, with the magic hand of chance;
> And when I feel, fair creature of an hour,
>   That I shall never look upon thee more,
> Never have relish in the fairy power
>   Of unreflecting love;—then on the shore
> Of the wide world I stand alone, and think
> Till love and fame to nothingness do sink.

The poem is more proleptically elegiac than any single sonnet he has composed thus far. Much of the elegiac tone comes from the verbal echoes of Shakespeare's sonnets 12 ("When I do count the clock that tells the time"), with that poet's worry of "lofty trees I see barren of leaves," and 107 ("Not mine own fears nor the prophetic soul / Of the wide world dreaming on things to come . . .").[49] Keats had already employed the agricultural metaphor in various poems as a trope for receptivity; but through Shakespeare, Keats deepens it into a seasonal metaphor that associates images of natural growth not only with literary production but also with death. The force of potentiality palpable throughout Keats's sonnets thus far is figured as grain "teeming" with life, ready to be "garnered" like "full ripen'd grain" by the harvesting pen.[50] In the second quatrain in the poem, Nature itself becomes a kind of writing carrying the symbolic message the poet is after. But the legibility of that message is, as usual for Keats, difficult, the book of nature obscure.

The "fears" of Keats's poem may have nothing to do with literal death—Bate insists that it is unlikely that Keats even suspected at this time that he had contracted tuberculosis, while other critics disagree—but in any case the "fears" certainly *do* have to do with anxiety over both secondariness and obscurity.[51] Keats's awareness of and thematization of his own belatedness—now anticipated as an early death—forms the nexus of this sonnet, in a manner similar to Shakespeare's sequence. That vision of early death is, however, remarkably transformed in the closing couplet of "When I have fears." The close actually begins in line 12, with a punctuated break in the text: "—then on the shore / Of the wide world I stand alone, and think." The powerful enjambment between those lines attempts to destroy the boundary between the liminal or threshold figure that reappears here, and the "wide world" that lets one, remembering Shakespeare, dream "on things to come." That affirmation appears to undo itself in the final line—but on second look, perhaps not. For while the last line does describe a peculiar sort of early death, it is not the death of the poet, exactly, but of poetic ambition. The "thinking" in which he engages empties out of him the anxieties of secondariness and obliterates the past by reducing "fame," the memory of that past, to nought.

Both the Lear and "When I have fears" sonnets concern themselves with a before-ness, a prolepsis that will somehow *not* be a mere repetition. The trap of form has become relentless *because* Keats himself so relentlessly identifies his subjectivity with literariness. Like Shakespeare himself, Keats's insight into his own visionary poetics tends toward nostalgia and to what Joel Fineman calls a "retrospective visuality, a poetry of belated re-turn rather than of simple turn."[52] Alienation from vision is marked by the fact that so many of his poems are linked to the act of reading: intelligibility itself is linked to experience-as-reading. Keats's consciousness of that prolepsis is part of *his* particular originality—an originality by which literary understanding (reading, writing) begins to resemble a sense perception as radical as physical sight.

Nevertheless, Keats's later sonnets do not overcome a concern with secondariness, and that failure once again becomes the occasion of composition. While "To Homer" (1818; published 1848) meditates upon that great original (and possibly, again, more crucially upon Milton), I suspect that the second, "Read me a lesson, Muse" (1818; published 1838), also called "Written on the Top of Ben Nevis," has behind it the shadow of Wordsworth, whose home Keats had just visited. Unlike previous sonnets, "To Homer" *opens* with the threshold figure standing at the shore and looking out onto those vast widenesses:

> Standing aloof in giant ignorance,
> Of thee I hear and of the Cyclades,
> As one who sits ashore and longs perchance
> To visit dolphin-coral in deep seas.
> So wast thou blind;—but then the veil was rent,
> For Jove uncurtain'd heaven to let thee live,
> And Neptune made for thee a spumy tent,
> And Pan made sing for thee his forest-hive;
>
> (Lines 1–8)

The octave fashions the radical connection—a figural substitution—between the literally blind Homer and the figuratively blind Keats. But the trope of vision is complicated by the trope of *hearing*; the implicit problem is again the relation of voice to vision: "continuity between singing and listening is desirable in both senses: if to be able to listen is to be able to sing, then Keats's own position in literary history—listening to older voices—is a favorable one."[53] The sestet, once again, opens the poem out toward a visionary potentiality that is figured by a prophetic radiance more typically available to Shelley:

> Aye on the shores of darkness there is light,
> And precipices show untrodden green,
> There is a budding morrow in midnight,
> There is a triple sight in blindness keen;
> Such seeing hadst thou, as it once befel
> To Dian, Queen of Earth, and Heaven, and Hell.
>
> (Lines 9–14)

The most technical aspects of these lines underscore the poem's lyric plot. Line 11's stress shift from *mid*night to mid*night*, due to that word's rhyming position, draws attention to *both* root morphemes, thus emphasizing the temporal liminality of that moment as the pivot between night and morning, dark and light; the alliteration of "*m*orrow" and "*m*idnight" figures that proleptic movement. Furthermore, the assonance of "sight" (line 12) with respect to the rhyme-words "light" and "midnight" (lines 9, 11) also tropes the poem's plotting from darkness to edge of vision.[54] Finally, the striking oxymoron, "blindness keen" (we usually think of "keen sight"), underscores the paradox of poetic insight for Keats, a paradox that has less to do with the actual relationship of imagination and reality than with some power of imagination that is explicitly intertextual. If the octave's image of the rent veil of heaven, from Matt. 27:51 ("And, behold, the veil of the temple was rent in twain from the top to the bottom. . . .") is meant to suggest that the poet himself shall receive a new testament to imaginative vision, the poem's "budding morrow in midnight" reemphasizes that Keats is still left, like Forster's boy in the short story, on the shore's edge with the conviction that he has still only "seen it coming. Light and a wind." Despite the weakly traditional diction of Keats's lines here—the prosaic Forster is more direct—the rhetorical move at the end of "To Homer" is a grand one; the poet claims a cosmic vision for Homer and, by the logic of metaphoric substitution, for himself.

The poem written on top of Ben Nevis in Scotland (which Rossetti called "perhaps the most thoughtful [sonnet] in Keats") makes more explicit the imaginative nearsightedness that Keats still experiences:

> Read me a lesson, Muse, and speak it loud
>   Upon the top of Nevis, blind in mist!
> I look into the chasms, and a shroud
>   Vaprous doth hide them; just so much I wist
> Mankind do know of hell: I look o'erhead,
>   And there is sullen mist; even so much
> Mankind can tell of heaven: mist is spread
>   Before the earth beneath me; even such,
> Even so vague is man's sight of himself.
>   Here are the craggy stones beneath my feet;
> Thus much I know, that, a poor witless elf,
>   I tread on them; that all my eye doth meet
> Is mist and crag—not only on this height,
> But in the world of thought and mental might.

The same configuration of tropes is there: being read to—as hearing; a veil or mist or "shroud vaprous"; chasms and precipices, a sublime landscape of imaginative struggle (a figure, surely, of the "mental might" of the just-visited Wordsworth); and the three-level division of vision that corresponds temporally to past, present, and future. The poem's repetitive diction of "measurement" suggests that the poet is defining as precisely as possible the limits of his imaginative vision: "just so much," "even so much," "even such, / Even so." He knows what he does not know.

The closing lines remind the poet that, as in his earlier sonnet on the Elgin Marbles, his eye meets only "mist and crag," obscurity and struggle, not only literally "on this height" but metaphorically, "in the world of thought and mental might." This sublime landscape, which should have suggested to him the boundlessness of the imagination, instead deflates him, reminds him only of how bounded his own abilities are. With even the force of natural light obscured, the poet calls on the intermediary muse that speaks through language.[55]

Whereas for Wordsworth and Shelley this scanty plot of ground was a launching pad to a visionary realm, for Keats it was more like quicksand, the problem of closure and its associated tropes and themes turning the sonnet into a formal trap. The sense of enclosure or entrapment in these poems is a negative end of Wordsworth's employment of the form as a receptacle for his visionary poetic; the introspection and involution he handled so powerfully is an ideal that Keats rarely achieves. His final love sonnets, in fact, turn away from visionary poetics altogether, becoming true emblems of entrapment within the self—poems of frustrated desire in which the Shakespearean couplet the poet so disliked closes the stanza shut with a vengeance.

The cataloging that has long characterized his sonnets and their effort to resist closure takes over the entire poem in "The Day is gone, and all its sweets are gone" (1819), where the conventional Renaissance blazon is turned inside out. A device that creates by a figurative sculpting an idealized figure of the absent lady, the blazon in this poem has the simultaneous effect of negating her image, with the word "Faded" opening every line of the following quatrain. In Keats's very last sonnet, "I cry your mercy—," too, the effort to condense "all" into this bound form creates a poem in which, as Curran has accurately put it, "syntax, logic, conjunctive language [are] all displaced," and the poem's fullness "collapses of its own weight into inanition, a vacuum that swallows every element of the catalog in a dying fall suggestive of Wordsworth's practice."[56]

Indeed, the literariness of Keats's notion of subjectivity, as I have described it throughout this chapter, appears to effectively close him off from the stance of poetic potency and originality that he obsessively seeks in and through the sonnet form. The Miltonic "wild uproar," for all Keats's disclaimers, still sounds in his mind's ear. If Nicholas Roe is right, even the last sonnet Keats worked on, "Bright Star," is not simply about Fanny Brawne, as everyone agrees, but is also more generally about the problem of Milton and Wordsworth. Roe's reading, among the first to widen our view of this well-known poem, connects the poem's primary figure, the star, to the very constellation of star images I have traced in earlier chapters, from Milton to Wordsworth to Shelley, for whom it signified "virtue," or strength, ethical as well as poetical. For Roe, Keats's "bright star" is instead a figure of the drive for originality and permanence in art, not just about frustrated love; the key is, once again, the need to locate a poetic authority that claims kinship to those predecessors, without being overpowered by their influence.[57]

Therefore, the strategy of "Bright Star," also written in 1819 but revised in 1820 on the boat to Italy,[58] is once again resistance to closure. The very sounds of the sonnet's first lines linger on throughout the rest of the poem, through Keats's use of internal rhyme and "vowel melody." The steadfastness of the star "hung aloft," eternally watching and sleepless, attempts to suspend temporality altogether from the octave. Nevertheless, the poet's desire for the actual rather than the ideal forms the pivotal conflict of the poem:

> No—yet still stedfast, still unchangeable,
>   Pillow'd upon my fair love's ripening breast,
> To feel for ever its soft swell and fall,
>   Awake for ever in a sweet unrest,
> Still, still to hear her tender-taken breath,
>   And so live ever—or else swoon to death.
>
> (Lines 9–14)

The sestet's compulsive repetition of "ever" and "still" acknowledges that after the "No—" that negates the star-speaker analogy that has been set up, the poem can only struggle to *keep* time suspended, and closure at bay, until the sonnet must snap shut with its "swoon to death," incapable of harboring the desired suspension. The fullness of the poem's expression is ultimately deflated by the imagined erotic fulfillment (assuming an allusion in the last line to the old Elizabethan pun); thus even Keats's last sonnet tropes this poet's frustrated idealism.

IV

There is in all of this poet's sonnet work one poem in which he appears to escape the claustrophobia of form and the pressure of literary-historical voices that echo in his own imagination. This neglected poem is a rare blank-verse sonnet, "O thou whose face has felt the winter wind," which appeared in a letter to Reynolds dated 19 February 1818 (published 1848):

> "O thou whose face hath felt the Winter's wind;
> Whose eye has seen the Snow clouds hung in Mist
> And the black-elm tops 'mong the freezing Stars
> To thee the Spring will be a harvest-time—
> O thou whose only book has been the light
> Of supreme darkness which thou feddest on
> Night after night, when Phoebus was away
> To thee the Spring shall be a tripple morn—
> O fret not after knowledge—I have none,
> And yet my song comes native with the warmth
> O fret not after knowledge—I have none,
> And yet the Evening listens—He who saddens
> At thought of Idleness cannot be idle,
> And he's awake who thinks himself asleep."[59]

What is unusual about the poem—in addition to the absence of rhyme—is a feeling of freedom in its occasion. Unlike all the sonnets previously looked at, this one confronts most radically the problem of the past, not by worrying over the memory of something already seen, already read, already heard, but by discovering in the imagery of nature a way of evading the poem's textuality—and thus a way of evading the closure of literary history itself. That is, the poem offers a reprieve from that history, such that the speaker can dwell in the comfort of a suspended moment of lyric. There are no voices here other than the speaker's (about whom more shortly), not even as whisperings or echoes. The temporality of this poem is not defined by retrospection, but by a strategy more powerfully proleptic than any we have yet seen.

A reading of this poem must begin, however, with a look at the extraordinary letter, of which the poem is, in fact, a distillation. Its primary theme is once again the "work" of poetry, and the relationship of perception, memory, and thought to poetic conception. Excused by the poet finally as "mere sophistication . . . to excuse my own indolence," the letter returns to the scene of poetic labor visited early in this essay. The letter passage begins to explain Keats's idiosyncratic revision of the Wordsworthian notion of poetic "work" and the power of the active subject; in contrast to that sort of active intensity, Keats argues for a "delicious diligent Indolence," "voyages of conception" that can be accomplished as well during a "doze upon a Sofa" as by reading a book. Indeed, the letter explicitly denigrates the need for coping with "noble Books" and their writers—and with the literary memory that he regards, here as in so many of his poems, as the writer's particular burden:

> Memory should not be called knowledge—Many have original Minds who do not think it—they are led away by Custom—Now it appears to me that almost any Man may like the Spider spin from his own inwards his own airy Citadel—the points of leaves and twigs on which the spider begins her work are few and she fills the Air with a beautiful circuiting: man should be content with as few points to tip with the fine Webb of his Soul and weave a tapestry empyrean—full of Symbols for his spiritual eye, of softness for his spiritual touch, of space for his wandering[,] of distinctness for his Luxury— . . .

These sentences highlight Keats's continued evasion of literary history in their assertive denial of (literary) memory as "knowledge." He attempts to return to a view of art in which nature supplies the materials—*or* in which reading becomes merely, as suggested earlier, a kind of sixth sense, as if words and ideas, like sights and smells, were understood through equivalent modes of perception.

The very notion of a work of art transforms into something like a natural process: a spider spinning its web. This figure of form is rather different from the trope of limitation seen in those "boughs pavillion'd"; it is now an "airy Citadel," its "circuitry" not rooted in the earth like those boughs but barely attached to the leaves and twigs. The poem is still troped as a "text," a weaving together of lines—but here the materials and shape of the tapestry are from the poet's own *"inwards"* (emphasis mine), a word with fascinating paradoxical force: from the poet's "inwards" a visionary world is built *out*wards. We have seen this paradox before—in the globelike eye of the poet-Cortez, the inward intensity of his vision troped as the vast wideness of the sea. "Custom," the knowledge and strictures of tradition, need not concern such explorers, who already sit at the edge of the known world.

Still thinking about "knowledge" and the process of poetry, Keats continues this fascinating and complicated letter by describing a reciprocality of objective and subjective that requires passivity rather than Wordsworth's more aggressively "egotistical" interactions. Indeed, the following passage of this letter has behind it the same Wordsworth images (from his sonnet on the sonnet) that "On Solitude" does:

> It has been an old Comparison for our urging on—the Bee hive—however it seems to me that we should rather be the flower than the Bee—for it is a false notion that more is gained by receiving than giving—no the receiver

and the giver are equal in their benefits—The f[l]ower I doubt not receives a
fair guerdon from the Bee—its leaves blush deeper in the next spring—and
who shall say between Man and Woman which is the most delighted? Now it
is more noble to sit like Jove that [*sic*] to fly like Mercury—let us not therefore go hurrying about and collecting honey-bee like, buzzing here and there
impatiently from a knowledge of what is to be arrived at: but let us open our
leaves like a flower and be passive and receptive—budding patiently under
the eye of Apollo and taking hints from eve[r]y noble insect that favors us
with a visit—sap will be given us for Meat and dew for drink—I was led into
these thoughts, my dear Reynolds, by the beauty of the morning operating
on a sense of Idleness— . . .

Keats's image of the Wordsworthian bee is not one of tranquility, "murmur-
[ing] by the hour in foxglove bells," but of impatience, "from a knowledge
of what is to be arrived at." It is likely that despite the allusion to Wordsworth's figure of the sonnet writer, Keats clearly recognizes this impatience
in *himself*, one motivated by his own knowledge of "what is to be arrived
at"—literary fame, and the sounding of his own voice over all others.[60]

Thus right before he begins his poem, Keats affirms the value of his
idleness with his refusal to *read*: "I have not read any Books," he says; "—
the Morning said I was right—I had no Idea but of the Morning and the
Thrush said I was right—seeming to say—." The poem that follows is spo-
ken, significantly, not in the voice of the lyric "I" but of a thrush, a "natural
agent" of song, not unlike the spider and its web. This displacement re-
lieves the pressure of his own subjectivity, a pressure we know from other
letters that he felt keenly, almost as an oppression. Having displaced the
importance of books, Keats appeals to nature's own cyclical temporality—
which always promises a future in the spring, or in the morning—to defuse
that impatience and to release him from the threat of literary history's closure before him. The passage's lapse into sexual imagery describes
figuratively a fulfillment, achieved not through aggression but through passivity, a receptivity that counters an egotistical appropriation of experience.
The gender metaphorics of this passage are, indeed, significantly different
from those of Wordsworth's letter to Lady Beaumont explicated in chapter 1.
This letter's proleptic rhetoric toward the issues of literary memory and
knowledge, idleness and work, nature and literature, rules the movement of
the sonnet itself. In the octave, the winter merely anticipates the spring,
which by a grandly proleptic sweep is called "a harvest-time." The darkness is not a time of deprivation, even though Phoebus, associated mythi-
cally not only with the sun but also, of course, with poetry, is absent; the
darkness anticipates both the morning and the spring, a conflation of the
two cyclical regenerations of nature.

In the poem's sestet, the problem of literary memory and knowledge—
"I have not read any books"—is quieted by its assertion, anticipated in the
letter passage, that poetry is "native," a word used in its rarer sense of "natural" or "according to nature." Keats finally imagines a moment when the
intellectual work of a poem can hardly be distinguished from perception
itself; poetic intuition and natural sensation are simultaneous. The work of
poetry is displaced as a form of idleness, giving Keats a fictional moment
of poetry that indeed appears to come as naturally as leaves to the tree and
to achieve a vision of voice that comes "native." Keats finally discovers his
own "intensity" in the sonnet—but of a character quite different from
Wordsworth's. The intensity lies not in concentration so much as in an apparent immersion of self in the present moment of receptivity. In this the
sonnet interestingly anticipates the later ode, "To Autumn," equally proleptic in its strategies.

The absence of Keatsian claustrophobia is mirrored by the freedom of
the sonnet form itself, the fetters of rhyme loosened altogether in the blank-
verse scheme. The sonnet's conventional divisions are clearly indicated,
however—not by line endings but by line beginnings, the anaphora that
marks quatrains and tercets. Even the pressure of closure is eased. While
the last two-and-a-half lines, marked by the poem's only feminine endings,
stand in the place of a terminal couplet in a Shakespearean sonnet, the
"elegiac" force of such a close is short-circuited by a final proleptic strategy, beginning with line 12's anticipatory announcement: "And yet the
Evening listens—." Like his earlier sonnet, "Great spirits are now on earth
sojourning," with its blank half-line, this poem ends with Keats's insistence
that we, his readers, *listen*. The logic of this poem and its letter, however,
represses entirely the voices of the past that haunted his earlier poems; our
ear is sharpened in anticipation of the figure left us at the poem's end—a
poet who "sleeps" with his visionary eyes open, on the verge of rising to
great things.

There are, predictably—perhaps necessarily—deep ironies in this let-
ter/poem's effort to escape the literary. Textuality intervenes inevitably, not
least in the text's own allusiveness to Wordsworth and to the wider tradition
of lyric poetry; the sonnet's claim of coming "native with the warmth" is at
once underscored by its framing fiction of being uttered by a bird, a "natural" agent, and undermined by the poet's displacement of the utterance from
himself to the most traditional of literary figures for the voice of lyric poetry. Most ironic is the poem's echo in lines 5–6 ("O thou whose only book
has been the light / Of supreme darkness which thou feddest on") of
Wordsworth's *Excursion* (published 1814), 6:886–87: "how far / His darkness doth transcend our fickle light!" For the very thrush that Keats "hears"

comes precisely from this same *Excursion* passage. In book 6, the Vicar
character is telling the story of the abandoned "Ellen," who, during a solitary complaint against her lover, hears a thrush singing, as she imagines,
"for delight / Of his fond partner" sitting silently in the nest (lines 867–68).
Wondering why her own partner was not as faithful as the bird, Ellen urges
the absent lover to "hear him!", how the bird sings "As if he wished the
firmament of heaven / Should listen" (883–84); hear, she says, "the proclamation that he makes, how far / His darkness doth transcend our fickle
light" (886–87). As the thrush sings for the hapless Ellen, declaring in his
song God's transcendent mystery, so it may be for Keats, whose thrush at
once proclaims the transcendence of "natural poetry"—and acknowledges
that proclamation as a poetic fiction.

   However carefully Keats would displace all threats to this scene of self-
authorization, tradition will out—with Wordsworth knocking loudest at that.
These paradoxes all point to this sonnet's central effort to free this poet of
his sense of inhabiting an imaginative space crowded with the sounds of
previous voices, shadowed by tradition. This was an experiment Keats did
not repeat—and yet one detects in it the shift out of the sonnet's too-con-
stricting form, and into the ode form, where he seemed finally to discover a
vehicle better suited to his own particular genius.

From Sonnet to Ode:
The Latency of Tradition and "To Autumn"

   H. W. Garrod, in 1926, was the first to make the connection between
Keats's "Dull Rhymes" sonnet and his ode form.[61] Bate has given most
careful and remarkable attention to this connection, and he asserts that after this sonnet, the form became "only an incidental and casual form for
Keats. If his poetic temper was still mainly lyrical, it was becoming too
richly weighted to be couched in the brief space of the sonnet." Bate explains elsewhere that "If by Dull Rhymes," the last of three experimental
sonnets ("To Sleep" and "How fever'd is the man" are the others) may have
given the poet the idea for a new lyric form that was more "malleable and
capable of extension."[62] The ten-line ode form—*ababcdecde*—is an amalgamation of the Shakespearean and Petrarchan sonnet forms, a truncated
sonnet-stanza, that gave him "a more richly capacious form than the sonnet
(or, for that matter, the song and the ballad)"[63] and avoids the problems he
had named in his letter prefacing the "Dull Rhymes" sonnet.

   The move from sonnet into ode form remarkably parallels Shelley's,
and the reason could lie in these poets' recognition of what is odelike in the

sonnet—its vision of voice, an aspect of the form highlighted by Milton and followed by Wordsworth. All these poets recognize the sonnet's concern with a particular set of tropes: emptiness and fullness; space and miniaturization; silence and voice. And Shelley and Keats, especially, discover an anticipatory motive in the sonnet that is related, as this and the previous chapters have shown, to the sonnet's own awareness of its formal need to close.

But Keats is not Shelley, and their solutions are not as similar as would at first appear, even if their overall patterns of development are. While Shelley's ode takes on a mode of sublimity, Keats's odes are generally thought to demonstrate mastery of his own mode, negative capability, a form of subjectivity divorced from what Keats named the "egotistical sublime." For Wordsworth and Shelley the strength of the sonnet lies in the excess of power generated by the mind's efforts of concentration or intensification into an "egotistical sublime." The expansiveness of the private voice in the Wordsworth visionary sonnet, however, fails in the sonnets of Keats, which strain against the sonnet as against a prison-house of poetic form. According to Woodhouse, Keats's view of the "highest order of Poet" was that he would possess

> so high an imag[ination] that he will be able to throw his own soul into [the] any object he sees or imagines, so as to see feel [&] be sensible of, & express, all that the object itself wo[uld] see feel [&] be sensible of or express—& he will speak out of that object so that his own self will with the Exception of the Mechanical part be "annihilated"—and it is of the excess of power that I suppose Keats to speaks [sic], when he says he has no identity—.[64]

The oppressiveness of identity for Keats is connected to the oppressiveness of this particular form, with its conventional affiliation with the *propria persona* and its Miltonic "vision of voice." Keats had not yet developed his *own* vision of voice, nor an aesthetic psychology fully devoid of the idealizing egotism of Wordsworth.

If developing the new ode form was an effort to escape the constraints of the sonnet form, along with the "traps" of literary tradition and of subjectivity that accompany it, it should be instructive to look at what happens to this problem of belatedness in the ode. I have chosen the ode "To Autumn," partly because it is his last, partly because the form there is itself a modification of the ode form that Keats himself had developed. While the Keatsian ode form usually had ten lines, in this last ode Keats adds an eleventh line—creating a couplet not at the end, but right before the end (*ababcdedcce* in the first stanza, *ababcdecdde* in the second and third). The stanza of "To Autumn" (1819; published 1820), with its extra line after the couplet, signals a kind of stanzaic excess, among the other kinds of excess the poem describes.

The creation of a sort of *penultimate* couplet has, as a strategy, a familiar feel to it. The new ode form grapples with the old problem of closure in the sonnet by bringing here a haunting reminder of that couplet-closure— and suspending it. "Suspension" in previous Keats sonnets had meant something like a "gesture of incompleteness"; here, it means something else: a "principle of continuation." The autumn harvest is over, but there is more:

1

Season of mists and mellow fruitfulness,
  Close bosom-friend of the maturing sun;
Conspiring with him how to load and bless
  With fruit the vines that round the thatch-eves run;
To bend with apples the moss'd cottage-trees,
  And fill all fruit with ripeness to the core;
    To swell the gourd, and plump the hazel shells
  With a sweet kernel; to set budding more,
And still more, later flowers for the bees,
Until they think warm days will never cease,
    For summer has o'erbrimm'd their clammy cells.

2

Who hath not seen thee oft amid thy store?
  Sometimes whoever seeks abroad may find
Thee sitting careless on a granary floor,
  Thy hair soft-lifted by the winnowing wind;
Or on a half-reap'd furrow sound asleep,
  Drows'd with the fume of poppies, while thy hook
    Spares the next swath and all its twined flowers:
And sometimes like a gleaner thou dost keep
  Steady thy laden head across a brook;
  Or by a cyder-press, with patient look,
    Thou watchest the last oozings hours by hours.

(Lines 1–22)

Keats is no longer imagining what is to come, as he did so compulsively in his sonnets, but rather what is already stored up. This is different from the potency in the poems of Wordsworth and Shelley, and different from the *potentia* discussed earlier in this chapter. It is instead a latency,[65] like the survival of the last line following the couplet in this stanza. There is the promise, formally as well as thematically, of something more that is already there, stored up, "spare."

Whereas I have so far described form as a figure of containment, in this poem form becomes something that is almost overwhelmed by its own fullness. Images of containment in the poem are filled up, not to the breaking point, as in Keats's final sonnets, but to the point of overflow: "For summer has o'erbrimmed their clammy cells"; "Thou watchest the last oozings hours by hours." Time is prolonged; in the first stanza, flowers keep budding and become "later flowers"; the bees are made to forget that in fact summer has left and warm weather will cease. Summer, in its lateness, has usurped the place of winter, for which all harvests are preparations. Everything in the poem goes beyond its conventional boundaries.

This strategy of overfilling things is powerful, suppressing winter and death in the first two stanzas. But the suppression "will out," as it were, as is evident in the images of latency in these lines, in the undercurrent of obscurity: the "mists," the "close"-ness, the "conspiring," the charged juxtaposition of the words "still more" in line 9, the deception of the bees by lateness. The pressure of oxymoron is palpable here. And then there is the deathlike stasis of the autumn goddess herself, whose forgetting, by the "fume of poppies," of her labor is so complete that all labors threaten to halt. So near-complete is this forgetting that Autumn is said to be "sound asleep," as if sound itself, the constitutive trope of the third stanza, is hushed.

In lines 16–18, however, the poem resists the leaning toward death: "Or on a half-reaped furrow sound asleep, / Drowsed with the fume of poppies, while thy hook / Spares the next swath and all its twined flowers." In the word "spares" Keats yokes together both its senses, of "forbearing death," allowing grain and flower to go unharvested and presumably to reseed and regenerate, and the sense of "surplus" or "extra," so that the word "spare" looks backward and forward. The force of suspension in the poem allows the word "next" to suggest something always about to be.

The rest of the poem is governed by this sort of temporal double vision and by the problem of survival after death. In the final lines of the stanza, the poet gives an alternate vision of the goddess as, once again, a laborer; her "patient look" carrying a sense of enduring, of the temporal prolongation that has characterized the stanza. But she also shows, in the midst of this excess, a sense of nostalgia, as she watches her own season come to a close. The nostalgia implicit at the end of stanza 2 is realized in the first line of stanza 3: "Where are the songs of Spring?"—clearly a line uttered from a belated world.

The peculiarity of what follows, however, is that although autumn implicitly bears thoughts of loss and death with it, these thoughts are suppressed in the next lines: "Think not of them, thou hast thy music too,— / While barred clouds bloom the soft-dying day, / And touch the stubble-plains with rosy hue" (lines 24–26). As Bloom and others have noticed, there is no mention of winter here; it is willfully forgotten. The turn in line 24 is based on another forgetting—of one's past songs. That act of willed forgetting, here as in the poems discussed earlier, is crucial, because the latency in the poem—the inhalation of "poppy fumes"—deactivates the self and its resistances, and activates sheer receptivity. The landscape is no longer "sound asleep"; rather, sound is awakened, and becomes the major trope of the last stanza.[66]

To a remarkable degree, this latency dissolves the trap of memory for Keats, because it evades the necessity of death by opening out of the present moment, during which one can forget about passing time and simply continue to produce.[67] The middle stanza revolves around past and future as indeed the season does; the poet summarizes this double vision in the word "store" in line 12, recalling not only of what has been stored up, the culmination and accumulation of the past growing season, but also what is *in* store, with the sense of futurity invoked. The earlier image of forgetfulness, the flowering poppies of stanza 1, informs and invigorates the final stanza; the poppies are figured grandly in the barred clouds, which have not only themselves bloomed but seem actively to cause the day itself to bloom, though "soft-dying."[68] The entire landscape is brought to a new flowering and to a new dawn, "with rosy hue."

The poem turns upon its own images and temporal double vision. It begins to embody, formally and imagistically, the cycle of the year, of which autumn is the culmination and synecdoche.[69] The final seven lines of the poem carry this double vision to its end:

> Then in a wailful choir the small gnats mourn
> Among the river sallows, borne aloft
> Or sinking as the light wind lives or dies;
> And full-grown lambs loud bleat from hilly bourn;
> Hedge-crickets sing; and now with treble soft
> The red-breast whistles from a garden-croft;
> And gathering swallows twitter in the skies.
>
> (Lines 27–33)

In "mourn" (line 27), "borne" (line 28), "lives or dies" (line 29), and "bourn" (line 30), we have various reminders of both life and death: In "mourn" we can hear "morn," in "borne" and "bourn," "born." In the "full-grown lambs" we see an almost oxymoronic image of adulthood and childhood; in "hedge-crickets" we hear fall coming, yet in "red-breast" we think of that first robin.

The stanza as a whole has been one of receptivity; the poet for the first time looks at an actual landscape rather than musing upon the idea of one, naming each element of nature as he sees or hears it. Helen Vendler reads these final lines as a forgetting or annihilation of subjectivity: "Both loss and its compensatory projections . . . are forgotten in an annihilation of subjectivity and a pure immersion in the actual."[70] Subjectivity is still present, but no longer a source of resistance. The forgetting of subjectivity (Keats's "negative capability," in other words) allows the poet's "pure immersion" in the actual, but it is his very subjectivity that records the perceptions. This is an intensity that is akin to Wordsworth's; both of them privilege the moment and its fullness, discovering power in that fullness, but Keats lacks Wordsworth's compulsive reappropriation of such moments in retrospective temporality.

The ode's final line, "And gathering swallows twitter in the skies" is the most difficult to interpret, perhaps because it is the only one that openly remembers what has been submerged throughout, the winter, and death. Almost ironically, the self-forgetting that has rendered the poet (negatively) capable of "immersion" in his subject has led him to the realistic acceptance of autumn as an ending. The gathering swallows are the poem's starkest image, for even the stubble plains are touched with color. And yet the birds are also the most hopeful image as well. Harold Bloom argues that Keats finds in the "predeparture twitterings of the gathering swallows an emblem of natural completion";[71] however, Bloom and others do not consider the importance of the adjective "gathering." One sees Keats preparing for flight into the world beyond like the congregating swallows—but in the word "gathering" Keats turns us back into the poem itself and the gathering that takes place there. This poem, like the "store" of line 12, is Keats's gathering of his own ripened grain and also a storing up for winter, when the landscape is dead.[72]

"To Autumn" is a final answer to his "When I have fears," with its explicitly literary worries about power and subjectivity. Here, those literary anxieties are quieted by metaphor. Following that earlier sonnet's agricultural metaphor, "To Autumn" is both an increase of and a gathering from Keats's store of poetic musing and production. The excellence of the ode is in the poet's recognition of a metaphor for his own natural and poetic life that offers both a structure for completion, and also a promise of something more. He himself becomes the very subject and subjectivity of the ode; his own identity, self-forgotten, blends into the figure of the autumn reaper, conspiring with the sun god, Apollo, the traditional god of poetry.[73]

The principle of continuity he had so obsessively sought in his sonnets is discovered.

At the opening of this section, I asked why Keats should have developed the ode form out of the sonnet form. I answer here that what Keats tried to accomplish in the odes grew out of what he perceived to be a failure in his sonnets. Keats would certainly have understood Dante Gabriel Rossetti's description of the sonnet as a "moment's monument," for he could not break out of the temporal bind of a poem that commemorates the death of a moment any better than Rossetti could. His effort in the sonnet was always to open out that moment, and only in the odes did he accomplish that—often, as in "To Autumn," evading the finality of death by suggesting, even formally, with that extra line, that something survives. Only here does the nearly pathological formal anxiety in the sonnets toward closure, silence, and death ease, and the proleptic motive that informed Keats's sonnet writing achieve a fully compensatory effect.

4

"Sonnettomania" and
the Ideology of Form

By the time Shelley and Keats had died, the romantic renaissance of the sonnet form was apparent from the sheer number of poems that appeared, both singly and in anthologies, through the end of the century. William Going's *Scanty Plot of Ground*, a 1976 study of the Victorian sonnet, includes an appendix compiling a partial listing of sonnet sequences in the eighteenth and nineteenth centuries; he numbers them at "some 260 . . . containing almost 4800 sonnets."[1] This is a list that could be greatly expanded, as he acknowledges—and it does not include the multitude of sonnets published singly. Wordsworth's sonnet on the sonnet, "Nuns fret not . . . ," had already spawned similar efforts: in 1807, the year of its publication, we also find Capel Lofft's ingenious, if mediocre, *corona* of sonnets on the sonnet. In the first lines of Lofft's series the bee of "Nuns fret not . . ." has wandered into new territory: "HERE end, industrious BEE, thy lov'd career; / Enricht from many a flowret's honied veins" (1.1–2).[2] Another minor poet, Thomas Doubleday, contributed his own sonnet on the sonnet in 1827, a rather clumsy effort with imagery, sentiments, and even an argument that clearly echo that same Wordsworth poem:

The Poet's Solitude

Think not the Poet's life, although his cell
Be seldom printed by the stranger's feet,
Hath not its silent plenitude of sweet.
Look at yon lonely and solitary dell;—
The stream that loiters 'mid its stones can tell
What flowerets its unnoted waters meet,
What odours o'er its narrow margin fleet;
Ay, and the Poet can repeat as well,—
The fox-glove, closing inly, like the shell:

The hyacinth; the rose, of buds the chief;
The thorn, be-diamonded with dewy showers;
The thyme's wild fragrance, and the heather-bell:
All, all, are there. So vain is the belief
That the sequestered path hath fewest flowers.[3]

The infectious nature of the literary response to Wordsworth's sonnets, which of course he continued to publish steadily over his lifetime, led in 1821 to one anonymous critic in the *New Monthly Magazine and Literary Journal* warning the reading public of what he called "sonnettomania," a "species of disorder" most akin to "the bite of a rabid animal."[4] Despite—or because of—the popularity of the form, the sonnet suffered a considerable "public image" problem, as the neologism "sonnettomania" alone suggests.

The *New Monthly Magazine's* literary alarmism was countered, however, by more sober observers of literary trends, and from the middle of the century onward "The Sonnet" became a topic for numerous scholarly and/ or journalistic discussions. Between the publication of Capel Lofft's *Laura: An Anthology of Sonnets* in 1814, with its lengthy and idiosyncratic preface on the history and construction of the form, and Reverend Matthew Russell's 1898 anthology of sonnets on the sonnet, a remarkable number of essays, review articles, and book prefaces appeared on the subject,[5] often to redeem the sonnet from the poor opinion in which it was still held:

> Whatever erroneous notions have prevailed among the less cultivated, there are few scholars who will not cordially sympathize with the warm and indignant protest of Mr. Aubrey de Vere against the loose and uncritical judgment out of which the unpopularity of the Sonnet has grown.[6]

The century-old judgment of Samuel Johnson continued to form academic and public opinion, it was felt, and Procrustes' bed was still rolled in whenever the sonnet form came under scrutiny:

> Although the writings of a distinguished living poet [Wordsworth] have done much towards diminishing the inveterate prejudice that once existed in this country against the Sonnet, I am afraid that the stern and haughty dictum of Dr. Samuel Johnson, who pronounced it incompatible with the genius of the English language, still continues to influence no inconsiderable portion of what is termed "the reading public."[7]

Some of these essays or "defenses" were published as introductions to anthologies of sonnets, some as prefaces to collections of contemporary lyric poetry in which the sonnet predominated over other poetic forms.

Other essays appeared as prefaces to volumes of sonnets by single authors (Thomas Doubleday or Wordsworth, for example), and still others were written as "histories" of the form for review articles covering a number of recent sonnet publications from England and abroad (France and Germany, primarily).

But the crucial question is why this topic should have provoked so much interest in the first place. Why anyone would bother to defend the sonnet at all? Because the answer to the question links my discussion of Wordsworth and his mode of romantic sonnet to the Victorian context that will follow, the present chapter is included as a transition from the analysis of romantic poets' sonnets to those of exemplary Victorians.

Sonnet Legislation and Formal "Morality"

The nineteenth century was, as Laurel Brake points out, a period "when literature [was] linked publicly with responsibility for national morality and salvation."[8] And what a retrospective look at these essays reveals is a multifaceted argument regarding not simply the renaissance of the sonnet form but also regarding the emergence of an aestheticist poetic and of a politics of literary form itself. The argument over form is best understood as part of a broader effort over the course of the second half of the nineteenth century to define a national aesthetic and a national morality with respect to literature—with Wordsworth as a "new Milton" and with the sonnet, a tool of both those poets, as a privileged form.[9]

These critics, the majority of them publishing after 1860, were well aware that it was primarily Wordsworth they were writing about; there are actually relatively few references to other contemporary sonnet writers, except in passing, and no serious discussions of the parallel development of women's sonnet writing during the century, even after the publication of Elizabeth Barrett Browning's *Sonnets from the Portuguese*. It is obvious enough rereading them now that the essays are part of an overall effort to hold up Wordsworth and his particular poetic. The critics do more than recognize the relation of the sonnet to subjectivity and to the interiority of experience; not missing the link with Milton, they also recognize—and insist upon—the integrity of Wordsworth's claim of a visionary poetic linking the private experience of the solitary poet to that of the public bard, a "man speaking to men."

The defense of Wordsworth's poetic genius and his cultural status is displaced by these writers onto issues of sonnet *form*, often at quite a technical level. For example, the matter of poetic "licences and liberties" is a persistent issue in the essays, for while the critics are committed to defending the strengths and virtues of the sonnet form, some recognize the need to allow for change in any poetic form and others recognize a need to justify the changes of the Petrarchan form by English authors. Either way, the consensus is that a "relaxation" of the rules is in order, since, from a practical standpoint, a "purist" would find rather few modern sonnets that would meet his standards. Although it is common to speak of "sonnet legislation,"[10] some commentators propose that poets and readers alike think of the properties of the sonnet as governed by a set of "rules" rather than "laws," for rules are bent and broken with less "damage" than laws are.[11]

The subtext of these frankly pedantic and overly technical discussions, however, is a nascent literary ideology evolving out of theories of form and of genius best brought together by Coleridge, who argues, for example, that no

> work of true genius dares want its appropriate form, neither indeed is there any danger of this. As it must not, so genius cannot, be lawless: for it is even this that constitutes its genius—that of acting creatively under laws of its own origination.[12]

Dublin archbishop Richard Chenevix Trench, a man of letters and obvious admirer of both Wordsworth and the sonnet, reminds his reader that poetic form is, in fact, a *choice*. He and a number of the other critics had learned from Wordsworth that the sonnet "no prison is" and that there is a freedom in simply having chosen confinement, or what D. G. Rossetti's companion Thomas Hall Caine calls "amplitude in confinement."[13] Aubrey de Vere, the son of Wordsworth's friend and fellow poet, adds that far from extinguishing poetic inspiration, the difficulty of the form "stimulates power where real power exists, and the spontaneity of poetic genius accepts the bracing discipline and survives within it."[14]

What this attention to formal restraint and formal choice shades into, furthermore, is a concern with a literary morality, of which *form* is the moral measure. The argument is that the poet who is content with the sonnet is more disciplined, not only intellectually but also morally. Thomas Hall Caine, for example, notes that the sonnet form's fourteen-line parameters must have been "accepted merely for disciplinarian purposes, in order to curb the insatiate demand for room, which was then, as it is now, the mark of a restless intellect."[15] Henry Reed, in a published lecture, elaborates most fully on this point, using diction that recalls repeatedly Wordsworth's own comments on the sonnet form:

The complaint of the narrowness of the limits of the sonnet appears indicative more of the character of the mind of him who makes it than of anything else. Writers vary wonderfully in the room they require: some can breathe freely in no space narrower than a modern state paper, while others are more considerate. The former are not the men to write sonnets: we commend them to the epic. But is there not in this craving for space something that does not accord very well with true poetic temperament? If a writer be indeed worthy of his calling, if he do indeed belong to that creative class who make the world they inhabit, what need has he of calling for more ground? Is it not enough that he has a spot to rise from? The peak of a broken crag, or the point of a blasted branch, would be sorry quarters indeed for a bear or a buffalo; but the majesty of the eagle claims no wider sovereignty for his footing, when he is springing from the earth to bathe his wings in the floods of the sun. Or, when the lark soars, like a sick man's hope, to meet the coming dawn, the home he leaves is wrapped in the little circumference of a tuft of grass. To these the spirit of true poetry is kindred. The insatiate demand for room is the symptom of a restless and licentious intellect,—of feelings undisciplined.[16]

This fascinating passage returns to Wordsworth's "scanty plot of ground" image for the sonnet but also speculates about the "poetic spirit," which, inhabiting a writer "worthy of his calling," needs a form no larger than a sonnet from which to launch itself from the earthly realm to the purer atmosphere of poetry. Reed ingeniously draws out romantic figurations of the poet as a bird—a "majestic" eagle, a skylark—for whom form is a "grounding," a station from which to rise into poetical flights, and to which one gratefully returns at the end.

Reed drives home this general point by providing the (almost predictable) negative example: Lord Byron, who once scornfully dismissed the form as "the most puling, petrifying, stupidly platonic composition"[17] (though he in fact wrote several good ones). "[Byron's] head," says Reed, "and his heart and his tongue were all undisciplined . . . How much is it to be deplored that Lord Byron was too disdainful habitually to lay his restless head in the lap of nature!"[18] Byron's penchant for epic and other long narrative forms was just the sort of "craving" for room that Reed regarded as inappropriate to the "true poetic temperament."

What is more surprising is that the moral undertone to Reed's thoughts is given a political twist as well: "But we greatly err if the sonnet be not a favorite abiding-place for him who, whether as a writer or a reader, joins to an intellect well disciplined a heart nursed in the spirit of genuine freedom."[19] Three years later, in his 1866 lectures, Archbishop Trench picks up this connection among formal discipline, morality, and political freedom by returning to a theme mentioned earlier with particular reference to Wordsworth: that "free will" and "free choice" alone dictate a poet's choice of forms. Obviously this argument stems from the preference for the form by Milton and by Wordsworth for the defense and promotion of religious and political liberty.[20] The sonnet form allowed Milton and Wordsworth, Hall Caine remarks, to be "faithful to [their] English intellect";[21] intellectual and creative "responsibility" and political freedom go hand in hand.

The moral and political tinge of these essays colors as well some commentators' responses to the problem of the sonnet's supposed "incompatibility" with the language, a charge that many of the writers are especially determined to refute. They do so by attempting to neutralize the form's admittedly alien origins. Numerous defenses attempt to "prove" that the sonnet, though originally Italian, is no longer a "foreign" form, but is, in fact, a "naturalized" one. Robert Fletcher Housman, in 1835, notes that "With us . . . [the sonnet] has never been completely naturalized,"[22] and Reed warns thirty years later that there is an "*un-English* feeling" found "to be creeping about the heart" when one reads a sonnet, because "the fancy is filled unconsciously with thoughts of Petrarch and images of Laura and Vaucluse. . . . [We hear] our own mother-tongue, but tuned to a strange note; we hear its glorious words uttered through a foreign instrument. That is not as it should be."[23] So too William Sharp, an anthologist and poet, in his summary of the form's history in England:

> Surrey, again, evidently found his task over-difficult of satisfactory performance, and so constantly experimented with a fourteen-line sonnet-mould—like a musician who, arriving in his own land, finds his countrymen's ears not easily attuned to the melodies of the new instrument he brings with him from abroad, and so tries again and again to find some way of making his novel mandolin or lute-sounds attractive to ears accustomed to the harsher strains of fife or windpipe.[24]

These statements concentrate on the technical aspects of the form, justifying the rhyme changes, for example, by the first English sonneteers, even though that modification threatened the delicate balance of octave and sestet in the Italian form;[25] Reed attributes these technical changes to "a characteristic temper" in English poets, who, "with Shak[e]speare as their leader, have . . . claimed greater freedom."[26] Even the transformation of the genre in England since Wyatt and Surrey, then, is attributed to a *national* impulse toward freedom that is consistently troped by the form itself.

Following an alternate metaphor of generic evolution, both Archbishop

Trench and John Dennis describe the "transplantation" of the sonnet, as of an exotic flower, into English soil,[27] and Sharp picks up the figure, observing that Spenser, "unable to acclimatise the new vehicle," created a new, modified form, in a "transitional stage of development which a tropical plant experiences when introduced into a temperate clime. In this case the actual graft proved short-lived, but the lesson was not lost upon cultivators, in whose hands manifold seed lay ready for germination."[28] Just as the Italian sonnet "instrument" is "retuned" for the English ear, so is the sonnet's scanty plot of ground *English* ground now, not Italian. Expressing an attitude of poetic "territorialism" (he uses the word himself),[29] Reed proposes, in a passage tinted by legalistic rhetorical color, that English poets assert their "nation's claim to any form of composition":

> It may be shown that the sonnet is a form of poetry fairly introduced in the literature of England, fully sustained, and now, without reserve or qualification, by the law of letters it is our own. . . . The domain of letters is no more susceptible of private exclusive domain than is the open sea.[30]

These vindications of the sonnet tend to take on, in other words, a distinctly patriotic cast; a certain nationalistic claim sounds very sharply along with the sonnet claim.[31] Thomas Doubleday, himself author of a book of sonnets, attempts to locate the faults of English sonnets not with English poets but with the original Italian ones: "Capel Lofft, in the preface to his *Anthology of Sonnets,* enumerates tinsel, conceit, frigidity, and metaphysics, amongst the many heavy accusations against the Italian muse; and these unpleasant symptoms are supposed to have shown themselves most inveterately in her offspring, the Sonnet."[32] Caine concludes that the Shakespearean sonnet is "wholly indigenous and, within itself, entirely pure."[33] Thus would both writers vindicate the form from the "allegation that our sonnet literature is a bastard outcome of the Italian."[34] The so-called illegitimate, or English, form has become as "legitimate" as the original Italian form; therefore, it should no longer suffer under the negative implications of being a "bastard form." The commentators pick up these figures and invent others in order to more fully describe the transcendent "perfection" of the English sonnet. For example, whereas the Italian sonnet is compared to an acorn, which can "fall asunder" into unequal parts,[35] the English sonnet is figured most often as a sphere, clearly a version of Wordsworth's "dew-drop" image.

In 1881, Theodore Watts-Dunton introduced a new figure of form in a sonnet on the sonnet that appeared in the *Athenaeum* on 17 September 1881:

The Sonnet's Voice:
(A metrical lesson by the seashore.)

Yon silvery billows breaking on the beach
    Fall back in foam beneath the star-shine clear,
    The while my rhymes are murmuring in your ear
A restless lore like that the billows teach;
For on these sonnet-waves my soul would reach
    From its own depths, and rest within you, dear,
    As, through the billowy voices yearning here
Great nature strives to find a human speech.

A sonnet is a wave of melody:
    From heaving waters of the impassioned soul
    A billow of tidal music one and whole
Flows in the "octave"; then, returning free,
    Its ebbing surges in the "sestet" roll
Back to the deeps of Life's tumultuous sea.[36]

Reminiscent of Keats's "dying fall" description of the form, the image of the wave is a shift, because it emphasizes the binary aspect of the sonnet form, rather than the unitary (troped by the star, the sphere, the dewdrop); earlier chapters have shown that it is the overcoming of binary structure that empowers Wordsworth's sonnets and gives them that visionary momentum. But the wave model was taken up enthusiastically by both Caine and Sharp, for according to them, D. G. Rossetti himself endorsed this description of the form. Caine used the figure to distinguish the excellence of the contemporary sonnet from its Miltonic and Shakespearean forebears:

> Its merit and enduring popularity consist in its being grounded in a fixed law of nature. The natural phenomenon it reproduces is the familiar one of the flow and ebb of a wave in the sea. . . . For the perfecting of a poem on this pattern the primary necessity, therefore, is, that the thought [is] chosen to be such as falls naturally into unequal parts, each essential to each, and the one answering the other. The first and fundamental part shall have unity of sound no less than unity of emotion, while in the second part the sonnet shall assume a freedom of metrical movement analogous to the lawless ebb of a returning billow. The sonnet-writer who has capacity for this structure may be known by his choice of theme. Instinctively or consciously he alights on subjects that afford this flow and ebb of emotion. Nor does he fail to find in every impulse animating his muse something that corresponds with the law of movement that governs the sea.[37]

An earlier figure of form will have been implicit in this outline of the "wave theory": the sonnet as musical instrument, or, in keeping with its name, as itself "a piece of music."[38] Sharp comments, for example, that the sonnet is a "natural instrument," designed to express "certain radical laws of melody and harmony, in other words, of nature."[39] He goes on to describe the appearance of the new, wavelike contemporary sonnet as an event similar to "a harpist discover[ing] that with another string or two he could greatly add to the potential powers of this instrument,"[40] by which he means the discovery of new rhyme-sound distribution rather than number of lines. It was generally asserted that the sonnet is "essentially musical, and essentially founded on the harmony of sound,"[41] a "musical and imposing formula for the expression of a single or a prominent thought." The preference for commenting upon the supposed "musical" nature of the form is most clearly visible in Housman's remark that a fine sonnet concludes in such a way that the "very silence becomes musical."[42]

What *all* of these figures—whether the anglicized sonnet "ground," the "retuned" instrument, the wave—point to is not merely an impulse toward a generally organicist view of form inherited from romantic contemporaries or predecessors.[43] It is also a figural solution to the problem of "naturalizing" the sonnet by attempting to remove the discussion of the form from national prejudices altogether. This symbolic strategy effectively mutes the voices of the past, whether Italian or English; the wave and song images preclude discussions of the form's historical nature by suggesting the form is both "natural" and "eternal" and transcendent, rather than highly artificial and grounded in a long tradition.[44] The shift toward "naturalized" figures is symptomatic of the more general shift toward a view of the sonnet, and of lyric generally, as highly self-reflexive and disconnected to social concerns. Yet these essays are fascinating for their *recognition* of the link between lyric modes and the legitimization of social norms and literary ideology, even as they attempt to suppress that link. This move is only typical of a romantic ideology that defines a poetic self capable, as Marlon Ross puts it, of "appearing to capture the word for itself, appearing to father the world."[45]

THE ROMANTIC STAR, TRANSCENDENT FORM, AND AESTHETIC WITHDRAWAL

In addition, then, to betraying a surprising aspect of Victorian literary nationalism, these defenses also betray the degree to which the visionary claims of Wordsworth's sonnet writing shade into the century's deepening commitment to an idealist formalism that emerges with nineteenth-century aestheticism. As the century goes on, these defenses focus less on the technicalities of the form and more on its metaphorics, its figurations of form, and on what Caine calls the "intellectual plotting of a sonnet":[46] its simplicity of conception, its complexity of development, and its compression and unity of overall structure—"fundamental brain-work," as D. G. Rossetti described it. The most striking similarity among the defenses in this regard is the emphasis on unity and completeness, on miniaturization or concentration, on constraint and discipline. What was true of Wordsworth's sonnets was true of all sonnets: that their "greatness" lies in the ability of the poet to overcome "littleness" of size by largeness of conception.[47] Clearly these writers follow Wordsworth in asserting that although the form is limited in size, it is "of infinite compass," perfect:

> It is a special advantage of this form of composition, that it necessitates the precision of language and the concentration of thought which are of priceless value in poetry. In the sonnet every word should have a meaning, every line add to the beauty of the whole; and the exquisite delicacy of the workmanship should not lessen, but should rather assist in increasing the stability of the structure. A sonnet, brief though it be, is of infinite compass. What depth of emotion, what graceful fancy, what majestic organ notes, what soft flute-like music, is it not capable of expressing?[48]

The success of Wordsworth's poetic is evident in the way the "commonplace" and finite find themselves, in a "great" sonnet, lifted into a sublimer territory:

> Condensation of thought, precision of language, unity of design, are among its first requirements; but in a good Sonnet these qualities are accompanied by a dignity and grace which raises them beyond the sphere of [the] commonplace, and redeems them from that formal and didactic tone which is fatal to the genuine poetic character.[49]

The greatness of the Wordsworth sonnet, in other words, is that within this small form he can in effect dissolve all boundaries. This definition of formal "perfection" parallels Pater's distinction between good and great art: the former is bounded by formalism, the latter "transcends" it. Thus, summarizes Pater, "it is on the quality of the matter it informs or controls, its compass, its variety, its alliance to great ends, or the depth of the note of revolt, or the largeness of hope in it, that the greatness of literary art depends."[50]

The previous section of this chapter has already outlined the critics' and the poets' various figures of form for defining the nature and function of the sonnet. These critics, then, describe in their figurations precisely the emergence of form and meaning that I discussed in the first chapter as so central to Wordsworth. Most interesting from this perspective is the younger Aubrey de Vere's definition of the sonnet as a form whose "essential" oneness produces *"the development of a single thought so large as to be, latently, a poem."* By this account, the "incompatibility" between a form and "its preformal sources, the incompatibility between meaning and the meaningless," as Miller puts it, is transcended.[51] De Vere is describing what I have been calling the "visionary sonnet," in which one poetic moment becomes an apocalyptic moment containing all moments, in which the smallness of the form itself opens out through largeness of conception.

This also recalls the trope of "radiance" in the Wordsworthian sonnet, and indeed that important figure, the romantic star—which I have previously traced from Milton to Wordsworth, and then to Shelley and Keats—does make its appearance in this set of essays as well. Archbishop Trench, for example, explains the advantages of so prescribed a form in this way:

> Why has the Sonnet been, with poets at least, for I speak not now of their readers, so favourite a metre? They have, in the first place, felt, no doubt, the advantage of that check to diffuseness, that necessity of condensation and concentration which those narrow limits impose. Oftentimes a poem which, except for these, would have been but a loose nebulous vapour, has been *compressed and rounded into a star.*[52] (Emphasis mine)

The momentum implicit in the figure is captured by Caine, who describes the beauty of the Miltonic sonnet as "the absence of point in the evolution of the idea, whose peculiar charm lay in its being thrown off like a rocket, breaking into light and falling in a soft shower of brightness."[53] Caine is also identifying the way in which the Miltonic-Wordsworthian sonnet—as we have seen—typically *opens out* at the end, a public voice and vision projecting from the private voice of the poet.

This description is midway between the star figure and another that is also prominent in the defenses: the sonnet as gem or jewel. This figure I take to be a later version of the romantic star, a notion borne out by its use in a sonnet on the sonnet by the prolific and interesting Victorian poet Charles Tennyson Turner (brother of the Laureate), who clearly learned his trade from Wordsworth:

> Oft in our fancy an uncertain thought
> Hangs colourless, like dew on bents of grass,

Before the morning o'er the field doth pass;
But soon it glows and brightens; all unsought
A sudden glory flashes thro' the dream,
Our purpose deepens and our wit grows brave,
The thronging hints a richer utterance crave,
And tongues of fire approach the new-won theme;
A subtler process now begins—a claim
Is urged for order, a well-balanced scheme
Of words and numbers, a consistent aim;
The dew dissolves before the warming beam;
But that fair thought consolidates its flame,
And keeps its colours, hardening to a gem.[54]

In this self-reflexive sonnet, called "The Process of Composition: An Illustration," inspiration is figured in the octave as radiance; indeed, as it is "before the morning," one can surmise that this glowing or brightening of thought that gathers into a "sudden glory," "flash[ing]" into "tongues of fire," is actually being compared to the rising of the sun.[55] The title itself suggests something of the ekphrastic nature of the sonnet—the way it frames itself *as* a description of its own composition—which Tennyson Turner might well have learned from Wordsworth, too.

While the octave describes poetic inspiration, the sestet turns to the formal impulse, the "subtler process" of ordering and molding, of balancing feelings and "hints" of ideas into words and numbers, octaves and sestets. Tennyson Turner's gem image in the poem's final three lines is a significant revision of Wordsworth's dewdrop trope. The figure is no longer wholly natural, not just there "like dew on bents of grass." The dew has "dissolved" in the process—but the heat that has burned it away is not, like the sun, something *outside* the poet. By a subtle conflation, the heat comes from "that fair thought" itself, "consolidating its flame": the flame that was inspiration, making visible to the poet the meaning of the once "uncertain thought," is now a figure for the thought itself. The "process of composition" Tennyson Turner describes, then, is a process by which inspiration, which seems so often to the poet to come from somewhere else, is internalized and made his own *as* it becomes a poem. The mind's tempering "hardens" thought into some kind of order; the poet's craft tempers thought into form. Tennyson Turner's sonnet on the sonnet is thus yet another description of the transcendence of the incompatibility of form and preform, or of meaning and meaninglessness.

For the commentators, as for Wordsworth, it is Milton who has "made [the sonnet] shine newly, as if he had cut his diamond in such a way that only one luminous light were visible to us"; as Sharp, echoing Wordsworth, adds:

He [Milton] considered—so we may infer—that the English sonnet should be like a revolving sphere, every portion becoming continuously visible, with no break in the continuity of thought or expression anywhere apparent.[56]

For some romantics, the "radiant" poem is imagined illuminating politically troubled countries with an explosion that scatters knowledge and notions of liberty and revolution abroad. For some Victorians, basking in the poetic authority offered by Wordsworth, the sonnet is also conceived of as a gem, a valuable thing to be discovered, polished, and worked upon, and collected in anthologies and "treasuries," as they were often called, of "hand-crafted" poetical objects to be held up and admired (or "appreciated," to borrow Pater's term) as works of art.[57] (Caine, in fact, wrote Rossetti requesting any "sonnet treasure" he might be able to offer for his anthology.) The sonnet is called "the most exquisite jewel of the Muses,"[58] with a concentration of thought and a precision of language that are "of priceless value in poetry."[59]

Leon Chai's chapter entitled "The Triumph of Form" is highly relevant to this mania for "collecting" poems (as well as so many other artistic and even scientific artifacts) in Victorian culture. Through a reading of James, Chai argues that "to collect" is more than "to possess." It is something deeper: "the impulse to possess in a collector of the highest type is at bottom a desire for form. In seeking this, the collector attempt to discover some principle of coherence to which one might subordinate all individual objects. The discovery of that principle marks the perceptions of form."[60] Chai's cultural observation here goes a long way toward explaining why so many of these essays were being written in the last few decades of the 1800s. The interest in the sonnet as a form is *itself* a synecdoche for a broader cultural interest (of a certain highbrow segment of the reading population) in form generally, in finding a "principle of coherence," a "type." The obsession with sonnets and with *collecting* them, resulting in the appearance of many of these defenses as introductions or appendices to sonnet anthologies, is material evidence of an aestheticist ideology permeating the literary culture and narrowing literary interests into an abstract idealism of form. What lies at the heart of this conflation of interests in collecting and in sonnets is an attempt to define a unifying vision of the mind's experience of reality. This is a vision that Wordsworth offers so powerfully in his sonnets (so much more succinctly than his grand epics)—and that motivates the admiration of his sonnets later on.

The shift of figure from radiant light or star to gem I have traced in this section also signals an implied acceptance of the withdrawal of the poet

figure from the political world. While Wordsworth and his followers composed perhaps as many as half of their sonnets to express political ideas
(with Keats the significant exception) the political motivation grows less
powerful as Wordsworth's self-authorizing poetic becomes the kind of or-
thodoxy these critics promote. Of course one does indeed find political
sonnets, even by Dante Gabriel Rossetti, by Christina Rossetti, by their
brother William Michael (whose *Democratic Sonnets* were written at his
brother's urging), and by Tennyson and his brother Tennyson Turner, not to
mention Arnold and Swinburne. But the sonnet is not as primary an arena
for politics in the late nineteenth century as it had been previously. The
"value" attributed to sonnets now is based more on the formal transcendence of the commonplace or "actual world" than, say, on the urgency of
voice that trumpets forth an imaginative and political Truth. It is no accident that it became a favorite form for aesthetes and symbolists later on.

If these sonnet defenses evade the conflict between a vision of the sonnet as a private-public mouthpiece and a vision of it as a meditation on
aesthetics, their authors are only reflecting a reluctance to address a dilemma that was implicit in the discussion of Keats in the previous chapter,
and that will be pursued more aggressively by D. G. Rossetti. The withdrawal into interiority and the simultaneous challenge to the visionary mode
that the form tropes so often in Keats is also registered in these defenses by
the critics' growing interest in the matter of the sonnet's temporal paradox—a theme that I argued Wordsworth could evade but that, starting with
Keats, becomes increasingly unavoidable. William Davies, writing in 1873,
anticipated Rossetti's 1880 "moment's monument" formulation with his
assertion that the sonnet "is capital for embalming the moods of a moment—those sentiments and feelings which contain a sort of completeness
in themselves."[61]

It is impossible not to associate comments like this, as well as the late-
century frequency of the diamond or gem figure, with Pater's *Renaissance*
"manifesto" that we should "burn always with this hard, gem-like flame, to
maintain this ecstasy," describing the aesthetic life as a concentration of
"the splendour of our experience and . . . its awful brevity, gathering all we
are into one desperate effort to see and touch. . . ."[62] But Rossetti in particular, for all his effort to achieve precisely that "completeness in itself" in
each of his sonnets, would be troubled by temporal paradox, the immediate
passing of such "eternal moments." The hardening of the romantic trope of
radiance into gem reflects the privileging and, ultimately, the monumen-
talization of "the moment" that Rossetti, unable to escape the consequences
of progressive temporality, highlights in his introductory sonnet to *The House
of Life,* and that he thematizes throughout that haunted sequence.

5

"A Moment's Monument":
Revisionary Poetics and the
Sonnets of Dante Gabriel Rossetti

Probably the earliest interesting critical remark regarding the sonnets of Dante Gabriel Rossetti from a formal standpoint came from his friend, the sonnet enthusiast Thomas Hall Caine. In his typically adulatory *Recollections* of the poet's life, Caine describes Rossetti's sonnets as

> almost peculiar to themselves among English sonnets. Rossetti was not the first English writer who deliberately separated octave and sestet, but he was the first who obeyed throughout a series of sonnets the canon of the contemporary structure requiring that a sonnet shall present the two-fold facet of a single thought or emotion. This form of the sonnet Rossetti was at least the first among English writers entirely to achieve and perfectly to render.[1]

Much of what I want to say about Rossetti's sonnet writing has emerged from considering the ramifications of Caine's comment, for it highlights the fact that although Rossetti's work *is* clearly a return to Italian forms, it partakes of the revisionary poetic this study has been tracing from Wordsworth. Rossetti's place in this study thus has more to do with his indebtedness to Wordsworth's and Keats's visionary sonnets than with his obvious and complicated relationship to the Italian tradition.

While Richard L. Stein has remarked that the Petrarchan form works with "remarkable appropriateness for his interests" and that "the form implies a world in which the contradictions of his art are accepted and reconciled,"[2] where that reconciliation actually takes place in Rossetti's poetry is unclear to me. Rossetti's preference for the strict Petrarchan form, with the clear division between octave and sestet, is significant in this context, for I suspect it is that revisionary ratio built into the sonnet's "deep structure," as it were, that interested the poet. The asymmetry of the 8-6 structure can, as we have seen for example in Keats, help to thematize *failure* and belated-ness, rather than resolution. Rossetti's particular engagement with the son-net is fueled by the same resistance to the temporal and spatial limitations of the form that I have examined in his romantic forebears—but his son-nets, like Keats's, often succeed in their expression of a perceived imagina-tive failure. The Petrarchan form's built-in but imbalanced binary structure is suited to explore the deep conflicts in Rossetti's art between the sensuous and the ideal, the visual and the visionary.

What emerges forcefully in his sonnets is the same sense of disjunc-tion we saw between the experiential moment and the aesthetic moment and between those kinds of moments and the occasion of writing a poem. For Rossetti that occasion is not so much a visionary as a re-visionary moment, literally a reseeing of experience, and even of his habitual aes-theticization of those experiences. This is both an aesthetic and a temporal problem; my notion of this problematic aligns with Robert Langbaum's description of the relationship between the century's schism between art and nature, and his so-called "doctrine of experience"—that "imaginative apprehension gained through immediate experience is primary and cer-tain, whereas the analytic reflection that follows is secondary and problem-atic."[3]

That revisionary moment of "analytic reflection" is at odds in Rossetti with the visionary moment that the sonnet had troped in Wordsworth. In a large majority of the poems in his sequence, *The House of Life*, upon which the first half of this chapter will focus, Rossetti uses the Petrarchan struc-ture of the sonnet to accomplish the revisionary attitude (to return to a Burkean term I used previously) that revolves around the issues of tempo-rality and of poetic occasion.

I

Rossetti's famous sonnet on the sonnet reveals that the tension of the revisionary stance underlies his very notion of the "conception of the qual-ity and function of the sonnet as a form of poetic invention and composi-tion," as his brother William Michael Rossetti put it.[4] The disjunction of experience and art comes to the surface with crucial implications for his view of his art:

> A Sonnet is a moment's monument,—
> Memorial from the Soul's eternity
> To one dead deathless hour. Look that it be,

Whether for lustral rite or dire portent,
Of its own arduous fulness reverent:
   Carve it in ivory or in ebony,
    As Day or Night may rule; and let Time see
Its flowering crest impearled and orient.

A Sonnet is a coin: its face reveals
   The soul,—its converse, to what Power 'tis due:—
Whether for tribute to the august appeals
   Of Life, or dower in Love's high retinue,
It serve; or, 'mid the dark wharf's cavernous breath,
In Charon's palm it pay the toll to Death.[5]

From the poem's opening line, the figure of the sonnet hovers between
two possibilities: the sonnet as a *temporal* figure and as a *spatial* figure.
The tension of the words "moment's monument" inheres primarily in its
claim—an ancient one for poetry and best known in Horace and
Shakespeare—that even the moment can endure eternally.[6] But beyond that,
this sonnet recalls that in a postromantic time, the moment is *worth* preserving. In the tradition of sonnets on the sonnet, this poem focuses its
attention on both "strictly" formal matters—the constraints of the rhyme
scheme, octave-sestet division, the fewness of lines—and on the matter of
occasion. As Hollander reads it, Rossetti describes the sonnet as "the monument *of* a moment, *to* a moment," which is "only made to outlast its moment by being married to the sonnet's own occasion, the absolutely unique,
revolutionary event of the occasion of its being written, the occasion which
Wallace Stevens called poems 'the cry of.'"[7] Furthermore, the opening oxymoron is weighted by the alliterative difficulties of the *m*'s, *n*'s, an inter-
weaving of sound that James Richardson suggests is typical of Rossetti's
effort to imitate the prolongation of the moment—the "dead deathless
hour"—that his poetry so often describes.[8] The important distinction to
make here is that Rossetti's sonnet self-reflexively tropes the Horatian/
Shakespearian topos by making that monument *to* the moment, rather than
simply *of* any particular moment.

The oxymoronic nature of those opening lines lies, however, in its
figuration of temporality as space. As a "moment's monument," the sonnet
is conceived of first as a place, figured as a physical structure left behind,
converting the Wordsworthian trope of the mental workspace; the sonnet is
no longer the space in which the "work" of poetry is done, but is a product—a monument, a crest, a coin—that is *visible* ("let time see"). It may be
that Rossetti proposes the materiality of language as a stay against the essential ephemerality of the moment, of experience, indeed of the poem

itself. Therefore, although the "arduous fulness" of the octave has been generally understood to refer to the "workmanship" of the inscribing artist, it is thereby also understood to refer to the very style of the poem itself.

Not the least of the tension inheres also in its difficulty as a text—what even the earliest critics recognized as Rossetti's characteristic obscurity,[9] especially in *The House of Life*. The term "arduous fulness" recalls descriptions of Rossetti's own method of sonnet composition; he evidently revised endlessly, arduously, replacing and rearranging words until the texture of the poem could become no denser.[10] Although Swinburne felt, according to William Michael Rossetti, that his friend's "whole system of composition [was] somewhat over-elaborate,"[11] he nevertheless recognized the significance of the poems' density, and defended it in print:

> He is too great a master of speech to incur the blame of hard or tortuous expression; and his thought is too sound and pure to be otherwise dark than as a deep well-spring at noon may be even where the sun is strongest and the water brightest. In its furthest depth there is nothing of weed or of mud; whatever of haze may seem to quiver there is a weft of the sun's spinning, a web not of woven darkness but of molten light. But such work as this can be neither unwoven nor recast by any process of analysis. . . .[12]

It has always been difficult for critics to avoid using terms like Swinburne's—words like "density," "depth," "haze," "web" and "weft" to discuss his style—terms, in other words, that highlight the textuality of the poems themselves. The "fulness" of the Rossettian sonnet is attributable not only to the weight given to the description of the moment but also to the density of the language itself, the arduousness of which creates the texture of the poem, the illusion of materiality being worked in or through it.

Beyond describing the intricacy of the textual *surface* (the trope of space as *design*), the "arduous fulness" also recalls the spatial trope that we have seen to be conventionally and imaginatively associated with this form, as if the sonnet were filled to the core with language. The sestet revises the Horatian trope of the carved monument by reducing it to the figure of the coin and examining through this trope the binary, revisionary relationship between octave and sestet in the conventional sonnet form. But as Hollander points out, the sonnet's acknowledgment of poetry's "continued insistence" that it can "outlast its moment" is "remarkable in bringing back the trope of the material carving again, rather than asserting the greater durability of uncrumbling words," as Horace and Shakespeare do.[13] The spatial flatness of the figure is somewhat at odds, though, with the gloomy image of the "dark wharf's cavernous breath"—a strange and paradoxical image that suggests either a mouth without voice, *or* a sort of echo chamber or whispering gallery. While these figures highlight the "materiality" of the poem itself, though, it is the peculiar deadness of the material that is striking, as that second oxymoron—the "dead deathless hour"—suggests. Even the "flowering crest," the only sign of life in the poem, is hardened by being "impearled and orient."

There is not in this poem, as there are in previous sonnets on the sonnet, any obvious figure of instrumentality or voice—unless it emerges only in a moment of syntactical obscurity in the final line. The word "toll," a noun meaning "payment," can be momentarily taken, merely by association to the following word "Death," to mean the "toll"-ing sound of some funereal bell—the living foxglove bell of Wordsworth hardened once again into a cast instrument. In any case, that which may be gained by creating poems, a compensation which I take to be behind the sestet's use of the coin image, is a kind of currency of the moment; the price, however, is the consciousness of that moment's death by writing.

It is important to remember that the introductory sonnet to the *House of Life* sequence was not published with the text until 1881. The poem is not only a metacommentary on the sonnet form generally but also on this sequence specifically; it is much more a look backward than a look forward, fitting for a poem that can be best characterized as "retrospective" and "elegiac."[14] It is fitting too for a sequence with an overall movement I would call "revisionary," again in the literal sense of the word. As with the individual sonnets, it is no coincidence that textual revision and rearrangement played a crucial role in the history of the sequence; each new completion of the text offered a new opportunity for reconsidering this artifice, revising, and reworking its shape and surfaces.[15]

Rossetti understands the sonnet to be a kind of death in life, a formalized stasis.[16] The isolation of the moment holds no revelatory vision, because revelation for Rossetti is obscured by temporality and therefore by thought, memory, and artistic form itself. The act of "formalizing," of writing a poem, places the "intense" moment in the temporal progress of thought and overshadows the poetic fiction of the "sonnet-as-present-moment," of composition as "instantaneous" with the act of creative perception, with an almost Keatsian sensation of loss.

The effect is not the intensity of Wordsworth's apocalyptic conjunction of moments and the achievement of a poetic "presence"; instead, the poem's emphasis on materiality and textuality only emphasizes the disjunction between experience and art that the poem represents. Experience is inscribed and thereby encrypted; Rossetti, like Meredith, literalizes William Davies's definition of the sonnet form as one that "embalm[s] within its tiny limits" the "moods of a moment"[17] by emphasizing the act of writing itself. That process, however, is a kind of fashioning, a revision—or, to create a term from the title of one the *House of Life* sonnets, a *superscription*—of the moment.

In Rossetti's vision of the sonnet, a form that Rossetti once described as "condensed and emphatic,"[18] tension inheres in the intensity of temporal instantaneousness and its troubled relation to poetic form. Although this poem follows in the tradition of sonnets on the sonnet I have been tracing throughout the book, it differs from them in its shifting and darkening of the figuration of form. Gone are the tropes of instrumentality and voice found in the earlier examples, blacked out are the images of light that flicker and finally radiate through them. The figure of form is no longer the romantic "radiant star," with its analogous tropes of explosiveness and of small spaces opening out; that figure suggests, as I have shown earlier, that the perfect form emerges simultaneously with the sensation of "aesthetic shock." Rossetti's poem departs from that tradition in limning the sonnet form no longer in light, but in shadow. The monument-poem is a form that houses absences rather than presences, that looks backward rather than bursting out and forward into time.

II

The temporal interests of Rossetti's poetry have received extensive critical treatment. It is almost a commonplace to speak of "intensity" in the poetry of Dante Gabriel Rossetti, and to relate it to Pater's "profoundly significant instants" and "exquisite pauses in time, in which, arrested thus, we seem to be spectators of all the fulness of existence, and which are like some consummate extract or quintessence of life."[19] Clearly Rossetti participates in the Pre-Raphaelite celebration of the "special moment," which the poet himself called "the momentary contact with the immortal which results from sensuous culmination and is always a half conscious element of it."[20] More recently, John Dixon Hunt's excellent article on the relationship of Pre-Raphaelite poetry and painting ties Rossetti's sonnet writing to a tradition of "Romantic fascinations" with "the personally perceived the hugely redolent moment [*sic*]" in which there is an apprehension condensed to an insight—"[t]he apprehension of infinity within time, of perfection within imperfection, of large within small."[21] It is not difficult to find poems that match this description of Rossetti's art; one thinks most quickly of well-known *House of Life* poems like "The Kiss" (sonnet 6), "Nuptial Sleep" (sonnet 6a) or "Mid-Rapture" (sonnet 26), which do best at capturing the self-involution of the sensuousness, and at gaining the fiction of the fullness of the moment as something transcendent that postpones progressive temporality.

But few critics have been able to leave the matter in terms so unproblematic. Even William Sharp's early reading was not without depth in this matter; he perceived, as Pater did, the undercurrent of the "weird and ominous" in Rossetti's work, noting in *The House of Life* especially a jangled strain of "foreboding . . . which again and again comes in throughout the sequence like some deep mournful chord of Handel in a solemn music—a sense of inevitable loss, an anticipated regret, anticipated despair."[22] As we have seen, the "intensity" of Wordsworth's sonnets inheres in their visionary function, the apocalyptic condensation of this form, whereby the one moment represented by the short poem becomes a synecdoche for all moments. As a sonneteer Wordsworth was successful in this process of intensification, this "narrowing into now," as Jarrell put it, the conjunction of past, present and future in the creative moment (note even in Jarrell's formulation the interesting conflation of figures of space and time). For Rossetti the romantic visionary moment, and the momentum accompanying it, is always a deferred moment, and becomes a revisionary one, for celebrating or reproducing a moment must mean necessarily that it is already lost. "Aesthetic distance," formerly a mark of the self-conscious power of poetic transformation, is now a mark of impotence. What Wordsworth called "the pleasure of poetic pain," what Ross describes as "the pleasure of being able to discern the *architecture* of the experience,"[23] is for Rossetti the pain of an ever-growing alienation from the iconic presence he seeks in art.

In few poems, even in the early part of the sequence, is the "special moment" described *without* apparent consciousness of its ephemerality. While the "presence" of Rossetti's sonnets gives us the sensuality for which he is well known (and for which Buchanan in particular excoriated him), the poem's effort to create an "eternal moment" rarely succeeds, and most often its undermining comes in the sestet of the sonnet. Rossetti frequently uses the two-part structure of the sonnet form to trope the temporal slip. In "Lovesight" (sonnet 4), for example, the collapse of the experiential or sensuous into some eternalized moment is undone in the sestet:

> When do I see thee most, beloved one?
>   When in the light the spirits of mine eyes
>   Before thy face, their altar, solemnize
> The worship of that Love through thee made known?
> Or when in the dusk hours, (we two alone,)
>   Close-kissed and eloquent of still replies

Thy twilight-hidden glimmering visage lies,
And my soul only sees thy soul its own?

O love, my love! if I no more should see
Thyself, nor on the earth the shadow of thee,
  Nor image of thine eyes in any spring,—
How then should sound upon Life's darkening slope
The ground-whirl of the perished leaves of Hope,
  The wind of Death's imperishable wing?

The Keatsian turn of the poem darkens tropes of light into shadow; the reflexivity of lovers (highlighted by the grammatical ambiguities of "O love, my love!") is severed into subject and object. Placed early in the sequence, the sonnet is characteristic of so many in *The House of Life* in its troping of the turn from octave to sestet as a revision—of present as past, of presence as absence. Most strangely, the moment of love becomes a moment of death: the sonnet revises the poet's sensuous moment with his lover as an infernally Dantesque one, reminiscent of Paolo and Francesca's embrace.

Another particularly good example of this is "Severed Selves" (sonnet 40). While the octave describes the absolute union of "two souls" ("Such are we now"), the sestet overshadows the event with the knowledge that that moment of union is past:

                    Ah! may our hope forecast
Indeed one hour again, when on this stream
Of darkened love once more the light shall gleam?—
An hour how slow to come, how quickly past,—
Which blooms and fades, and only leaves at last,
Faint as shed flowers, the attenuated dream.

Even in sonnets famous *for* their evocation and attenuation of the moment, the poet often suggests that the representation of that moment, as a poem, is only possible because it no longer exists:

Your hands lie open in the long fresh grass,—
  The finger-points look through like rosy blooms:
  Your eyes smile peace. The pasture gleams and glooms
'Neath billowing skies that scatter and amass.
All round our nest, far as the eye can pass,
  Are golden kingcup-fields with silver edge
  Where the cow-parsley skirts the hawthorn-hedge.
'Tis visible silence, still as the hour-glass.

Deep in the sun-searched growths the dragon-fly
Hangs like a blue thread loosened from the sky:—
    So this wing'd hour is dropt to us from above.
Oh! clasp we to our hearts, for deathless dower,
This close-companioned inarticulate hour
    When twofold silence was the song of love.
                       ("Silent Noon," sonnet 19)

This is one of many sonnets in which one finds a conflation of spatial and temporal tropes, the "hours of Love," as Rossetti puts it in "A Day of Love" (sonnet 16), "fill[ing] full the echoing space / With sweet confederate music favourable" (lines 7–8). But the voice of the present in this poem is only a silent "song of love." The present is characterized by attention to the visual; indeed this is one of the sonnets in the series that resembles a Rossetti painting, which, as we will see, may well be called "visible silence." The sestet, however, with its echo of the introductory sonnet in line 12—"deathless dower"—contextualizes the "presence" of the octave in the passing of that moment. The tension of the temporal is registered in the oxymoronic image at the pivotal turning point of the sonnet: the "still hour-glass." While the octave captures the stillness of an hourglass at a particular moment, surely an hourglass, emblem of temporality and, metonymically, of death, is anything but still unless measured instant by instant—or unless time has run out entirely.[24] The "inarticulate hour" of pure experience is given voicing only by being framed as an instant that has passed and that can be therefore contemplated. Only then is such a moment able to be transfigured into *articulation*, or poetry.

What many call the "iconicity" of Rossetti's sonnets is countered by their inability to rest in that iconic relation to the experiential moment. Most recently, Carol Christ and James Richardson have written provocatively on the way the *House of Life* sonnets "dissolve" the moment,[25] focusing on the particularity and "presence" of the experience of the moment in order to prolong it and highlighting the "intensity" of the moment in order to generalize or idealize it. But both critics recognize the dialectical aspect of this effort to capture the material or sensuous experience at the same time as the poet idealizes it through art. The heart of the problem is just the poet's own subjective working on experience—that is, his radically subjective revision of it. The claustrophobic quality of nearly every *House of Life* sonnet can be traced to the way in which the rigidity of the sonnet form tropes the poet's psychological and temporal entrapment by his own subjectivity.[26] The hauntedness of these self-enclosed spaces is caused by the sequence's engagement in, and acknowledgment of, the context of time.

In this, Rossetti's use of the sonnet form is most akin to Keats's, for whom, as we have seen, the form did become a kind of trap for subjectivity and a scene of imaginative failure and frustrated vision.[27] It is therefore not surprising to see Rossetti following Keats in his handling of a particular aspect of the sonnet: its ending. Rossetti too thematizes the confrontation with imaginative failure, rather than resolution, in a sonnet's close; rather than achieving the powerful Wordsworthian expansiveness, with its tropes of radiance, Rossetti ends his poems with images of indeterminacy, pushing away from the iconicity of one moment and entering into the next moment.[28] A considerable number of these sonnets end in a question, a rhetorical resistance—even postponement—of closure:

> Each hour until we meet is as a bird
>   That wings from far his gradual way along
>   The rustling covert of my soul,—his song
> Still loudlier trilled through leaves more deeply stirr'd:
> But at the hour of meeting, a clear word
>   Is every note he sings, in Love's own tongue;
>   Yet, Love, thou know'st the sweet strain suffers wrong,
> Full oft through our contending joys unheard.
>
> What of that hour at last, when for her sake
>   No wing may fly to me nor song may flow;
>   When, wandering round my life unleaved, I know
> The bloodied feathers scattered in the brake,
>   And think how she, far from me, with like eyes
> Sees through the untuneful bough the wingless skies?
>
>   ("Winged Hours," sonnet 25)

In addition to the clear break between octave and sestet, marking the typical shift from presence to absence, the interrogative ending of the sestet marks Rossetti's typical movement away from the vision achieved at the end of the Wordsworthian sonnet and into the viewless skies of Keatsian indeterminacy. The interrogative and Keatsian endings point toward a failure to unite the physical and ideal or transcendental; a grimmer postromantic sonnet, with its silenced birdsong, is hard to imagine.

The extremes of the entrapment of the poet in such a duality is best figured in the sonnet "He and I" (sonnet 98), in which the poet's revisionary stance toward his own experience clearly reveals his own failure to himself:

> Whence came his feet into my field, and why?
>   How is it that he sees it all so drear?

How do I see his seeing, and how hear
The name his bitter silence knows it by?
This was the little fold of separate sky
    Whose pasturing clouds in the soul's atmosphere
Drew living light from one continual year:
How should he find it lifeless? He, or I?

Lo! this new Self now wanders round my field,
    With plaints for every flower, and for each tree
    A moan, the sighing wind's auxiliary:
And o'er sweet waters of my life, that yield
Unto his lips no draught but tears unseal'd,
    Even in my place he weeps. Even I, not he.

Here is a vision indeed, but only of the most dismal kind, a lyric poet's nightmare. It is a picture of past and present selves so alienated from one another that they both join the party of shadowy figures inhabiting *The House of Life*.[29] If this is Rossetti's *Vita Nuova*, by *this* sequence's end, where "He and I" appears, the new life has come to consist of a haunted present barely distinguishable from the past. It would be difficult to speak even of "foreboding" here, as temporal levels collapse more finally than in the early, sensuous sonnets.

The revisionary conflict between the moment as icon and the moment as simply "passing" is also highlighted by *The House of Life*'s very sequentiality. Appropriate to Rossetti as well is Archbishop Trench's assertion that Wordsworth was

> the first who conceived a poem made up of a succession of Sonnets, each complete in itself, but at the same time constituting, so to speak, a stanza of that larger poem whereof it formed a part; just as the bracelet made up of a string of cameos or mosaics, each may be a perfect little picture in itself, while at the same time contributing to the beauty and perfection of a larger whole.[30]

For Rossetti, as for the earlier poet, the central problem of the sonnet sequence, as a form, centers on the tension between the isolated moment that the sonnet monumentalizes or "frames" (to pick up Trench's very aptly Rossettian metaphor of the "perfect little picture") and the knowledge of the brevity of "the whole / Of joy, which its own hours annihilate" ("Secret Parting" [sonnet 45], lines 5–6). The tension between continuity and discontinuity is a central matter in the poem, as indeed it is to Rossetti's aesthetic, whether that is an "aesthetics of the moment," as John P. McGowan suggests,[31] or, as Christ and Richardson argue, an aesthetics of dissolution. Temporal disjunction is thus writ large in this sequence, where, according to Christ, experience is portrayed "as a succession of ephemeral moments, which dissolve even as we try to apprehend them."[32]

The handling of temporality in the poem guides the analysis of the overall structure of the poem. Early critics perceived no particular progression or unity to the work but saw instead simply a sequence of "moments" strung together—"a string of cameos" as Trench put it. The first to move toward a more complex argument was William Fredeman, who argued that the whole structure of *The House of Life* is actually a sonnet writ large, as it were; it is divided into two parts that are analogous to the octave and sestet division of the Petrarchan sonnets that make up the series.[33] The point of doing this, he asserts, would be to frame this house of life and to extend the argument of the introductory sonnet:

> The juxtaposition of Time in the octave with the figure of the sonnet as a monument of a moment suggests the wider interpretation of the moment as *movement*, as in momentum, referring to a course of events extending over a prolonged period of time, such as life itself. . . . The larger sonnet celebrates not the ephemeral and evanescent sensations stimulated by particular occurrences but the residual emotional recollections of a lived life.[34]

This argument left Fredeman open to criticism from those who tried to find exact correspondences or some precise logic connecting the two parts, as one tries to do in an individual poem. But taken in the most general sense, Fredeman's point is valuable: the two sections, labeled "Youth and Change" and "Change and Fate," *do* work in a revisionary relationship, creating something like "movements" in the series overall.

Without pushing the analogy too far, one can say that the first section, "Youth and Change," concerns itself more often with capturing those "moments of fullness" that critics so typically describe in Rossetti. These poems tend to push toward a representation of the presence of erotic and aesthetic experience;[35] one thinks of poems like "The Kiss" or "Nuptial Sleep" (sonnets 6 and 6a) among others. The second half, "Change and Fate," is more self-consciously about art, memory, and the relationship of those to experience, as if a sort of consciousness were injected into the sequence to remember and revise all previous moments and poems.[36]

David Riede interprets the relationship between the individual sonnets and the sequence as a narrative that edges toward the "string of cameos" model:

the poem itself exhibits a tension in which sequentiality suggests narrative, logical, rational development, but the parts, the individual sonnets, resist it. Each sonnet is an immortal artifact describing an eternal moment. The sonnets are removed from life into eternity, yet the sequence is a House of Life, not a mausoleum. The tension, perhaps, is meant to suggest time's point of contact with eternity, life's with art.[37]

While Riede identifies here the crucial tension between the temporal and the eternal, he eases the discomfort evident in the poem by downplaying it. Because the individual sonnets persistently *fail* in their effort to become eternal moments, such an idealized reading of the sequence becomes difficult; while the individual sonnet may well, as various critics believe, attempt to "dissolve" the moment by attenuating it, the sequentiality of the poem necessarily differentiates the moments. The sequence as a form thematizes the loss of every "intense" or "special moment" in progressive temporality.

Whether or not Rossetti learned anything about his notion of sequentiality from Wordsworth, it is notable that at least one trope that underlies *The House of Life* is the stream, an image of spatialized temporality that structures the *River Duddon* sonnets.[38] But there is no "radiant progress" in this sequence, as there is in Wordsworth's poem; instead, the revision is the looking back at the mutability of life, moment by moment. When Christ says that this sequence is all *about* mutability, she might have noted that the middle term in the progression from "Youth" to "Fate" in the poem's section titles is "Change"; others have noted the way in which moments become attenuated and are "more important," says Boos, "for their expansive reverberations in a later contemplation."[39] These "later contemplations" color, or shadow, the second section of the poem, "Change and Fate," the very title of which highlights a fatal causality in time that one can see retrospectively as being what George Meredith, in his anti-Petrarchan sequence *Modern Love,* would call "tragic hints" (sonnet 50, line 13). The result is similar: that sense of foreboding or "hauntedness," as Pater put it, that pervades the poem.

Perhaps the most remarkable commentary on the sequence's own structure is "A Superscription" (sonnet 97), a poem that is about the way memory writes over any single moment of the present by placing it in the past and contextualizing it there:

> Look in my face; my name is Might-have-been;
> I am also called No-more, Too-late, Farewell;

Unto thine ear I hold the dead-sea shell
Cast up thy Life's foam-fretted feet between;
Unto thine eyes the glass where that is seen
    Which had Life's form and Love's, but by my spell
    Is now a shaken shadow intolerable,
Of ultimate things unuttered the frail screen.

Mark me, how still I am! But should there dart
    One moment through thy soul the soft surprise
    Of that winged Peace which lulls the breath of sighs,—
Then shalt thou see me smile, and turn apart
Thy visage to mine ambush at thy heart
    Sleepless with cold commemorative eyes.

Boos reads this sonnet as a commentary on Rossetti's own dark vision of the sonnet form: "The remembrance that a sonnet is a monument to one dead, deathless hour now loses all but ominous associations."[40] The dead-sea shell, a figure for the poem itself, catches and makes audible past occasions, figured now only as absences. The poem is the most extreme example of the way Rossetti tropes the disjunction of moments, his temporal and imaginative alienation from them figured as those strange allegorical ghosts that parade before him in his mind's eye.[41]

Elsewhere in the sequence, the passage of time is described similarly as a kind of imaginative procession: "Stand still, fond fettered wretch! while Memory's art / Parades the Past before thy face, and lures / Thy spirit to her passionate portraitures" ("Parted Love," lines 9–11). At such reflective moments the sequence names itself as a parade, or as a "Wild pageant of the accumulated past" ("The Soul's Sphere," line 13). All these images of processional time are, like the river image in Wordsworth's *Duddon* series, spatial tropes for a progressive temporality that counters spatial tropes of the iconic moment.[42] Once again the paradox of the sonnet form is evident, the stillness of the moment the sonnet represents resisted by the "processional" appearance of the figures of time that haunt the poem.

Some critics have argued that with his accommodation of the processional attribute of temporality accounted for in his "aesthetics of the moment," Rossetti does create a fundamental unity among the poems that comprise the sequence: "It is precisely this lack of coherence in Rossetti's poem that makes it somewhat uninteresting as a sonnet sequence—but not as a group of sonnets. The unity is the unity of its theme—ramifications of sensual and spiritual love—and the unity of mood and language."[43] But the unity of the sequence lies also in its tropological structure—in an ever-sharper consciousness of its own revisionary procedure. As the sequence begins to

draw to a close, the sonnets are more and more often *about* the poet's failure to create what William Michael Rossetti called "the intimate intertexture
of a spiritual sense with a material form, small actualities made vocal of
lofty meanings."[44] The inconclusiveness of the sonnets highlights the ir-
resolution of the sensual and the spiritual, the material and the ideal, and
the poet's failure to find in secular moments the typological significances
that his romantic impulses would lead him to.[45] "The Landmark" (sonnet
67), a part 2 revision of the central "Willowwood" sonnets of part 1, highlights the failure of the visionary:

> Was *that* the landmark? What,—the foolish well
>   Whose wave, low down, I did not stoop to drink,
>   But sat and flung the pebbles from its brink
> In sport to send its imaged skies pell-mell,
> (And mine own image, had I noted well!)—
>   Was that my point of turning?—I had thought
>   The stations of my course should rise unsought,
> As altar-stone or ensigned citadel.
>
> But lo! the path is missed, I must go back,
>   And thirst to drink when next I reach the spring
> Which once I stained, which since may have grown black.
>   Yet though no light be left nor bird now sing
>   As here I turn, I'll thank God, hastening,
> That the same goal is still on the same track.

While the octave looks into the well of low wave, a trope of an exhausted
will, the sestet marks the absence of the common romantic images of light
and of birds; vision and song are replaced by paths that have been missed[46]
and by wells, earlier reflective surfaces and depths of which have turned
dark.

   The only compensatory strength of that failure is the consciousness of
its ramifications: that what the poet is left with is the material form itself,
the poem and its *linguistic* texture:

> When vain desire at last and vain regret
>   Go hand in hand to death, and all is vain,
>   What shall assuage the unforgotten pain
> And teach the unforgetful to forget?
> Shall Peace be still a sunk stream long unmet,—
>   Or may the soul at once in a green plain
>   Stoop through the spray of some sweet life-fountain
> And cull the dew-drenched flowering amulet?

> Ah! when the wan soul in that golden air
>> Between the scriptured petals softly blown
>> Peers breathless for the gift of grace unknown,—
> Ah! let none other alien spell soe'er
> But only the one Hope's one name be there,—
>> Not less nor more, but even that word alone.
>>>>> ("The One Hope," sonnet 101)

This sonnet, which Rossetti thought equal to his best ("or I should not have wound up the sequence with it"),[47] ends the poem with images of writing: the "scriptured petals" (flowers with writing on them, which William Michael explains as a reference to "the Greek fancy [that] assumed the hyacinth to be inscribed") and the "alien spell" (which appeared in the 1870 version as "written spell").[48]

The final attempt at a vision of completion and union in this sequence brings together the powers that have dominated this poem—not Life and Love, powers of spontaneity and sensuousness, so much as Art and Death. The writing alone is a kind of promise to the poet in this vision of death; these words, like *The House of Life* as a whole, become a monument to "Hope." This vision is the ultimate deferral in Rossetti: hope is only achieved in death, and so even here he cannot name the "one name" that would give his life any meaning. Foreboding is replaced by "Hope"—but either way, death appears, finally, to be the Power to which these sonnets are due. The binary structure of the introductory sonnet is not alleviated by the end of the sequence; the alienation from the phenomenal that both temporality and art have created is palpable.

III

The tension between the phenomenal and the transcendent, between the momentary and the sequential, in the Rossetti sonnet is most remarkably troped in that body of his poetry that has been receiving most recent attention: his sonnets on paintings. Much has been made already of the pictorialism of Rossetti's sonnets and the way in which these poems come as near to being visual artwork as the "Introductory Sonnet" could have suggested. Discussions of the relationship of poem to painting in Rossetti often start with a citation of Pater's essay—no doubt deeply influenced by his study of Rossetti—on "The School of Giorgione," in which Pater discusses "what German critics term an *Anders-streben*—a partial alienation from its own limitation, through which the arts are able, not indeed to supply the place of each other, but reciprocally to lend each other new forces."[49] Lucien Agosta, for example, reads the poem-painting as a work that "insists upon its own completeness," creating an "eminently fleshly form spiritualized by [the] meditative gaze and infused with an active consciousness as established in both painting and poem." The poem-painting, he argues, unites the flatness of the canvas and the depth of consciousness and language, and lifts the work of art from its iconic status. The viewer has the impression of simultaneity, boundaries of space and time dissolving into some timeless "alternate aesthetic realm," some "separate aesthetic space."[50] At their best the sonnets do become, as Rossetti writes in "A Sea-Spell," a "summoning rune" (line 12); the poem becomes "literally" the consciousness of the painting as the subjects "speak" to the reader/spectator.

It is the handling of temporality that most interests me. John Dixon Hunt suggests that the conjunction of sonnet and painting overcomes the temporal limitations of each form: "the sonnet does endeavor with some success to emulate the condition of the other art: what we read in time strives towards the instantaneity, the nontemporal sight, of the painting." Later Hunt adds that in many of the poem/paintings, "the momentary (appropriate to the painter's art) is imbued with the spirit of something larger; the iconic present, with the consciousness of meanings from past and future. . . . This use of a sonnet to emulate the instant mental apprehension of visual images was to become a characteristic effort of Rossetti's poetry."[51] He points out, finally, that it is a painting's ability to capture the instant in "visual time" that is "itself what many Romantic sonnets emulate—trying, like Rossetti's upon Giorgione, to offer a simultaneity of thought through fourteen lines."[52]

Hunt is right up to a point, for one of the most remarkable things about Rossetti's sonnets on paintings, as opposed to his haunted *House of Life* sonnets, is their extraordinary effort to establish a coordinate, as it were, of space and time, "in this place / This hour," as Rossetti writes of his drawing of "Cassandra." In several of these poems the word "here" appears, by which is often really meant, "here and now," the work of art *as* it is looked at:

> Behold Fiametta, shown in Vision here.
> ("Fiametta [For a Picture.]," line 1)

> What mystery here is read
> Of homage or of hope? But how command
> Dead Springs to answer? And how question here
> These mummers of that wind-withered New-Year?
> ("For Spring [By Sandro Botticelli.]," lines 11–14)

> Here meet together the prefiguring day
>   And day prefigured.
>   ("The Passover in the Holy Family [For a Drawing.]," lines 1–2)

The intention is to conflate the temporal instant and its spatial analogue. As Rossetti worked in this mixed medium, he assured the mutual presence of painting and poem by inscribing the sonnet on the canvas itself, rather than publishing it separately or trusting patrons to preserve the original frame where the poem was sometimes inscribed. Wendell Stacy Johnson argues that these picture-poems are an attempt to "relate or balance the temporal and the ideal," eternalizing the form of the painting.[53] And on rare occasions Rossetti did succeed. In the two-stanza sonnet sequence, "Mary's Girlhood," the poet "reads" the painting, identifying each element with precise deictics: "This is" (line 1) or "These are" (line 15). The first sonnet deals with the historical aspect of Mary's life, up until the "fulness of the time was come"; the second sonnet rereads the painting, explicating the symbolic aspects ("These are the symbols") that look forward to the events of Christ's life. The second sonnet comes full circle to Mary's role as that which completes what God has envisioned, tying historical and spiritual realms together:

> The seven-thorn'd briar and the palm seven-leaved
>   Are her great sorrow and her great reward.
>   Until the end be full, the Holy One
> Abides without. She soon shall have achieved
> Her perfect purity: yea, God the Lord
>   Shall soon vouchsafe His Son to be her Son.
>   (Lines 23–28)

The visionary completeness of the sonnet form, which I have been tracing through the romantic tradition in this century, is accomplished in poems like this one, in which the poet balances the binary structure of the Petrarchan form with the rounded completeness of the romantic visionary sonnet. Indeed, "Godlike completeness" was what Rossetti said he admired in painter Hans Memling's work—and he produced similarly successful poems to accompany two of Memling's paintings. The completeness Rossetti saw there is troped in the sonnets as "MYSTERY"—the word that begins each of the poems:

> MYSTERY: God, man's life, born into man
>   Of woman. There abideth on her brow
>   The ended pang of knowledge, the which now
> Is calm assured. Since first her task began

> She hath known all. What more of anguish than
>   Endurance oft hath lived through, the whole space
>   Through night till day, passed weak upon her face
> While the heard lapse of darkness slowly ran?
>
> All hath been told her touching her dear Son,
>   And all shall be accomplished. Where He sits
>   Even now, a babe, He holds the symbol fruit
>   Perfect and chosen. Until God permits,
>   His soul's elect still have the absolute
> Harsh nether darkness, and make painful moan.

The duality of Christ's life is highlighted by the sonnet structure in this poem, entitled "For A Virgin and Child [By Hans Memmelink]." While the octave revolves around the earthbound life of the newborn Christ and his future sufferings, the sestet emphasizes that everything about his future is already known and "shall be accomplished," the fulfillment of God's promise figured as the "symbol fruit / Perfect and chosen." This moment is chosen by the painter, the poem implies, because it is the beginning of that fulfillment, the beginning of the existence of God as Man, simultaneously spiritual and sensual or material. The "Mystery" of the scene in the Memling painting is the mystery of our own inability to comprehend God, rather than the sort of indeterminacy of *The House of Life*.[54]

In few others of these sonnets on paintings, however, does the effort to join the materiality of the moment to the visionary future succeed so well. One of Rossetti's best-known sonnets provides a characteristic example of the temporal disjunction that still underlies the genre:

> Water, for anguish of the solstice:—nay,
>   But dip the vessel slowly,—nay, but lean
>   And hark how at its verge the wave sighs in
> Reluctant. Hush! Beyond all depth away
> The heat lies silent at the brink of day:
>   Now the hand trails upon the viol-string
>   That sobs, and the brown faces cease to sing,
> Sad with the whole of pleasure. Whither stray
> Her eyes now, from whose mouth the slim pipes creep
>   And leave it pouting, while the shadowed grass
>   Is cool against her naked side? Let be:—
> Say nothing now unto her lest she weep,
>   Nor name this ever. Be it as it was,—
>   Life touching lips with Immortality.
>   ("For a Venetian Pastoral [By Giorgione.])

This sonnet was composed during Rossetti's trip to the continent with William Holman Hunt. Rossetti wrote to his brother that the painting (then erroneously attributed to Giorgione) was "so intensely fine that I condescended to sit down before it and write a sonnet." Rossetti then describes the picture briefly, noting that "in the centre two men and another naked woman, who seem to have paused for a moment in playing on the musical instruments which they hold."[55] The sonnet "takes place," of course, during that moment. Everything in the octave of the so-called *Fête Champêtre* sonnet tries to approach what John Dixon Hunt calls the "iconic present," the repetitive "nay's" and the imperative "Hush!" encouraging absorption in the presence of the day's high-noon fullness. The very shape of the sonnet participates in this effort to resist progressive temporality; it is one of a minority of Rossetti sonnets that is printed without the break between octave and sestet, the enjambed question, "Whither stray / Her eyes now . . . ?" (lines 8–9), overrunning the poem's conventional turn.

And yet in fact the sestet does, characteristically, threaten the integrity of the moment that the octave has described. As the sestet urges the reader to overgo the potential "turn" of the poem, it also brings to our attention the "straying" of the piping figure's eyes. Those eyes are the one image in the poem that does not continue this sonnet's self-involution, for no matter where they stray, they bring us out of the repletion of the moment by hinting at something outside the frame (whether of poem or painting), at a moment following this one. The sonnet, despite its exhortations to "Let be" and "say nothing" to disturb the "Immortality" of the moment, is centrally aware that the sun is at its height and will begin to decline, and that the moment is at its "brink" and will end. The straying of the eyes is the visual threat to the integrity of the moment; the poem tries to cut that threat off by denying its own binary structure.

Far from producing completeness, Rossetti once again ends up only highlighting in these painting-poems the incompleteness and indeterminacy of such moments. While many of these sonnets try to encompass past and future, the *subject* is itself typically *caught* in the moment, expecting fulfillment, but trapped "here." In "For the Holy Family [By Michelangelo.]," for example, in which, according to Rossetti's note, "the Virgin Mother is seen withholding from the Child Saviour the prophetic writings in which his sufferings are foretold," the poem is once again about resisting progressive temporality: "Turn not the prophet's page, O Son! He knew / All that Thou hast to suffer, and hath writ" (lines 1–2). The poem interprets the painting as an arresting or withholding of the visionary moment, which will reveal to Christ the historical fulfillment of his incarnation. Yet the sestet of the sonnet itself looks forward, revising the static momentariness of the octave with a vision of the preparation for his suffering:

> Still before Eden waves the fiery sword,—
>   Her Tree of Life unransomed: whose sad Tree
>   Of knowledge yet to growth of Calvary
>   Must yield its Tempter,—Hell the earliest dead
> Of Earth resign,—and yet, O Son and Lord,
>   The seed o' the woman bruise the serpent's head.
>
> (Lines 9–14)

The momentariness of the sonnet and the painting is at odds with the *narrative* that is the story of Christ—and which is troped by the mention of the prophetic writings in both poem and painting. The thrust of several of these sonnets is toward fulfillment, or toward vision, but as in *The House of Life*, that fulfillment is deferred.[56] The constraints of the sonnet can be exploited to catch its subject in that moment, the deferral becoming an entrapment in form similar to that which I discussed in the section on *The House of Life*.

Rossetti's "Cassandra [For a Drawing.]," another binary sequence, again revolves around the problem of prophecy,[57] and the awaiting of its fulfillment. The first sonnet describes the painting, setting the scene where "in this place / This hour thou bad'st all men in Helen's face / The ravished ravishing prize of Death to know" (lines 6–8), and ends describing Cassandra's words "beat[ing] heavily," which like Hector's shield "shall not save" (lines 12, 14). The second sonnet is itself a revision in the sense that Cassandra becomes the spectator, speaking words after Hector but also speaking to us. Both scene and words only emphasize the stasis of a moment that is a prelude to tragedy. Once again, it is the *incompleteness* of the moment that becomes the subject of the poem-painting.

IV

The effect of Rossetti's sonnets, derived partly from Keats and in reaction to Wordsworth's visionary mode of sonnet writing, is in their effort to control, in the binary structure of the Petrarchan form, the profound duality of experience and art. Rossetti's intention is directed at making compatible what he finally finds to be incompatible: a notion of art as visionary and an acknowledgment of art's artificiality. For this reason, the "presencing" that motivates (in the Burkean sense) the majority of Rossetti sonnets results in the highlighting of the "absenting" of the phenomenal moment they attempt to describe. This is only aggravated by Rossetti's apparent conception of the sonnet not "as the moment itself" but as a monument to it, a trope of it—a revision of it as a work of art. There is in much of his sonnet work a sense of a necessary alienation between experience and art—all the more striking when it is the juncture of those two realms that he is trying to achieve. If Rossetti accomplishes some unity in his poetry, it is not in a visionary mode but in a revisionary one, with the acknowledgment that art is possible only when the moment it would commemorate passes out of itself. The uncanniness of so many of Rossetti's paintings, particularly those of the various women, is caused by the same disjunction in temporality that induces the haunting of *The House of Life* sequence. The radical discontinuity between memory and representation or reproduction offers what Derrida, in his early discussion of temporality in *Speech and Phenomena*, described as a "nonpresent, a past and unreal present."[58] Although it is argued that the poem-paintings are designed to "give life" and "presence" to the figures, their statuesque deadness only highlights the artist's dilemma: in attempting to represent the figures at this "enduring" moment, the flow of time stalls and they are denied the possibility of animation.

Riede argues that "the real landmark for an artist without genuine faith [in art] is the well in which he sees his own image, which is, like the doubles of 'Lost Days,' a symbol of his inner self, the proper source of Romantic art."[59] In a remarkable passage from a review of Thomas Hake's *Parables and Tales*, Rossetti in fact describes the postromantic twilight in which he finds himself:

> Of [the highest] of poetry—the omnipotent freewill of the artist's mind,—our curbed and slackening world may seem to have seen the last. It has been succeeded by another kind of "finish," devoted and ardent, but *less building on ensured foundations than self-questioning in the very moment of action or even later*: yet by such creative labour also the evening and the morning may be blent to a true day, though it be often but a fitful or an unglowing one.[60] (Emphasis mine)

While Rossetti continues the tradition of using the sonnet as figuration of subjectivity, of consciousness itself, his sonnets' transfiguration of life into art scarcely lifts the poet beyond that reflecting well of the Willowwood sonnets. Rossetti's sonnets present a diminished[61] role for art. As it so often threatened to be for Keats, the sonnet for Rossetti is often a site for a failure of imaginative transcendence and a site for revising his stance on the poetic will.

6

"Charged with the Grandeur of God":
The Allegory of Form in the
Sonnets of Gerard Manley Hopkins

This book has traced the emergence in the nineteenth century of a "visionary" sonnet out of a developing revisionary poetics, and has studied the relationship of such a mode to a procedure of synecdoche and to a notion of temporality. The study has followed the consequent set of themes: the way Wordsworth revises the sonnet's motivation toward miniaturization and limitation into a poetics of presence that overrides those formal limitations (whether of time or space) with a figuration of imaginative vision; the manner in which this vision invests the private, lyric voice with a public authority; the Wordsworthian sonnet's vision of itself as a site for origination; the relationship between poetic form and representation or revelation, and the way that relationship highlights formality itself; and the paradox of temporality, and how the sonnet attempts to accommodate that paradox.

The study has also shown how, for some poets following Wordsworth and lacking his sense of authority though "self-possession," the sonnet becomes a site—not merely of impotence, but rather of potentiality—of potency sought after. My readings of Shelley, Keats, and Rossetti examine the relationship of each to the visionary function of the sonnet that Wordsworth offers. Their responses vary from acceptance of this visionary mode to ironic challenging of it and to introspective questioning of their own poetic wills through it.

The difficulty of characterizing Hopkins's sonnets is that they seem to fall at both extremes of that range of response. While many of the religious sonnets partake of Wordsworth's sublime vision of the form, with just the same expansion of imaginative vision and potency, there are others—particularly that body of poems critics call the "terrible sonnets"—that lack that visionary authority. This chapter offers a reading of Hopkins's analysis of the sonnet form that accounts for both of those possibilities. My argument is that Hopkins's most crucial perception with regard to the form lies in his "dogmatic" (his word) insistence on the division of octave and sestet, as well as in his recognition of the revisionary movement in the sonnet structure, a movement I will call the "trope of diminishing." Like Rossetti, Hopkins recognizes the revisionary relationship between octave and sestet in the sonnet form as one of "mirroring" or "analogy"; but, beyond that, he also perceives it to be one of *reduction*. The sestet, however much it is a "reflection" of the octave, is unlike it simply because it is smaller and because it comes after.

On the one hand, this trope of diminishing contributes to the claustrophobic space of subjectivity that characterizes the "terrible sonnets," just as it did for Keats and Rossetti. What is so interesting about Hopkins's sonnets, however, is that there we can also locate, in his engagement with the form's figurations of limitation, his own poetics of "accommodation." Conscious of the miniaturization of octave in sestet, Hopkins focuses on the turn of the sonnet, the *volta*—and finds in that turn a formal trope for the imaginative bridge between heaven and earth, between divine and human.

In the mode of Wordsworth, then, this analogical diminishing becomes a figure for an intensification or concentration, rather than for a mere lessening, of power. The sestet's revisionary relationship to the octave, in other words, becomes a paradigm for the poet's progress from cognition to revelation to composition; the *volta* marks a reperspectivizing of thought into poetic vision. Even more powerfully, however, this discovery offers Hopkins a formal analogy for what was the persistent subject of his sonnets: the presence of Christ in man, the accommodation of God in nature. Each of his religious sonnets can be read as an allegory *in* form, as the poet discovers in the sonnet a formal analogy for the incarnation of Christ. While the "terrible sonnets" partake of the sonnet's built-in figuration of diminishing, and thus of the thematics of entrapment and impotence, the strongest of Hopkins's sonnets use the form as a site for a sublime identification of the poet's own self with Christ—perhaps the most extreme version of Wordsworth's own synecdochic and visionary procedures.[1]

I

The approach to the trope of diminishing located in Hopkins's sonnets is best made by beginning, once again, with a consideration of the sonnet form itself. While Hopkins wrote no "sonnet on the sonnet" from which to launch the discussion, his interest in the problems of the form was, from his early years, sophisticated in its connection with the problems of poetic form itself. This simultaneous reflection upon the sonnet form and upon poetic form (the relationship of synecdoche that I have asserted earlier) is obvious in the radical experimentation with the form, for which he is best known.

Although the contemporary sonnet commentators discussed earlier appear to have created a favorable environment for sonnet experimentation at the time Hopkins was writing, the poet found in them neither encouragement nor justification for the kind of explorations he had in mind. "On the Sonnet and its history," he wrote to R. W. [Canon] Dixon on 29 October 1881, "a learned book or two learned books have been published of late and all is known about it—but not by me."[2] Hopkins is something of a paradox: on the one hand, radically experimental in the form, and on the other hand, unswerving in his insistence on the perfection of balance and unity in the conventional Italian sonnet. As he himself wrote to Bridges, "With all my licences, or rather laws, I am stricter than you and I might say than anybody I know."[3] That explanation notwithstanding, Hopkins's stylistic compression and formal complexity threw off even the devoted Bridges, who characterized Hopkins's poetry, in the "Notes" to the first edition,[4] as "obscure":

> in aiming at condensation he neglects the need that there is for care in the placing of words that are grammatically ambiguous. . . . Now our author not only neglects this essential propriety but he would seem even to welcome and seek artistic effect in the consequent confusion; and he will sometimes so arrange such words that a reader looking for a verb may find that he has two or three ambiguous monosyllables from which to select.[5]

Coventry Patmore (who received Hopkins's manuscripts by apologetically admitting to being the "worst *offhand* critic of really new works that I know")[6] considered the difficulty and overly "arduous" nature of this new style the result of "self-imposed shackles."[7] (Critics a generation or two after Bridges and Patmore—namely William Empson and F. R. Leavis—would have considerably less trouble with this characteristic; indeed, they would regard that ambiguity in Hopkins, as in Donne and other more "difficult" poets, as a strength.) But Hopkins himself, obviously aware of the sublime possibilities of the sonnet, observed to Bridges that there are "two kinds of clearness one shd. have—either the meaning to be felt without effort as fast as one reads or else, if dark at first reading, when once made out *to explode*."[8]

The center of Hopkins's originality *is* his technical experimentation—although it is not simply the fact that he so compressed and expanded the conventional form in his idiosyncratic curtal and caudate sonnets.[9] Leavis made the crucial point some time ago: "His bent for technical experiment can be seen to have been inseparable from a special kind of interest in pattern—his own term was 'inscape.'"[10] Claude Colleer Abbott, otherwise critical of the effects of the poet's prosodic experimentation, observes in a related comment that Hopkins's "persistent use of the sonnet form" may have "been because he had some hope of concentrating on, and finishing, a poem of this length that along with discipline of form gave scope for individual pattern."[11] Hopkins himself says as much in a well-known letter to Bridges that Abbott may have been thinking of:

> No doubt my poetry errs on the side of oddness. I hope in time to have a more balanced and Miltonic style. But as air, melody, is what strikes me most of all in music and design in painting, so design, pattern, or what I am in the habit of calling "inscape" is what I above all aim at in poetry. Now it is the virtue of design, pattern, or inscape to be distinctive and it is the vice of distinctiveness to become queer. This vice I cannot have escaped.[12]

It does not seem to concern him much that he has not; indeed he was acutely aware of his own individuality and defended it without the anxiety so palpable in someone like Keats: "Every true poet, I thought, must be original and originality is a condition of poetic genius; so that each poet is like a species in nature (not an *individuum genericum* or *specificum*) and can never recur. That nothing should be old or borrowed however cannot be."[13] I agree entirely with Paul Mariani, therefore, that Hopkins's interests lie less with what his predecessors did with the sonnet form than with the form itself and what more he himself could discover in it.[14] What does concern him is the "virtue of design, pattern, or inscape" in poetry and in the sonnet form. Hopkins's interest in the sonnet amounts to an exploration of implosion and explosion of trope and form, as seen in Wordsworth and Shelley in particular. But beyond that, Hopkins's restless stretching and contracting of the sonnet form is an effort to study the inscape, to use the poet's own terms, of the form itself. By measuring the sonnet's uniqueness *as* a form against what he finds to be essential to it—as if the sonnet too were like a "species in nature"—Hopkins discovers variants that still maintain the essential integrity of that form.

That integrity has to do with two features: the sonnet's characteristic parallelism—a principle of artistic beauty and of poetic structure or organization that Hopkins identifies in all beautiful forms, whether linguistic or material; and proportion. Both are properties he finds most perfectly embodied in the sonnet form. This we know from Hopkins's precocious undergraduate essay, "On the Origin of Beauty" (1865), supposedly written for Walter Pater.[15] Even at age nineteen Hopkins had already worked out the principles of form that would anchor his later comments on the sonnet form; indeed, he cites the sonnet several times in the essay to explain several of the notions under discussion. Attempting to define some principle of beauty that could be used for critical judgment, the Professor, Hopkins's mouthpiece, concludes that beauty is a contrast or "relation of comparison"—a "parallelism"—between regularity and irregularity, or "likeness tempered by difference."[16] This relation adheres to nearly every facet of poetic discourse: to overall structure, to development of metaphor, to rhythm, to rhyme,[17] to devices such as alliteration and assonance.

The problem of poetic form itself is discussed in terms of these relations; "beauty" in poetry supposes that there must be a balance between regularity and irregularity, between likeness and difference, with unity enforced upon these relations by form itself. Asked to explain how it is that "the highest literary efforts . . . have been made in verse and not in prose," the Professor responds that

> genius works more powerfully under the constraints of metre and rhyme and so on than without, that it is more effective when conditioned than when unconditioned. . . . the concentration, the intensity, which is called in by means of an artificial structure brings into play the resources of genius on the one hand, and on the other brings us to the end of what inferior minds have to give us.

"Greatness," adds the painter Middleton in agreement, "is measured by the powerful action of mind under what we look on as difficulties."[18] Poetic form is implicitly, then, a concentration of thought and craft, a struggle between ideas and the "antithetical shape"[19] necessary for their expression.

The speakers cite the sonnet form itself, not surprisingly from my perspective, as an exemplum, or synecdoche, for lyric poetry generally. The drift of this part of the argument is to "shew . . . that there is a relation between the parts of the thing to each other and again of the parts to the whole, which must be duly kept."[20] Proportion, then, becomes a crucial factor: the shorter the poem, the more emphasis each verse will carry. The speakers turn to the sonnet as the exemplary poetic form: its brevity requires strong structural connections, and the sonnet will suffer more than a longer form from excision. They look too at beginnings and endings, noting that beginnings set up a kind of "pleasurable expectancy" and that endings fulfill that expectation with the proper emphasis of feeling. The sonnet again is said to best illustrate the principle:

> Sonnet-writing demands this feeling you speak of. A sonnet should end, or at all events may very effectively end, with a vigorous emphasis. Shakespere's end with an emphasis of pathos impressed in a rhyming couplet. I would use these as a strong instance of the relative character of beauty. On the one hand the sonnet would lose if you put two other lines instead of that couplet at the end, on the other the couplet would lose if quoted apart, so as to be without the emphasis which has been gathering through the sonnet and then delivers itself in those two lines seen by the eye to be final or read by the voice with a deepening of note and slowness of delivery.[21]

This background helps to ground the comments on the sonnet form that Hopkins left later in his letters, particularly the one to Canon Dixon in which he roundly criticizes Dixon's own sonnets for being "unpardonably licentious in form," and then spells out what he takes to be the "sonnet proper." Hopkins insists, in a passage I must quote at length, on maintaining the distinctive proportions ("the division into the two parts 8+6, at all events 4+4+4+2") and rhyme scheme of the Italian sonnet, no matter what other licenses one takes:

> Now it seems to me that this division is the real characteristic of the sonnet and that what is not so marked off and moreover has not the octet again divided into quatrains is not to be called a sonnet at all. For in the cipher 14 is not mystery and if one does not know nor avail oneself of the opportunities which it affords it is a pedantic encumbrance and not an advantage. The equation of the best sonnet is
>
> $$(4+4) + (3+3) = 2.4 + 2.3 = 2(4+3) = 2.7 = 14$$
>
> This means several things—(A) that the sonnet is one of the works of art of which the equation or construction is unsymmetrical in the shape of $x+y = a$, where x and y are unequal in some simple ratio, as 2:1, 3:2, 4:3: perhaps it would be better to say $mx + nx = a$. . . . And I could shew, if there were time, that it would be impracticable to have a ratio of the sort required with numbers higher than 4 and 3. Neither would 4:2 do, for it wd. return to 2:1, which is too simple. (B) It is divided symmetrically too in multiples of two, as all effects taking place in time tend to be, and all very regular musical composition is: this raises the 7 to 14. (C) It pairs off even or symmetrical members with symmetrical (the quatrains) and uneven or unsymmetrical with uneven (the tercets). And even the rhymes, did time allow, I could shew are founded

on a principle of nature and cannot be altered without loss of effect. But when one goes so far as to run the rhymes of the octet into the sestet a downright prolapsus or hernia takes place and the sonnet is crippled for life.

I have been longer and perhaps more dogmatic than I shd. have been over this point.[22]

What is striking is how rigidly this explanation adheres to his undergraduate definition of the "beautiful" form, in which, as noted earlier, Hopkins observes in his concept of "parallelism" both a relationship of likeness (metaphor, simile, etc.) and a relationship of unlikeness (antithesis, contrast). The sonnet form, as the poet describes it in his equation, accommodates both relationships, delicately balancing likeness and difference by strictly maintaining the octave-sestet divisions and the rhyme schemes. However peculiar his "equation" looks, then, it is essentially a figure for the poet's conception of a form of perfect beauty, a form marked at each juncture by the principle of parallelism: like is associated with like, unlike with unlike, the two unequal parts associated by being in some sense versions of—and therefore "parallel to"—each other. That play of like and unlike gives the sonnet its characteristic turn, and for this reason Hopkins insists on that division.

Herein lies the insight of Hopkins that I posited at the opening of this discussion. While octave and sestet are "like" each other in their symmetrical structuring, rather like mirror images of one another, the images are not exact: the relation between them is one of asymmetry, in a ratio of 4 to 3; the "mirror image" on the "other side" of the division is "unlike" simply by being smaller. The sestet must also differ from the octave in merely being "after" it temporally—"(B) It [the sonnet] is divided symmetrically too in multiples of two, *as all effects taking place in time tend to be* [emphasis mine], and all very regular musical composition is:"—and "below" it spatially, and this too is a play of structure that Hopkins seems to consider.

Obviously the tropes of constraint and limitation I have been observing come into play here, and while Hopkins's abstract equation of the sonnet is provocative, one reaches quickly enough its limitation: that it cannot describe so precisely the figures of thought that develop parallel to that structure. If the sonnet form has a characteristic *volta* or turn, so too does the process of thought expressed there. That turn or trope is of limitation or reduction, a reperspectivizing of thought into a spark of vision. A key to Hopkins's sonnets, I suggest, is their conscious interest in that reperspectivizing. Many critics have examined the analogical nature of Hopkins's thinking and of the structuring of his poetry. However, it is more precise to say, in discussing his sonnets at least, that the analogy finally turns on the "diminishing" of great things into lesser ones, a kind of poetic accommodation of vision. In addition, the revisionary movement that Hopkins perceives within the sonnet takes into account the temporality of the poem's structure; that is, the sestet comes not only under or behind the octave, but after it.

For Hopkins, then, the binary structure of the sonnet becomes not only marked, as it is in Rossetti, but dynamic. The *volta* of the sonnet form is as "charged" as the close of the form is for Keats; just as Keats troped the ending of the poems themselves, so too does Hopkins trope the shift from larger to smaller, and from likeness to unlikeness. His recognition of the power of the diminishing of octave into sestet provides a characteristic thematization of the asymmetrical binary structure of the sonnet form. The effect of this movement, however, is, as I noted at the opening of this chapter, interestingly divergent: in some sonnets, the condensation or intensification that takes place in the sestet leads to tropes of "diminishing," inadequacy and belatedness; in others, however, this intensification leads to tropes of sublime vision or explosiveness, thus returning to the figures of Wordsworthian unity considered earlier.

II

A look at an 1877 sonnet, "The Sea and the Skylark" (originally "Walking by the Sea"), will show how forcefully Hopkins uses the analogical thrust of the octave-sestet turn that characterizes nearly all the sonnets of 1877 and afterward. The poem highlights its author's recognition of the repetition of the octave in the sestet—but more crucially, it also highlights his recognition that the diminishing is not only formal but tropological:

> On ear and ear two noises too old to end
>   Trench—right, the tide that ramps against the shore;
>   With a flood or a fall, low lull-off or all roar,
> Frequenting there while moon shall wear and wend.
>
> Left hand, off land, I hear the lark ascend,
>   His rash-fresh re-winded new-skeinèd score
>   In crisps of curl off wild winch whirl, and pour
> And pelt music, till none's to spill nor spend.
>
> How these two shame this shallow and frail town!
>   How ring right out our sordid turbid time,
> Being pure! We, life's pride and cared-for crown,

Have lost that cheer and charm of earth's past prime:
Our make and making break, are breaking, down
To man's last dust, drain fast toward man's first slime.[23]

The poem is a series of balances, beginning with the opening "On ear
and ear two noises too old to end," a line clogged with repetitions of words
and sounds. The octave imitates the sensation of *listening*, first to the "noise"
at the right ear: the rhythmic percussion of waves against the shore that
recalls to him the larger rhythms of the tides, with their various sounds and
volumes, and the influential control of the moon. Even in these four lines,
Hopkins has created a remarkably layered structure of parallel sound, image, and rhythm. Furthermore, the quatrain has nearly imperceptibly taken
the reader from the sea to the alternate (parallel) image of the moon, an
image that enlarges both the spatial and temporal contexts of the poem by
recalling the correspondence of the movement of the sea to this heavenly
body and by recalling the eternality of this "frequenting."

The second quatrain similarly imitates the poet's perception of the music
of the lark, which he *hears* (but does not necessarily see) ascend "left hand,
off land." The bird's music, like that of the sea, is described as a repetition—"re-winded, new-skeinèd score"—although in the repetition there is
something "rash-fresh," something quickening and original.[24] The octave,
then, sets up a counterpoint of sounds, one endlessly repetitive, the other
"free-form," a burst of notes and graces inspirited with a freedom of spon-
taneous movement that the ocean's tidal movements lack.

The profundity and originality of the sea and skylark (that well-con-
templated figure of the poet in romantic poetry) are contrasted with wound-
down existence of this poet and the men of the town nearby, and the larger
parallelisms of octave and sestet are obvious: in the octave, "these two," the
sea and skylark, are unlike "us" in being "pure," in being wholly part of
nature; the sestet examines man's belatedness, caught up in chronological
"time" rather than in cyclical "tide." While the images of the octave lead to
a repetition that is paradoxically original every time, the sestet depicts the
activities of men as leading to a breaking down rather than to a renewal.
Indeed, if there is a repetition for man, it is an ironic one: man is "past,"
caught in a sequence of time that breaks him down to his original state—to
the same biblical "last dust" that was "man's first slime."[25]

While the octave revolves around sounds of eternity, with "noises too
old to end," the sestet, necessarily coming after, revolves around the image
of a fallen world in which time inexorably breaks down the world and brings
it to an end. The poem contemplates a belated world in which man has lost his
original "cheer and charm," the glad countenance and song of the paradise

that once was nature. The very movement of the poem downward, from the lark's heavenward flight to the breaking down into dust, is imitated by the poem's rhythm, the octave's inspirited counterpoint degenerating into the monosyllables that "drain fast" towards the poem's close. The poem pivots, then, around the diminishing of our world from what it was and from what nature itself still is.

What becomes of the poet figure, who is implicitly present at the poem's opening? The poem seems to worry over the status of poetry, a "making" that may also be a breaking-down. Indeed, Hopkins regretted, like his romantic forebears, the loss of "freshness" in composing and working this poem.[26] In a November 1882 letter to Robert Bridges, Hopkins laments that in attempting to describe the movement of the bird,

> the saying of it smells, I fear, of the lamp, of salad oil, and, what is nastier, in one line somewhat of Robert Browning.[27] The sea and skylark are "pure," perfect in the sense. I felt even at the time that in endless labour of recasting those lines I had lost the freshness I wanted and which indeed the subject demands.[28]

Time and the conditions of "living in the world" make the perception, "perfect in the sense," less than what it originally was, and the attempted renewal—the poem itself—only a diminished version of the lark's song.[29]

The tropological diminishing from octave to sestet is most painfully employed in the so-called terrible sonnets of his later career. In these, the introspective character of earlier poems intensifies, and the poems turn ever more inward to become involutions, rather than simply evolutions, of thought. The diminishing of these poems reflects a kind of mental claustrophobia, in which the poet becomes "the heir / To his own selfbent so bound so tied to his turn" ("Ribblesdale," lines 10–11), and his efforts seem to him to remain almost unexpressed, "a lonely began" ("To seem the stranger," line 14). Perhaps no one of these "terrible sonnets" more clearly illustrates my point than his last, "To R. B. [Robert Bridges]" (1889):

> The fine delight that fathers thought; the strong
> Spur, live and lancing like the blowpipe flame,
> Breathes once and, quenchèd faster than it came,
> Leaves yet the mind a mother of immortal song.
>
> Nine months she then, nay years, nine years she long
> Within her wears, bears, cares and combs the same.
> The widow of an insight lost she lives, with aim
> Now known and hand at work now never wrong.

Sweet fire the sire of muse, my soul needs this;
I want the one rapture of an inspiration.
O then if in my lagging lines you miss

The roll, the rise, the carol, the creation,
My winter world, that scarcely breathes that bliss
Now, yields you, with some sighs, our explanation.

This poem, like the rest of the terrible sonnets, has a more Miltonic feel to it—though without either Milton's or Wordsworth's confidence in his vocation. In this respect these late sonnets are a return to Hopkins's beloved Keats, whose fears of early poetic impotence in the face of precursors fuel the same frustrated sonnet writing as Hopkins's late sonnets.

"To R. B." is characteristic in its despair over confinement within the human body and physical and temporal limitations—what he calls in one sonnet "our small durance" ("No worst," lines 11–12), and in yet another, echoing Milton, "drudgery, day-labouring-out life's age" ("The Caged Skylark," line 4). The formal diminishing here becomes a trope for his own imaginative diminishing. The octave does imagine a power of inspiration that "fathers thought," "impregnates" a fertile mind to leave it full, a "mother of immortal song." Its final lines describe a mind that still lives by the craft of poetry, by the "hand at work."

However, in a reversal of Wordsworth's gender metaphorics regarding the birth of imaginative power and authority, the sestet shows that inspired mind to be vacant, infertile, the "widow of an insight lost." This is almost pathetically marked by a shift of tone: just at the *volta,* at the point of tropological diminishing from the image of the fertile poet's mind to the empty "I" of line 10, the speaker *resists* by calling out—not even to the absent muse, but to an even prior source: "Sweet fire the sire of muse, my soul needs this; / I want the one rapture of an inspiration" (lines 9–10). Even before the muse herself, which "allows" vision to be formed into poetry, the speaker wants the original and originating spark that Milton and Wordsworth also called upon. The following lines of the sestet, then, lack the energy to go further, for the poet wants even poetic desire, the "rapture of an inspiration." Inspiration diminishes to a scarce breath, the poet diminishes to a soul that "wants," in two senses of the word. The strength of the masculine rhymes in the octave slip into the feminine rhymes of the sestet: the final line is a metrical example of the lagging lines and trailing sighs that mark his imaginative impotence.[30]

In poems such as these, the form becomes for Hopkins, as it so often did for Keats and Rossetti, a metaphor for self-limitation, for subjective entrapment, for the inability to see beyond one's self into any "belonging field," as Hopkins put it—that field of vision which surrounds the self-as-center. Thus is he also unable to resolve successfully what the poet called the "deliberate antithesis" of the form; the dialectics of the sonnet satisfy only the expression of internal conflict, without offering a resolution. Like Keats's sonnets, Hopkins's "terrible sonnets" possess an elegiac tone that anticipates the ending of a poetic career.[31]

Another particularly interesting example of this imaginative failure is Hopkins's curtailed sonnet, "To his Watch":

> Mortal my mate, bearing my rock-a-heart
> Warm beat with cold beat company, shall I
> Earlier or you fail at our force, and lie
> The ruins of, rifled, once a world of art?
> The telling time our task is; time's some part,
> Not all, but we were framed to fail and die—
> One spell and well that one. There, ah thereby
> Is comfort's carol of all or worst woe's smart.
>
> Field-flown, the departed day no morning brings
> Saying "This was yours" with her, but new one, worse,
> And then that last and shortest . . .

The brevity of the sonnet emphasizes the incompleteness of the poet's efforts, the triumph of time over life, the failure of the poet's artistic "force" over the threat of death's obliterating force. This sonnet is classified as a curtal sonnet, which I think is correct. It does not follow the "condensed" scheme of a poem like "Pied Beauty," because it maintains the full octave. But its sestet is simply *cut off*. The final short line, used so effectively to opposite effect in "Pied Beauty," emphasizes the dissatisfaction of the poet with his "hasting days," as Milton puts it in his early "How soon hath Time," a poem that I suspect lies behind this one. Time leads the poet here not to a promise of perfection and a sense of "the will of Heav'n," but to a sense of being "fram'd to die"; rather than feeling the "sweetest comfort" in the fact, the poet feels instead the "worst woe's smart." In such poems, the sonnet's tendency to trope its own self-enclosure becomes a poetic entrapment that mirrors the poet's claustrophobic vision of his world.

III

But this is, as I have suggested, only one side of the coin. The trope of diminishing is, when Hopkins is at his strongest psychologically and poetically, a powerfully charged and explosive trope for the sublime vision, as it was for the romantic sonnet writers before him. This is a link that Wordsworth's sonnets, in particular, had discovered already, as we have seen. To this extent, Hopkins clearly belongs to the line of sonneteers I have been following; while Hopkins could certainly claim seventeenth-century influences—Herbert, Donne, and, most importantly, Milton—his use of the sonnet form and the character of his voice would not have been possible without Wordsworth. He extends even Wordsworth's insights, however, by finding in the miniaturization of octave in sestet a formal trope for "poetic accommodation." For Hopkins there is not only an allegory *of* form, which this study has located in the self-reflexivity of the sonnet, but also an allegory *in* form, as he discovers in the sonnet a formal analogy for the sacrifice of Christ.

Such a conclusion is undoubtedly related to Geoffrey Hartman's more general observation that there is a "downing motion" in poems such as "Hurrahing in Harvest" (1877) or "The Windhover" (1877). Quoting lines 4–5 of the former poem, Hartman remarks that there is a "mimic and optative gesture that recalls, together with the distance between heaven and earth, the spanning mystery of the Incarnation."[32] Hopkins once called this event an "incredible condescension"[33] and seemed to see it as a sublime limitation of the infinite in the finite form. The poet's astonishment at God's willingness to sacrifice his Son in this way is behind some of most successful of the religious sonnets. As Wordsworth's sonnets are organized around and motivated by the "surprise" of the imagination's perception of the disjunction between nature and the poet's perception of divinity in it, so in Hopkins's sonnets do we find an aesthetic shock that also indicates a shock of faith.[34] In either case, this shock associates the imaginative power of the poet with the creative power of God. Its effect in the religious sonnets is to give the poet a feeling of liberation of self in the perception of himself in God.

In Hopkins's famous celebratory religious sonnets, the trope of diminishing that I have been showing in one light is employed to an opposite effect, creating a countermotion to those self-involutions as the poet discovers that creative identity with the divine. Most readings of poems such as "The Windhover" locate the power of these texts in that identity; Michael Sprinker describes that poem, for example, as a

poem that brings forth the paradoxical triumph through limitation that is Christ's peculiar achievement and the poet's destiny. By an act of willed limitation, the poet, like Christ, blazes forth in greater glory, his poetic "fire" shines "a billion / Times told lovelier, more dangerous."[35]

"Triumph through limitation" aptly describes the formal motivation of nearly all of Hopkins's sonnets. The tension of the octave is formed by a dialectic between constraint and freedom, figured by the stasis of the poet (the "heart in hiding") and the "ecstatic" motion of the bird:

> I caught this morning morning's minion, king-
>   dom of daylight's dauphin, dapple-dawn-drawn Falcon, in his riding
>   Of the rolling level underneath him steady air, and striding
> High there, how he rung upon the rein of a wimpling wing
> In his ecstasy! then off, off forth on swing,
>   As a skate's heel sweeps smooth on a bow-bend: the hurl and gliding
>   Rebuffed the big wind. My heart in hiding
> Stirred for a bird,—the achieve of, the mastery of the thing!
>
> (Lines 1–8)

That tension is supported by the poem's sprung and outriding rhythms, and by the relentless and startling enjambment of lines, which drives the octave forward to a final exclamation point, a punctuation mark that registers the poet's surprised recognition that by perceiving the bird he partakes of its freedom. The "achieve of, the mastery of the thing" refers to the bird's mastery of the poet's heart; its achievement is that the poet's heart is "Stirred for a bird," stirred to move outside itself into a "belonging field" of the self[36] and toward this object of nature, which the poet recognizes as so much more than that. Even the internal rhyme of "stirred" and "bird" supports that movement out; the sweep of one word to the other is joined by assonance. The expansive force of the poem[37] inheres, as others have noted, in the poet's recognition of the allegorical status of the bird. The bird's achievement is the spiritual and imaginative movements of the *poet* rather than simply his own perfect and pure physical movements, for those movements reveal to the poet the bird's allegorical potentialities.

The poem's sestet, then, will revise the physical description of the bird in new terms. The last six lines turn downward from the particulars of the scene to the components of the relation that Hopkins sees between the bird, himself, and also Christ, to whose grace he attributes these revelations:[38]

> Brute beauty and valour and act, oh, air, pride, plume, here
>   Buckle! AND the fire that breaks from thee then, a billion
> Times told lovelier, more dangerous, O my chevalier!
>
> No wonder of it: shéer plód makes plough down sillion
> Shine, and blue-bleak embers, ah my dear,
>   Fall, gall themselves, and gash gold-vermilion.

The poem's triumph is that perception of the likeness in the unlikeness— and of the *poet's* own achievement—the association of bird, self, and *Christ*. The "buckling" in line 10, then, is a sort of gravitational center in the poem, where the conflation of figural levels "here," in the poem itself, takes place as analogy is lifted to the level of allegory and interpretation. The octave of "The Windhover" is to a large degree *about* perception; the sestet, a formal revision of the octave, is also about re-vision—seeing again. Mere percep- tion has become a different kind of vision, the visionary. The poem's self- reflexivity is the triumph made possible by the limitation imposed by poetic form itself.

It is interesting to note that this "triumph," as Sprinker calls it, "brought forth" by the bird's "figural hovering in the first nine lines and its fall in line 10,"[39] is figured once again by a familiar romantic trope: radiance. The tension of the octave explodes in the sestet into images of light: the "fire that breaks from thee," the "shine" of the plough, and the igniting of the earth's "blue-bleak embers" into "gold-vermilion."[40] A kind of reversal or crossing over takes place here, whereby the downward motion that Hartman and others have been noting becomes an upward movement as well. The fire that breaks forth is metaphorical evidence of an energy one could de- scribe as elemental or universal in that it inheres in everything, "Brute beauty and valour and act," the glory of God.[41] That which is below becomes, by means of the metaphor, part of that which is above, and it is the figure of radiance that encompasses them both. In retrospect, it is evident that this light was prefigured in the octave's opening association of the windhover with the sunrise, "dapple-dawn-drawn Falcon"; even a tracing of the poem's light imagery reveals that the movement of the poem has been downward, only to make possible the radiance that figures the ascent at the end.

Motto argues that this act of revision is characteristic of what she calls a struggle in Hopkins between lyricism and design,[42] that is, between the exuberance of language that describes his witnessing of the external world and the impulse to impose order on those sometimes "too-engrossing" ob- servations. She adds the subtle and important point that "each act of revi- sion reach[es] deeper into the world beyond the particulars physically seen. And the re-vision of vision attests to the continuing search for the original, absolute, and primal design, *Ipse*."[43] This is the double movement of de- scent and ascent that I have been describing, and which finds a formal anal- ogy in Hopkins's use of the Italian sonnet form. In this way the revisionary structure of the poem makes manifest, as many have argued, what Hopkins calls "inscape." Jonathan Culler has defined the term inscape as "a moment of revelation in which form is grasped and surface becomes profundity";[44] such a definition has the advantage of highlighting the reversal of depth and height. While critics like to talk about the "mimetic" aspects of this poem, what is more important is the analogical (and allegorical) motive of the sonnet form and how that analogy of likeness and difference becomes a liberating figure of thought for Hopkins.

"God's Grandeur" (1877) displays a similar revisionary movement from octave to sestet, and once again the general movement is toward discovering a depth in which one will find a height and thus redirect the force of the poem outward:

> The world is charged with the grandeur of God.
>   It will flame out, like shining from shook foil;
>   It gathers to a greatness, like the ooze of oil
> Crushed. Why do men then now not reck his rod?
> Generations have trod, have trod, have trod;
>   And all is seared with trade; bleared, smeared with toil;
>   And wears man's smudge and shares man's smell; the soil
> Is bare now, nor can foot feel, being shod.
>
> And for all this, nature is never spent;
>   There lives the dearest freshness deep down things;
> And though the last lights off the black West went
>   Oh, morning, at the brown brink eastward, springs—
> Because the Holy Ghost over the bent
>   World broods with warm breast and with ah! bright wings.

The first end-stopped line, with its counterpointed rhythm and alliteration, strains to hold in the force of its own metrical momentum, as if the entire poem were also "charged" by that original sublime source. The octave modulates between two sets of images: first, the paradoxical images of "flaming out" and "gathering to a greatness," both condensing and expanding at the same time; second, the contrasting images of man's "wearing out" his existence. Hopkins's unusual metrical markings show us how carefully those stresses support his tropes: "gathers," for example, indicates that the poet wanted to imitate metrically what he describes, for the marking indicates that two syllables are to be drawn in, "gathered," to stand metrically for one.

While the octave runs itself out by describing, as in "The Sea and the Skylark," the ever-diminishing existence of humanity, self-involved in trade and other spiritually dulling activities, the sestet once again reverses that diminishing, even as it continues to probe it. There is a contrary movement taking place in the sestet, both a downward one, such as I have discussed before, and an upward one. The poet identifies in nature not the dreariness of man's daily life but the "dearest freshness deep down things"; the dullness of nature exists only because man has grown too "bleared" to see it, like the shod foot unable to feel the earth. The going "deep down" is also a "going up," as the depth of profundity becomes, in a sublime reversal, something high in addition to being something low. Thus from this depth, and from the "black West," can emerge a morning that springs from the east. Hopkins, always astonished by his perceptions of faith and of the presence of the Holy Spirit, rhythmically recreates that surprise in the punctuation and counterpointed rhythms of the final tercet, where surprise releases the gathering movement of the octave in the "Oh" of line 12, and the "ah!" of line 14. What Hartman calls "pure vocality" lifts the poet into a different register (supported by the final lines' evocation of Milton).

Not surprisingly, the trope of radiance is visible in this sonnet, as indeed it is in "The Windhover." Hopkins's spiritual notes suggest how the poet associated the glory of Christ with light in a passage that recalls "God's Grandeur": "All things therefore are charged with love, are charged with God and if we know how to touch them give off sparks and take fire, yield drops and flow, ring and tell of him."[45] So in this sonnet, where a descent into nature's freshness "deep down things" sparks images of light and radiance, the sunrise, and the "warm" breast and "bright" wings of the Holy Ghost.

Many of Hopkins's other sonnets repeat this octave to sestet pattern of limitation and release, of narrow vision and transcendent revision: "The Caged Skylark" (1877), for example, is organized in this way. The octave's description of the caged skylark and the dull spirit of man imprisoned inside his "bone-house, mean house," is replaced in the sestet by the promise of release, a promise figured by the rainbow in the last line. "As kingfishers catch fire" (date unknown) is a more subtle example, in which the octave describes how nature everywhere praises God simply by existing, thus "Crying," in words that echo Christ, "*What I do is me: for that I came*" (line 14). The sestet moves away from nature generally to man specifically, opening startlingly with the poet's voice:

> Í say more: the just man justices;
>   Keeps gráce: thát keeps all his goings graces;
> Acts in God's eye what in God's eye he is—
>   Chríst. For Christ plays in ten thousand places,
> Lovely in limbs, and lovely in eyes not his
>   To the Father through the features of men's faces.

The poet says "more" than nature can because the poet, like the "just man," can recognize the grace of God and act in accordance with, and in praise of, that grace. In doing so, Hopkins more than suggests, man can "become" Christ. Graham Storey usefully remarks that this poem is "the clearest statement in all Hopkins's poems of Duns Scotus's belief in the fulfilling of individuality, in 'selving' (Hopkins's word)." He also refers us to an entry in Hopkins's spiritual notes that shows how profound was Hopkins's sense of "identity" between the just or faithful man and Christ: "It is as if a man said: that is Christ playing at me and me playing at Christ, only it is no play but truth: That is Christ *being me* and me being Christ."[46] The mirroring of self and Christ in this remark explains the sestet's incessant reflexiveness of diction, which encourages the conflation of man and Christ: "the just man justices; / Keeps gráce: thát keeps all his goings graces; / Acts in God's eye what in God's eye he is— / Chríst." Indeed, Hopkins is writing again about the "incredible condescension" of Christ into the human form, where he "plays in ten thousand places . . . through the features of men's faces."

But like so many of the sonnets we have looked at, the poem is finally about vision. Not surprisingly, it is in the sestet that the poem's images conflate the "I" of the poet and the "eye" of God: both the poet and God hear in nonhuman creation praise to Christ; both see, in the sestet, the fulfillment of Christ in every created thing. Form for Hopkins seems to be the making visible of divine presence, in poetic form no less than in the forms of windhovers or pied things.

IV

In light of Hopkins's general use of the revisionary relation of octave and sestet, I would like to reconsider his two well-known formal variants. Generally speaking, it is said that Hopkins "discovers" the curtal and so-called heavy sonnets, condensing and stretching the conventional form. These experiments involve the challenge of accomplishing either the implosion or the explosion of the form into the curtal or into the caudate sonnet without disrupting the formal integrity he so adamantly insisted on; like Rossetti, Hopkins felt that the strength of the sonnet was in its proportions. The curtal sonnet is a variant that was waiting to happen. The sonnet's characteristic dialectic of constraint and freedom, and, more specifically, its effort to find *in* that constraint a freedom or explosion of meaning—that "apocalyptic thrust" looked at earlier—clearly revealed to this poet the form's sublime possibilities. Better than any other single revision of the sonnet form created during the Victorian period, it exemplifies the dictum (quoted by John Dennis) that the sonnet is a form of poetry in which style comes "under pressure." From the larger perspective of the history of the sonnet I have been tracing, it is one logical endpoint of its formal self-reflexivity. Gardner sees little purpose in this experiment, deeming the curtal sonnet "a perfect medium for expression of a lyrical impulse which is intellectually too slight to fill up the normal sonnet-mould";[47] my own reading tends toward the opposite conclusion. The curtal sonnet intensifies those tropes of space and of voice that mark the visionary sonnets previously considered, and of the few examples of this form that Hopkins composed, clearly the most skillful is "Pied Beauty" (1877). Miller's commentary on the poem explains that this most well-known of the curtal sonnets is

> like an ordinary sonnet, but different, and so the relation of this sonnet to the usual sonnet is another case of pied beauty. The poem's structure of rhythm and sound seems to be all for the purpose of making the poem a model in little of the universe it names.[48]

The trope of diminishing looked at so far reaches one logical end here. The poem is a "model in little" because any effort to contain or describe God's universe will necessarily be incomplete and inadequate. Put in another light, such a miniaturized sonnet is a model for just the synecdochic procedure toward which the sonnet form tends; the sonnet's exaggerated compactness is, in other words, analogous to the compacting of self that God performs when he "fathers-forth" the beauties of the world.

While maintaining the proportions and parallelisms of the sonnet form precisely—including the revisionary relationship of octave and sestet—the poem embraces the question of the form's diminishing or miniaturization. One would suspect in this case that the spatial trope of the sonnet would be operating here, and so it does. As Motto points out, "[T]he world space to which Hopkins responds most readily is filled space, space crowded with sensory impression."[49]

The proliferation of images in the poem is countered by the intensification of the sonnet form into ten and a half lines, emphasizing the divine accommodation necessary for containing the infinitude of the divine in the perceptible minutiae of nature. That tension is highlighted in the sestet's breakdown into adjectival paradoxes—"With swift, slow; sweet, sour; adazzle, dim." As one would expect in the sestet, those last four and a half lines gather the particular aspects of God's beauty into categories, delineated by the adjectives, that lift them out of their particularity and into the universal. God's comprehension of those paradoxes is his power, which therefore Hopkins describes in the next line, "He fathers-forth whose beauty is past change"; Lichtmann points out usefully that the "simple preposition, 'forth', indicates relation, manifestation to and in the world."[50] Motto has said of this poem generally that "the abstracting design here holds, enfolds, envelops, the lyricism, while the discrete images held are examples and embodiments of the stable design that frames them."[51] I take the sonnet form to be that frame and stable design, a literal image of the framing and stable design of God's creation.

More explicitly than perhaps any other single Hopkins poem, "Pied Beauty" shows us how form becomes what Valéry called "voice in action." "Pied Beauty" reduces even the basic function of poetic voice to a singular purpose: the praise of God. The poem's final half-line, "Praise him," condenses the poem into Hartmanian "pure vocality," reinvigorating the Miltonic/Wordsworthian trope of sonnet-as-voice that was considered earlier in this book and radically condensing the tradition of praising God that calls for rhetorical *amplification*. The poem is the formal opposite of a litany; it is itself the praise, the trumpet of fame for God's creation, and art liberates because of its ability to praise.[52] A search for the trope of radiance in this poem will locate it in two places: in the "fathering-forth" of God, and in Hopkins's own voice, in the outwardly directed act of "praising him" that creates Hopkins's own poems.

When Barbara Hardy pointed out that "[m]ore native to the poetry of Hopkins is the process of expansion,"[53] she was not talking about formal expansiveness but rather the movement from "the sensuous and phenomenal to the larger spiritual adventure"; one could extend her observation to the formal application. Two years after inventing the curtal sonnet, Hopkins wrote one in alexandrines, "Peace," in which he both contracts and expands the form at the same time; the dialectics of the sonnet are always so active in Hopkins that he gradually begins to try to capture the tendency to implode and the tendency to explode simultaneously. The expansive movement toward the spiritual that Hardy mentions and that this study has explored in Hopkins's sonnet form may have foreshadowed his experiments, as he sought formally to imitate that expansion or movement.

Hopkins outlined primarily metrical reasons for trying "long sonnets," as he called them. He felt that the English sonnet, written in the Italian structure, was shorter than its Italian counterpart because of the absence of vowel length and of Italian's frequent elisions. This shortness he considered a fault of the English version of a form that depends so much on precise proportion and balance. Hopkins therefore describes "Spelt from Sibyl's Leaves" as "longest by its own proper length, namely by the length of its lines; for anything can be made long by eking, by tacking, by trains, tails and flounces."[54] But having already composed sonnets in lines of six and eight heavy stresses, Hopkins became interested in the possibility of using a coda; his correspondence to Bridges includes a request for information on that device—"I shd. be glad however if you wd. explain what a *coda* is and how employed"[55]—and a dissatisfied thank-you for the little guidance Bridges evidently provided him.[56]

Of the several caudate sonnets[57] he did finally compose, the longest one, "That Nature is a Heraclitean Fire and of the comfort of the Resurrection" (1888) is also the most spectacular. Gardner has appropriately called this sonnet a "gargantuan offspring of the Petrarchan sonnet,"[58] with its alexandrines, caesurae, three codas, and "burden" lines at the end of each. Yet despite its expansiveness, the sonnet clearly preserves, as Hopkins always insisted, the crucial division of octave and sestet. The characteristic trope of diminishing is very much present; whereas the octave describes the infinite power and eternality of nature, the sestet, which is clearly marked by the full stop at the end of line 9, concerns itself with the diminished status of mankind. As Mariani puts it,

> Hopkins moves toward the realization that the distinctiveness of man may be swallowed up by death. His language precisely captures this loss of distinctiveness, this shading off of man into an indistinguishable mass, in his grouping of vowels and a soft *n* sound, which move down a scale until the words become all slack, without any pitch or sharpness. . . . The markedness of rhythm, the inscape of the sound, echoes the markedness of that part of the human inscape ("Manshape") which resists slack, and which cannot be lost or swallowed up.[59]

The trope of diminishing leads us even in the octave from heaven to earth, from clouds and "bright winds" (a Heraclitean image, but one possibly reminiscent of Shelley as well)[60] to ruts and dust. The further diminishing of the sestet is located primarily in the poem's major trope, fire; that is, the sestet reduces the universal "bonfire" (line 9) that is nature to the quickly extinguished "spark" (line 10) that is man. Images of light that gleam in the octave—the stars that "glitter," the "dazzling whitewash," the "Shivelights and shadowtackle," the "bright wind" (lines 2–5), are countered by images of unfathomable darkness, of drowning, of mankind extinguished by the "vastness" of the universe and by the force of time: "Manshape, that shone / Sheer off, disseveral, a star, death blots black out" (lines 13–14). That downward motion has led us to a kind of erasure of man, to an oblivion. By the end of the "sonnet proper," man is "[no] mark," without impression or significance, without "stark"-ness or power.[61]

If the poem had ended here, it would have resembled the several "poems of desolation" that are contemporaneous with it. What distinguishes this poem from those, or even from the other heavy sonnets, such as "Spelt from Sibyl's Leaves" (?1884) and "Tom's Garland" (1887) is that Hopkins finally discovers, no thanks to Bridges, that in the use of the coda exists the potential for both formal and thematic recovery: the caudate sonnet releases him from the movement downward that marks nearly all the other sonnets of this period. Barbara Herrnstein Smith would have been able to explain to Hopkins what Bridges apparently did not, that the poetic coda is "likely to appear when the thematic structure of a poem is paratactic, associative, or dialectic," and that it often offers a stability that may not be evident in the rest of the poem.[62] Hopkins, whose exploration of the dialectics of the sonnet was so varied and profound, discovered this for himself, and the turn to stability is what this poem's close accomplishes.

Thus in the first coda appears the crucial "second *volta*," as some have called it, in the word "Enough!" (line 16).[63] The Resurrection, immediately introduced in this coda, eliminates the need for pity and indignation; the word "enough" is an imperative that dismisses both emotions. The image of light, which had been extinguished by the end of the sonnet proper, returns in this coda: "Across my foundering deck shone / A beacon, an eternal beam" (lines 18–19). This light, which the poet distinguishes from the "world's wildfire" of the second coda, is no longer the light of the Heraclitean fire that is nature, but the light of Christ, the evidence of his power. As the poem moves toward its close, the saving beacon of line 19 becomes the flash of the Apocalypse, and as in romantic sonnets discussed in previous chapters, the sublime thrust of that vision fuses images of light, space, and voice. Figures of radiance and prophecy, the flash and the trumpet, return from the sonnets of Milton, Wordsworth, and Shelley (and, of course, from the original biblical sources); here, as for those poets, the sonnet becomes a site for an explosion of poetic force that accompanies the poet's recognition of his relation to divine power.[64]

Hopkins's recognition involves a final condensation of images, not simply of "man" and Christ but, much more specifically, of "me" and Christ. In the third and final coda, the radical conflation takes place, and while the movement is still downward—from Christ to "I"—the movement is simultaneously expansive and triumphant:

> In a flash, at a trumpet crash,
> I am all at once what Christ is, | since he was what I am, and
> This Jack, joke, poor potsherd, | patch, matchwood, immortal diamond,
> Is immortal diamond.

The perspective of the sonnet has gradually narrowed, from nature and the cosmic Heraclitean fire to mankind generally and to the poet himself. But the final emergence of the self is more a merging of the self in Christ. The "I am" at the opening of the final coda signals a breakdown of the metaphors that have formed the knotty texture of this poem into one final metaphor; by the poem's end, it is the likeness of the speaker himself in Christ that takes over the poem. The emphasis on "am" and "is" marks the poet as not only "similar to" Christ, but part of him, as he is redeemed and purified through him.[65]

The first downward movement of the poem, then, explodes out in the codas with the recollection of the Resurrection and its traditional images. This movement focuses downward again, however, in the bold conflation of earlier images—of man, poet and Christ—into the final image, another image of radiance: the immortal diamond. It is as if the light that has figured both mankind and Christ himself (that light that "across my foundering deck shone") hardens into the gem, with its many reflective facets. Hopkins supports the conflation aurally with the rhyme of "I am and" and "diamond."[66] The poet is no longer figured by sparks that are stamped out by time and nature but, now, by a material that is eternal, unbreakable, and radiant. Images of "vastness," light, and form, whether divine or human, are focused down into a single image of clarity.

The conflation of imagery seen in Wordsworth and Shelley is rehearsed here: space and time now do not blot out man, but are finally contained in him through the faith in his relationship to Christ. Knowledge of that faith lends a kind of anticipatory force to the images of light in the first part of the poem, all of which point toward the final apocalyptic radiance of the ending. There is in this poem in particular a near-collapse of metaphor, as comparison or parallelism breaks down into identity. The pressurized miniaturization characteristic of the post-Wordsworth sonnet leads to a final figure in which the metaphor of form seems nearly to break down as well. The constraints of shape and space are eliminated by the figure of radiance; the boundaries of inside and outside are no longer distinguishable. The triumph of this poem is the concretion of significance around this radiant moment, leaving a figure not of dissolution but of permanence, the "immortal diamond." Monumentality has been transfigured in this poem as eternality.

Nowhere are the consequences of the sonnet's strain against its own form clearer than in the sonnets of Hopkins. His work in this form often reminds me of Valéry's remark that "the true condition of a true poet is as distinct as possible from the state of dreaming. I see in it only willed inquiry, suppleness of thought, the soul's assent to exquisite constraints, and

the perpetual triumph of sacrifice."[67] If poetic form is a figure of thought—
and it has been my assumption throughout this study that this is the case—
for Hopkins, perhaps even more than for the other poets discussed here, the
structure of the sonnet offered a way of thinking about not only his major
"subject," the sacrifice of Christ, but also about the parallel sacrifice of the
poet—his "assent to exquisite constraints." When Hopkins can see his work
in such a light, as in the celebratory sonnets looked at earlier, the sense of
triumph is palpable. Like Wordsworth, with whom these sonnets resonate,
Hopkins perceives the visionary function of the sonnet form: the dialectics
of octave for sestet become for him, as for that earlier poet, a figure for the
dialectic of the sublime that charges or "animates" (to use a word that
Wordsworth suggests in his "Scorn not the sonnet") the form itself.

But then like Keats as well, Hopkins fought against the narrowness of
a form that all too easily became a figure of claustrophobia and dissatisfaction. In Hopkins's terrible sonnets, he seems to lack the will necessary to
break the constricting shape of the sonnet as he is able to do elsewhere.
Indeed, the peculiar "dialect" of poetic voice that we associate with Hopkins
falls away in these poems. These sonnets become "stripped down" versions
and sound more Miltonic—as if Hopkins could find a source of strength by
returning to the mode of a poet who handled the dialectics of the sonnet so
well as to defeat crisis with vision.[68] Gardner writes that Hopkins is "trying
to reconcile freedom and necessity in artistic creation";[69] sonnet dynamics
recreate this struggle in all of the sonneteers we have looked at, but perhaps
nowhere is that struggle more evident than in Hopkins's work. The poetry was
itself a freedom that Hopkins was not sure he should allow himself; he was not
sure that his avocation and his vocation were even morally compatible, and
once called poetry writing a "luxury." This was a particularly troubling issue,
as we know clearly from his letters to Dixon, who so persistently urged him to
publish. In his late poems Hopkins loses not the willingness to sacrifice
himself but the ability to see any longer the triumph of his sacrifice.[70]

Robert Bridges was absolutely correct in concluding that "it was an
idiosyncrasy of this student's mind to push everything to its logical extreme, and take pleasure in a paradoxical result."[71] This chapter has attempted to refine that statement, to identify where it was that Hopkins pushed
and how that paradoxical result was achieved. But another early critic, Barker
Fairley, can be credited with recognizing the direction of Hopkins's explorations into another kind of formal dissonance—even as far as choosing
musical terms Hopkins himself might have employed: "Hopkins's disharmonies are the studied disharmonies of one who continues to use the old
scale, his concern being to extend its expressiveness, not to reject it or
change it. The tradition may be jolted, but it is never upset."[72]

"What to Make of a Diminished Thing": Speculation and Survival in Robert Frost's Sonnets

From one perspective, a history of the post-Wordsworthian sonnet and the revisionary poetic that it highlights could halt with Hopkins, under whose hand the sonnet experiences both a compression and a dilation beyond which it would be difficult to go without either abandoning the form once again for the ode, as Shelley and Keats did, or collapsing it altogether into epigram, to which early historians of the form presumed the sonnet to be originally related. Few poets since Hopkins have so fully explored the various kinds of formal implications the sonnet offers. Hopkins also draws together the various major themes of this study: the impact of Milton and Wordsworth on English sonnet writing; the question of formal "legislation" and experimentation; and formal self-reflexivity and the emergent figures of form. All of these merge in Hopkins, as they had not done since Wordsworth, in that spectacular figure of the "immortal diamond."

The previous chapter also, however, traced the divergent thematics of Hopkins's sonnet work, which is as likely to thematize poetic impotence as potency. The authoritative stance that Wordsworth mastered in his own sonnet work, particularly its conflation of the private and public roles of the poet, was, on the one hand, an ideal model for a Jesuit celebrating the presence of God by searching him out in his own experience of the world; Hopkins had so much to gain from accepting Wordsworth's claims for the form and the apocalyptic vision one could achieve within it. On the other hand, Hopkins rarely achieved the dissolution of boundaries and form implicit in the trope of radiance; the fiction of "the moment," whether the apocalyptic moment of Wordsworth or the aestheticized "special moment" of postromantics, was rarely as persuasive for Hopkins as it was for Rossetti or for his real poetic mentor, Keats. But at least Hopkins does enjoy a level of faith, in God if not in art, that makes the visionary occasion *possible*, as in his "Heraclitean Fire" sonnet. In the divergent results of Hopkins's sonnet work, then, the paradox of Wordsworth's sonnet poetic is apparent, for it appealed to the poet who would, at the same time, speak for all men and withdraw into the experience of the self alone.

If the aestheticism of the latter half of the nineteenth century more successfully popularized a depoliticized vision of the visionary sonnet, that would not remain the case. The story of the Wordsworth visionary sonnet and its revisionary poetic is still only partially told, as the form has enjoyed consistent attention throughout our own century despite (or perhaps because of) the pressure on the very concept of form itself. There has remained a persistent postromantic interest in the deconstruction of the moment, in the attention to and troping of the disjunction between past and present, between experience and representation, between the iconic moment and the temporal progression into which that moment dissolves. Above all, writers have returned particularly to the significance of "the moment" *as* a historical—*historicized*—moment. The examples here, from England and America, are many, and a study of them would make up another book: Aiken, Auden, Berryman, cummings, Heaney, Hollander, Lowell, McClatchy, Merrill, Millay, Moore, Murray, Owen, Ransom, Robinson, Seth, Stickney, Wilbur, Yeats—and so many others. Whether the subject is the lyric moment or the narrative of "real-life" (social or autobiographical) events, the self-conscious return to the historicity of the moment—as the *subject* of the poem or the sequence—is the distinctive aspect of the form's evolution in this century. Wordsworth's late sequences in particular, exemplified in this study by the *River Duddon* sonnets, lie behind that evolution.

At the same time, the twentieth century has brought with it a skepticism regarding artistic form and formalisms that has severely complicated the handling of this most self-consciously formal and traditional of poetic genres; many concur with a contemporary sonnet writer, Reynolds Price, who describes his "suspicion" of the sonnet's participation in a "near-metabolic unity with the western mind's rate of experience and reflection."[1] Such skepticism underlies the argument of this entire study, which at once holds up Wordsworth's visionary sonnet poetic and yet also locates within its revisionary poetic the challenge to that very stance. The difficulty with the Wordsworthian conception of the sonnet, with its romantic, synecdochic vision of the closed circle of time, is its assumption of the possibility of some coherent final vision, one that can be reached via the poet's imaginative linkage of his own private insight with the order of the world at large. For the post-Wordsworth authors in this study, the belief in, even the yearning for, the *possibility* of that linkage is there. But the anticipation of the imagination's *failure* from Keats onward points at a crisis of faith in art that lies at the center of the challenge to the Wordsworthian vision of the sonnet.

In a study focusing on British poets in the last century, it may seem an argumentative sleight of hand to conclude with a look at Robert Frost, an American poet from this century. The rationale lies, however, not only in the implicit thematic and philosophical connections of Robert Frost's sonnet work to the post-Wordsworthian themes just summarized but also in the *explicit* debt to Wordsworth's sonnet writing that Frost himself acknowledges. In a letter to Lewis N. Chase in July 1917, Frost recalls the writers and poets whom he "read for myself and read all to pieces" in his formative years. He mentions Poe, Robert Browning, E. R. Sill, Arnold, and T. E. Brown; he remembers a "great time with Emerson. . . . Oh and there was Keats minus Endymion." He also read *Palgrave's Treasury* "literally to rags and tatters." Frost concludes, however, with this: *"But before all write me as one who cares most for Shakespearean and Wordsworthian sonnets"* (my emphasis).[2]

Frost's postromanticism is evident in so many ways.[3] As for previous authors, the sonnet tradition offers Frost tropological terms with which to argue out problems of form and representation. His sonnets participate directly in the Wordsworthian sonnet line insofar as they invest the experiential moment with a significance that the poet's consciousness—the "work" of art—attaches to it, and insofar as they attempt, at least, to assert the moment's synecdochic relation to a teleologically directed notion of temporality.

In one crucial respect, however, Frost's sonnets radically differ from Wordsworth's: they acknowledge that this lyric moment, this emergence into form, is only a momentary victory—a "momentary stay," as Frost famously described poetic form generally, "against confusion." Frost's sonnets thematize not vision but *speculation*, sometimes doubting pessimistically whether the transformation is even possible,[4] other times wondering, more optimistically, how such a transformation is achieved—and for how long. These are the obsessive themes of Frost's sonnets, and a reading of them reveals that Frost's stated suspicion of the sonnet is provoked by the apprehension that lyric plot emerges either out of the threat of discontinuity and incoherence, or even out of the discontinuous gaps themselves. For all his conservatism, his admiration of traditional forms and traditional poets, Frost's sonnets register a profound skepticism toward the Wordsworthian visionary mode, in light of what his sonnets present as the unintelligibility of the phenomenal world.

Although his demand for form in art was as insistent and as consistent as Hopkins's, Frost too had once called the sonnet form "suspect," explaining that its very formality worries the writer over whether he will "outlast or last out the fourteen lines—have to cramp or stretch to come out even—have enough bread for the butter or butter for the bread."[5] The poet is indicating not only the sonnet's characteristic difficulty (the old "Procrustes' bed" complaint), but also something more complicated—something about survival ("outlasting") and about the poetic will (the "lasting out") that Hopkins had lost.

Frost's speculative notion of poetic form has clear connections with the conception of formality that this study explores. The dialectic of the conventional sonnet, I have been arguing, has been troped as the lyric plot of poetic representation itself. While in earlier sonnets, however, the notion of "strain against form" has signaled the poet's own assertion of will against the artifice of form and against literary tradition, Frost's intention is different. Critics often note a general feeling of threat in Frost—not least because of his oft-quoted remark in the letter to the *Amherst Student*:

> The background is hugeness and confusion shading away from where we stand into black and utter chaos; and against the background any small man-made figure of order and concentration. What pleasanter than that this should be so?[6]

Indeed, Frost directly connects the problem of form to this environment of threat:

> there are no two things as important to us in life and art as being threatened and being saved. What are the ideals of form for if we arent [*sic*] going to be made to fear for them? All our ingenuity is lavished on getting into danger legitimately so that we may be genuinely rescued.[7]

The insistence on form[8] has therefore been properly interpreted by critics as a fundamentally conservative gesture against that threat. Frank Lentricchia, for example, notes that a "characteristic movement of the imaginative man in Frost's poetry is one of advance and retreat: out to confrontation with the confusions of experience; back inside to enclosure before it is too late."[9] That same pattern of advance and retreat characterizes accounts of Frost's political involvements as well; often accused of being a reactionary by left-wing foes and by friends alike (Louis Untermeyer was particularly irritated by his position—or evident lack thereof—during and after World War II), Frost once stated that it "is not the business of the poet to cry for reform." Elsewhere he added that "Wordsworth and Emerson both wrote some politics into their verse. Their poetic originality by which they live was quite another thing."[10]

But Frost "wrote some politics" into his verse as well, however implicitly, and the Wordsworthian mode of sonnet serves Frost just here. Offering the controlled dialectic of constraint and freedom as well as the visionary stance of the poet that Wordsworth learned from Milton, Frost's sonnets take on as their central theme the same confrontation between public and private experience, between social and private time, even if the historical situation is drastically altered. In Frost's early- to mid-twentieth-century America, the threat of confusion or chaos creates pressures from outside the boundaries of spatial and temporal dimensions in the form. These tensions are palpable in sonnets both early and late: look at "The Flood" (published in 1928; "Blood has been harder to dam back than water") and "Once by the Pacific" (1926), both nightmare visions of form utterly overwhelmed— to the extent, in the latter poem, that the light of the phenomenal world would be extinguished with God's countermand, *"Put out the light."* In the late sonnets in particular, such as "No Holy Wars For Them" (1947) or "Bursting Rapture" (1949), the context is the clear and present danger of global annihilation.

All these poems treat with irony the apocalyptic thrust of the Wordsworthian mode of sonnet: while seeking a pattern for history, the speaker, himself threatened by the prospect of the atomic bomb, imagines a moment that would contain the possibility of not continuity but the literal *dis*continuity of time after a nuclear apocalypse. Even in the sonnetlike "On Looking Up By Chance At The Constellations" (1930), a poem (with a Keatsian title) that takes care to remind the reader what a diminished thing a man is in the universe, with his "particular time and personal sight" (line 15), the final line threatens, offhandedly, that the calm of heaven "seems certainly safe to last the night" (line 16).

Frost's sense of a historical, changing universe challenges the kind of revelatory collapse of time and space—that moment of unmediated vision or presence—that Hopkins, at his best moments, could glimpse and that Wordsworth found often enough. Hopkins spoke of a "field of belonging," a conception of a ever-expanding field of vision the limits of which are only possible to perceive with the perspective of God himself. But Frost's field of vision[11] in the phenomenal world is frankly limited, and the challenge in his sonnets is that confrontation of the poet's own will for order with the randomness of nature and experience. More often than not, however, his sonnets record incomplete visions. They are poems typically about the effort to *contextualize*, or to recontextualize, in order to remedy the incoherence of the present moment itself. What is "present" to Frost is the incompleteness of experience, the mind's incomprehension, the invisibility of pattern.

In "Design" (1922), for example, the poet's own perception of the coincidence of white sets his poetic, metaphor-making faculties to work. The octave is constructed out of observation and out of trope, each object's blind whiteness countered by the mind's immediate effort to look for meaning in the likenesses:

> I found a dimpled spider, fat and white,
> On a white heal-all, holding up a moth
> Like a white piece of rigid satin cloth—
> Assorted characters of death and blight
> Mixed ready to begin the morning right,
> Like the ingredients of a witches' broth—
> A snow-drop spider, a flower like froth,
> And dead wings carried like a paper kite.[12]

(Lines 1–8)

In addition to the attribution of metaphor to each object, the octave sets about trying to contextualize this (random?) coincidence, as if, taken together, these could be seen as "ingredients" whose interrelationships, whether physical or metaphoric, contribute to some final end, some transformation effected by the work of a controlling mind. But even the image of the witches' brew evokes a coherence, a "design" or intention structuring that moment, that the sestet undermines:

> What had that flower to do with being white,
> The wayside blue and innocent heal-all?
> What brought the kindred spider to that height,
> Then steered the white moth thither in the night?
> What but design of darkness to appall?—
> If design govern in a thing so small.

(Lines 9–14)

Playing off the metaphors of darkness and light as tropes of intelligibility, what appalls is the incomprehensibility of the event, even as the mind itself tries to find to locate some centered, coherent, "kindred" order. The sonnet's structure, following a conventional 8-6 division, is typical of Frost: the octave setting up the problem to be meditated upon, the sestet offering the poet's interpretation or at least his effort to recontextualize the problem so that *something* can be understood. But the poem's final couplet ironizes even this. Line 13's move toward the assumption of some intelligibility is cut short by the dash at the line's end—and by the acknowledgment that that assumption may be wishful thinking. The offhand tone of the final line points at the more appalling possibility that the poet's own final afterthought (represented by the poem itself) has more of "design" than the event that it describes.

It is remarkable just how many of Frost's sonnets concern themselves with an unintelligibility whose source is each human being's limited perspective, his boundedness in a particular time and space that is troped by the conventional rigidity of sonnet boundaries. The dialectic that motivates Frost's sonnets is the poet's resistance to what appears to the speaker to be the possibility of a universal chaos. The challenge to chaos and confusion is launched, not surprisingly, simply by thinking itself. In "Time Out" (1972), for example, the relentless and potentially meaningless passage of time is countered by the poet's insistence on the "moment to reflect": "It took that pause to make him realize / The mountain he was climbing had the slant / As of a book held up before his eyes / (And was a text albeit done in plant)" (lines 1–4). This poem's lyric plot, like a Wordsworth sonnet's, is motivated by "that pause"—and while its conclusion takes us only as far as the act of reflection itself, even the act of realizing the metaphor of mountain and book implies an ordering of temporality, a mental narrative, an "intellectual history."[13]

As so often has been the case, however, that moment, a peculiarly static one as the poet reflects inward, is typically figured by the form itself: once again a figure for "mental space," the sonnet is the site for interpretative/creative work. The feeling of stasis that often adheres to Frost's sonnets differs in kind from the stasis of the Wordsworthian and post-Wordsworthian sonnet, and the difference is related to this notion of perspective. The stasis of the sonnets considered in previous chapters was most often related to the sonnet's monumentality, its effort to freeze the present moment and create out of it a significance that comes of reflecting upon it. In Frost's sonnets, however, it is caused more by his attempt to perspectivize, to dwell momentarily at a single vantage point—while being fully aware that no claim for the permanence or mythic significance of such moments *can* be made. In this attempt, these sonnets can be said to be similarly ekphrastic. The sonnet is, characteristically, describing the process—the plotting—of its own appearance.

However, the stasis here has an ironic force as well. Against the background of that appalling darkness, insight in the Frost sonnet is typically concealed or obscured. The stasis tropes the mind's own dwelling in and on the ambiguity, its effort to read and interpret. The quietude of these poems inheres less in form's monumentality than in the hesitation of one who suspects he is lost. The poem itself records the moment at which either a decision or choice is made regarding an approach to that concealment,[14] or at which the poet, like a traveler unsure of which fork in the road to take, hesitates at the revelation of mere ambiguity.

This is why so many of Frost's sonnets concern themselves with what the poet obscurely calls "the thing," or "something" or "it"—without very clearly defining what the "thing" or the "something" or the "it" is. So in "Mowing" (1923), in which he asks, "What was it it whispered? I knew not well myself; / Perhaps it was something about the heat of the sun, / Something, perhaps, about the lack of sound—" (lines 3–5). So too in "Time Out," the second half of which recalls the Keatsian procedure of troping interpretation of the phenomenal world as *reading*::

> But the thing was the slope it gave his head:
> The same for reading as it was for thought,
> So different from the hard and level stare
> Of enemies defied and battles fought.
> It was the obstinately gentle air
> That may be clamored at by cause and sect,
> But it will have its moment to reflect.
>
> (Lines 8–14)

Frost's unwillingness or inability to define is evident in line 8's strange ambiguity: "But the thing was . . .", the line begins—and we hear there the colloquial "The thing is" that prefaces our attempts to clarify our own position (as in "The thing is, I feel that . . ."). But Frost's colloquialism is deceptive here, in that he *literalizes* that stock phrase. "But the thing was" is no throwaway, but a definition of the poem's obscure subject—"But the thing was the slope"—that certain downward slant of the head that "means" reading, interpretation, the effort to comprehend the book of nature, whose own temporal order, troped by the "flowers fading on the seed to come," is "followingly fingered" by the poet as he climbs. The temporal process of interpretation itself is what is revealed; here, as in "Design," figuration "fuses with fact," as Cameron put it, "interprets it, and what we initially called the confusion of the two now makes sense in the context of divination."[15]

But divination is exactly what Frost denies himself. I cannot help thinking that Rossetti's "The Woodspurge," with its protagonist's desperate slant of the head, lies behind this poem; here, as there, the insight has something to do with the facticity of the phenomenal world. But this poem, unlike that one, concerns itself much more obviously with the dilemma of immediacy.

The "it" in the poem does not, like the woodspurge, merely "mean" what it "is." While it is difficult, even grammatically, to make that "it" correspond to any one antecedent, "it" seems to be finally the context in which the "moment to reflect" will take place, the current state of existence that "will have its moment to reflect." There is, indeed, "confusion" here, located in the determination of whether the "it" refers to the speaker's own will or to the will of something outside himself, some "design" of nature. The poet's very effort to identify and define that confused, indeterminate "it" is what makes reflection possible and necessary, what leads the poet upon this quest for intelligibility.

An interesting companion poem to this one might be the sonnet "Acceptance" (1930), which considers how in nature, unlike in the realm of humanity, "No voice in nature is heard to cry aloud / At what has happened. Birds, at least, must know / It is the change to darkness in the sky" (lines 3–5). From this perspective, the horror of incomplete vision is quieted; darkness is not a figuration of chaos but only "what is"—the unthinking "fact" of nature:

> At most he thinks or twitters softly, "Safe!
> Now let the night be dark for all of me.
> Let the night be too dark for me to see
> Into the future. Let what will be, be."
>
> (Lines 11–14)

The creature not alienated from nature is safe in its darkness; not so ourselves, whom the darkness "appalls."

The sonnet's association with "the moment" is thus profoundly complicated by Frost, whose sense of temporality is figured most problematically in "On A Bird Singing In Its Sleep" (1934) as "the interstices of things ajar / On the long bead chain of repeated birth" (lines 10–11), a figuration of temporal progression that points at the true dilemma of even referring to "discrete moments" in the flow of time. The figure suggests incoherence, gaps paradoxically located within the chain itself. The poet wonders whether the tune slipped through one of those interstices and whether meaning can in fact be located at that point of incoherence, thus evading him: "It ventured less in peril than appears," he suggests, some teleology or design not "apparent" to the poet directing the bird's action.

If the literal world is so difficult to decipher, if the direction of time's events are so obscure—if such a direction exists at all—then what becomes important to Frost's effort to make that world intelligible is "perspective," the vantage point of the speaker at any particular moment. The matter of

perspective has been implicit throughout this book, emerging most promi-
nently in the discussion of Keats, whose sonnets Frost occasionally echoes,
and of Hopkins, whose notion of a "field of vision" I have already recalled
in this chapter.

Given the potential blankness of Frost's universe, the only fact that the
poet can assert is the fact of "myself." In one of his most powerful poems,
"Acquainted With the Night" (1928), the speaker can only assert his own
subjective existence, his own facticity, so to speak, within the context of an
"unearthly height" against which "one luminary clock" (which I take to be
the stars themselves) "Proclaimed the time was neither wrong nor right."
This is a kind of "self-possession," but a diminished one: this speaker's
perspective upon the heavens is a far cry from Wordsworth's "subliming"
of his poetic power *as* Hesperus.

The logical octave-sestet structure typical of Frost's sonnets breaks down
into a series of terza rima tercets in this one, each tercet recording a different aspect of his quest for intelligibility: "outwalking," walking down, and
standing still—which is where he leaves himself. The identity of the first
and last lines, "I have been one acquainted with the night," provides an
almost tautological conclusion, suggesting that the poem merely records
the one "fact" that he (reminiscent once again of the subject of Rossetti's
"Woodspurge") can say: "I have been one acquainted with the night." Beyond that there is nothing that explains, no divination.

Frost's sonnets are therefore often moments that try out different perspectives, sometimes in the course of a single sonnet. In "The Vantage Point"
(1913), for example, the octave presents a field of vision in which the speaker
is diminished; the sestet, on the other hand, records not only the turn of his
body but also a shift into a perspective of a kind of gigantism. Paul Fussell
notes that the poem's two-part structure "coincides wittily with something
like a literal turn of the head or body."[16] Each perspective is neither "wrong
nor right," and there is no conclusion. The center of the poem is simply the
seeing "I" in the landscape: "Myself unseen, I see." This poem registers a
definite movement of time, from dawn to noon, but there is no correspond-
ing movement from the dawn to the fullness of insight.

"Lost In Heaven" (1935), a "curtailed" Shakespearean sonnet, takes
up an almost self-mocking perspective on his own limited sight, as he finds
himself unable to identify any familiar patterns of stars through an opening
in the storm-clouds, and thus is like a sailor lost at sea, unable to locate
himself: "Seeing myself well lost once more, I sighed, / 'Where, where in
Heaven am I? But don't tell me! / O opening clouds, by opening on me
wide. / Let's let my heavenly lostness overwhelm me'" (lines 9–12). The
irony of this final line is quite profound, as it suggests that his very "lostness"

is, like the "offering" (line 2) of the rent in the clouds, itself "heavenly," an offer of a potentially sublime revelation. But clearly what lies behind this exultant apostrophe is less the welcoming of the sublime than the horror of nonidentity, of being, as Hopkins put it in the "Heraclitean Fire" sonnet, blotted "black out." Again, it is a far cry from the Wordsworthian constellation shining over all.

Cameron speaks on a similar point in Dickinson's poetry, and refers to what she sees as an underlying "despair" in the lyric moment generally:

> Lyric poems insist that coherence be made of isolated moments because there is no direct experience of an alternative. They suggest, too, that meaning resides neither in historical connection nor in the connection between one temporal event and another. Meaning is consciousness carved out of the recognition of its own limitations. They insist that meaning depends upon the severing of incident from context, as if only isolation could guarantee coherence.[17]

I would agree with this generally, but for Frost it only works up until the last sentence, as he ultimately refuses that severing. His lyrics tend to acknowledge context rather than to sever it, even if the only context that can provide meaning is his own subjective experience of time—that is, of his own experience of past (memory), of present, and of the future (anticipation, fantasy). Cameron's suggestion that "it is the speaker's words that matter, not her past"[18] does not fit neatly with Frost's imaginative procedure, for it is in the mind's ability to reflect and *interpret* experience that Frost finds his own sense of authority. "For Once, Then, Something" (1920) is a sonnetlike (fifteen-line) poem that plays with problems of perspective, limited vision, and the potentially narcissistic self-reflexivity *of* the reflective "me myself":

> Others taunt me with having knelt at well-curbs
> Always wrong to the light, so never seeing
> Deeper down in the well than where the water
> Gives me back in a shining surface picture
> Me myself in the summer heaven, godlike,
> Looking out of a wreath of fern and cloud puffs.
>
> (Lines 1–6)

In a passage that recalls Rossetti's "Willowwood" sonnets, this lyric's plot records a near-visionary breakthrough, the disruption of the next moment breaking his self-parodying "godlike" perspective from which he admittedly can see nothing but himself:

> *Once*, when trying with chin against a well-curb,
> I discerned, as I thought, beyond the picture,
> Through the picture, a something white, uncertain,
> Something more of the depths—and then I lost it.
>
> (Lines 7–10)

A typically Frostian event, such a glimpse is short-lived—if it is really even discernible: the ambiguity of "as I thought" suggests that this appearance was not a certain one but one he *believed* or thought that he saw. But whether there or not, the discernment of thought (or of a different sort of reflection than the narcissistic sort) brought "something," if only the crucial awareness of something beyond himself. This poem returns to the vagueness of that blind "whiteness," of "it" and "something," and it ends with half-serious, half-mocking questions concerning the magnitude of his apprehension (it remains too vague, perhaps, to call it an "insight"): "What was that whiteness? / Truth? A pebble of quartz? For once, then, something" (lines 14–15). The final line surviving beyond the usual fourteen-line boundary of the form at once acknowledges the utter incompleteness of the poem's vision, but closes the poem with the satisfaction of having "for once, then, something" survive beyond the mere fact of "me myself."

It is difficult to talk about anything permanent or mythical in Frost; instead, one can talk about survival. This is an overt, literal concern in some of the poems mentioned already—how it is that the bird singing in its sleep survives, how it is that man can deem himself "safe" at least for tonight. But "survival" is, not surprisingly, also a figural concern, indeed a concern of figuration, of poetry. Perhaps the way to get at this is to consider again the problem of perspective in Frost. "The Master Speed" (1936) is yet another sonnet about perspective—the ability of "you" not only to "climb / Back up a stream of radiance to the sky, / And back through the history up the stream of time"—but also to "have the power of standing still— / Off any still or moving thing you say" (lines 8–9). "Standing still" allows one, if only momentarily, the ability to look *through* time. Thus while the stream of time is what makes intelligibility seem impossible in some poems, in others it also offers the poet the one thing that might create a kind of coherence: the possibility of memory and the recognition of the "traces" of the past.

The narrative of traces and poetic survival recalls recent accounts of signification—what Derrida would call *différance*; such accounts of "spacing" and "temporalizing" are certainly relevant. For as we have already seen in previous chapters, it is just that coincidence of the immediate present and the "experienced sense of lack, the constructed emptiness, the nothing, the gap"[19] that is the motivation of the sonnet (and arguably of any lyric poem). In Frost's sonnets, that "constructed emptiness" is most often troped as sound, which Frost, in this a true descendent of the nineteenth century, described as "pure form."

It is not surprising that the group of poems that concern themselves most deeply with poetic survival include some of his most famous sonnets—"Never Again Would Birds' Song Be The Same" (1946), "The Oven Bird" (1923), "Mowing" (1913)—nor that Frost's consistent figure for this is "voice." "Hyla Brook" (1923), for example, another fifteen-line sonnet, is a poem that Frost describes as being "about the brook on my old farm. It always dried up in summer. The Hyla is a small frog that shouts like jingling bells in the marshes in spring."[20] While Cameron regards the lyric voice as "a disruption" to the linear sequence of events, with the lyric poem thus becoming a stay against temporality,[21] voice can also, from another perspective, become a figure not of disruption but of survival—insofar as the voice can be remembered. There are various physical traces of the brook, particularly the dried-up jewelweed leaves that blanket the brook's bed with "a faded paper sheet / Of dead leaves stuck together by the heat—" (lines 10–11)—and that therefore become traces of texts. But these "texts" are legible "to none but who remember long" (line 12). While the poem "takes place" at a particular temporal standpoint (the Hyla frogs are said to have shouted "a month ago"), it opens out from lines 10 through 14 into memory and into the future that memory gives to what has already past: "This as it will be seen is other far / Than with brooks taken otherwhere in song. / We love the things we love for what they are" (lines 13–15)—but "what they are" includes both what they have been and will be. The brook's song and frogs' shouting are clearly figures of temporality itself—they inevitably begin in spring and disappear by June—but what interests the poet are their "ghosts," their echoic traces in memory.[22]

Of the other three famous sonnets mentioned above, "Mowing" probes most profoundly the relationship of voice to memory and to the problem of poetic survival. The poem appeared in his first volume, *A Boy's Will*, in 1913—and therefore it is not coincidental that this poem, with its voice that "whispered" and its description of this scene as "no dream of the gift of idle hours," always reminds me of Keats:

> There was never a sound beside the wood but one,
> And that was my long scythe whispering to the ground.
> What was it it whispered? I knew not well myself;
> Perhaps it was something about the heat of the sun,
> Something, perhaps, about the lack of sound—

And that was why it whispered and did not speak.
It was no dream of the gift of idle hours,
Or easy gold at the hand of fay or elf:
Anything more than the truth would have seemed too weak
To the earnest love that laid the swale in rows,
Not without feeble-pointed spikes of flowers
(Pale orchises), and scared a bright green snake.
The fact is the sweetest dream that labor knows.
My long scythe whispered and left the hay to make.

Even more remarkable than the survival of Keats here is the echo of
Marvell's mutability poem, "Damon the Mower." The very details of "Mowing" are ghosts of the previous lyric: the heat; the hay; the speaker's labor
and "earnest love"; the snake; the thistles. The language of Frost's poem is,
characteristically, evasive, with its repeated "perhaps" and "something" and
"it." For what the sound of the scythe whispered was nothing less than the
echo of Marvell's words: "Perhaps it was something about the heat of the
sun" surely alludes to Marvell's "Oh what unusual heats are here." Frost
even borrows Marvell's "sigh / scythe" pun; the confusion of sound and
instrument in the earlier poem is clearly at work here as well. As in Keats's
early sonnets, where the voices of the literary past sound too loudly in the
poet's inner ear, memory here speaks with a ghost's voice, heard now by
this poet with an uncanniness that prompts the darkly ambiguous "I knew
not well myself." Indeed, as for Keats, the problem in this early poem is
poetic identity and the power of memory's presence, and the poem's eva-
siveness is crucial if this mower is to resist the fate of his predecessor.

The apprehension of poetic sound can become as "real" as any other
sense perception, a sort of sixth sense for him who remembers long, to
recall "Hyla Brook." The sound of the scythe-through-hay whispering, with
its presencing of memory-echoes of Keats and Marvell, is the poet's best
evidence of poetic survival. I take "the fact," the antecedent of which is
(typically) obscure, to be the presence not only of sound but also of the
scythed rows laid, like lines of poetry surely, with labor and "earnest love."
With (again typical) irony, though, the laboring poet "knows" that while
the act of making is "the sweetest dream," the "fact" of physical nature has
therefore become something other by itself, something of the poet's own
mind.

This mower is thus not as simpleminded as Marvell's, who, as Cameron
rightly says, makes the mistake of "failing to distinguish between phenomenal and psychological worlds";[23] this speaker is well aware that memory,
the "whispering," has indeed confused the two worlds. His recognition of
the uncanniness ("I knew not well myself") therefore prompts him to ask

questions, sets his mind to work. This insistence on the process of know-ing,[24] on probing the difference between the metaphorical laboring in sound that he makes and the ghost scythe-sound that he momentarily identifies with, is an insistence on the poet's own identity that is ultimately the claim on the world that every Frost sonnet makes. That process of knowing is the process of metaphor itself, as Frost passionately argues in "Education by Poetry." Frost's mower is "smarter" than either Marvell's or Keats's, be-cause of what he "knows" about metaphor and survival—but perhaps this mower also had the advantage of learning from those earlier poets.

This stubbornly hopeful assertion of identity—of will—motivates nearly every Frost sonnet we have looked at. "Will" becomes Frost's particular "authority," to return to a term used to describe Wordsworth's own discov-ery of his originality. Frost's poetics diverge from Wordsworth's, inasmuch as Frost's poetry refuses the visionary relation of the moment to a teleo-logical history, as his predecessor claimed. Despite that fundamental dif-ference, these two poets are finally joined by several (interrelated) beliefs: the belief in the subjective self; in the imagination's ability to locate signifi-cance in the mundane, however temporarily; and in the ability of poetry to *encompass* the contradiction between "social time" and "private time" that Sharon Cameron calls the "generating impulse" of all lyric.[25] Far from los-ing faith in art, Frost's confrontation with the world leads back to what is strongest in Wordsworth's sonnets: the *authority* of imagination—that is, of metaphoric thinking. "Life should be broken up and interrupted," Frost asserts, "and then be brought together by likeness, free likeness."[26]

Michael Cooke has pointed out that in this poetry "No act, no person is innocent of thought (this is one source of Frost's incessant symbolizing), and no thought is innocent of incompleteness. (This is the other source of Frost's incessant symbolizing.)"[27] Many of the authors covered in this study employ a symbolic function for the sonnet form itself that is related synec-dochically to the narrative of poetic insight and representation, and even to the poet's particular engagement with the problem of literary history. In-completeness or resistance to closure was a trope that inhered in many of these sonnets—a strategy of resistance to the very demand for closure and containment that the sonnet conventionally demands. What is unique about Frost's sonnets is that, with rare exceptions (such as "Lost In Heaven"), formal closure is not resisted but actually *sought* after because of the con-textual threat of disorder that pressures the poem's boundaries, or even threat-ens the dissolution of those boundaries.

This seeking after closure relates to Richard Poirier's apprehension that "Much of what can be said of 'home' in Frost can also be said of literary forms, at least in the way he thought of them. . . . 'Home,' like any literary form, involves relationships that work themselves out internally and under the aegis of decorums which can contain and therefore even encourage excesses of expression."[28] Indeed, this is the best explanation for the delicate adjustments Frost made to the sonnet form in his fifteen-, sixteen-, and twenty-one-line sonnets, none of which can be easily classified as caudate. As Poirier's remark above intimates, it is the confinement of form itself that comes to *mean* freedom: "The almost incredible freedom of the soul enslaved to the hard facts of experience,"[29] as Frost wrote to Edward Garnett in 1915, is gained through the exercise of form. This easily recalls a familiar dialectic for sonnet writers, one that Wordsworth addresses in his "Nuns Fret Not"—the dialectic of freedom and imprisonment in form. For Wordsworth, form was a choice. So it is for Frost,[30] but the "freedom" the former poet associates with the form is a diminished concept.

The figure of sonnet-as-synecdoche reaches its premiere spokesperson in Frost, whose own definition of poetic form parallels, from a modern perspective, those of the nineteenth-century sonnet defenders surveyed earlier. Not insignificant here, of course, is Frost's labeling of himself as a "synecdochist; for I prefer the synecdoche in poetry—that figure in speech in which we use a part for the whole."[31] Each "little poem" tries to achieve what Frost hoped for all poems: "Each poem clarifies something. But then you've got to do it again. You can't get clarified to stay so: let you not think that. In a way, it's like nothing more than blowing smoke rings. Making little poems encourages a man to see that there is a shapeliness in the world. A poem is an arrest of disorder."[32] There is in this very definition a recognition that temporality—history—inherently threatens form itself. So much the better, given his dark suspicion of the "confusion," that form is still possible to Frost: "To me any little form I assert upon it is velvet, as the saying is, and to be considered for how much more it is than nothing. If I were a Platonist I should have to consider it, I suppose, for how much less it is than everything."[33] Herein Frost locates how far from the "grace" of a faith in art poetry has fallen. While Frost at least is jealous of the dead leaves of poetry, he is never less than brutally honest about the ephemerality of *any* stance he would take regarding poetry or nature or experience, much less the relation of the one to the others. Although art is that which defeats meaninglessness by creating an image of the mind's working upon the world, Frost acknowledges ironically that the synecdochic power of form is only a shadow of the *idea* of order.

Frost's remark above is ultimately subversive of the authority upon which the sonnet has made its claim since Wordsworth. If the sonnet is troped as a "star" by Wordsworth and his followers, Frost's trope is *"something like"* that Wordsworthian star—more than nothing, but less than everything.[34] But that very subversiveness is what has allowed the form to continue. While Wordsworth's recovery of a visionary function for the form may be countenanced, if at all, with skepticism by sonnet writers of our own century, from Auden through J. D. McClatchy, the dialectics of the sonnet are well able to accommodate such dilemmas regarding coherence and form. Post-Wordsworth sonnet writers have shifted the terms of Wordsworth's visionary poetics to lesser and greater degrees, but the shift, and the strain against form, was possible when they discovered the revisionary poetics implicit there. That accommodation, along with poets' persistent hope for, if not claim for, the permanent significance and value of art generally, motivates the continued tradition of this form. It may be paradoxical to speak of the "flexibility" of the sonnet form—and yet it is the trope of the revisionary, built into the very structure of the form, that creates that flexibility, whether within the structure of a single sonnet or through the shifting narrative perspectives of the sonnet sequence. The dialectic of form and its subversion has always been built into sonnet dynamics, and it is poets' awareness of that fact and of its implications that allows them to reanimate this form time and time again.

Bibliographical Listing of
Nineteenth-Century Sonnet "Defenses"

The full list of essays I have been able to locate runs below in chrono-logical order:

Lofft, Capel. Preface to *Laura; or, An Anthology of Sonnets, (On the Petrarchan Model,) and Elegiac Quatorzains.* London: B. and R. Crosby & Co., 1814.

Doubleday, Thomas. *Sixty-five Sonnets; with Prefatory Remarks on the Accordance of the Sonnet with the Powers of the English Language: also, a Few Miscellaneous Poems.* London: Baldwin, Cradock, and Joy, 1818.

"Sonnettomania." *The New Monthly Magazine and Literary Journal* 2 (1821): 644–48.

Dyce, Alexander. Introduction to *Specimens of English Sonnets.* London: W. Pickering, 1833.

Housman, Robert Fletcher, ed. Preface to *A Collection of English Sonnets.* London: Simpkin, Marshall & Co., 1835.

White, Joseph Blanco. "The Sonnet." *The Christian Teacher,* n.s., 1 (1839).

Woodford, A. Montegu. Introduction to *The Book of Sonnets.* London: Saunders and Otley, 1841.

"On the Sonnet," *Christian Remembrancer,* n.s., 2 (1841): 321–29.

Reed, Henry. "Miscellaneous Essays on English Poetry: Essay I. English Sonnets." In *Lectures on the British Poets.* London: John F. Shaw, 1863.

Trench, Richard Chenevix, D.D. (Archbishop of Dublin). "The History of the English Sonnet." In *The Sonnets of William Wordsworth.* London: Suttaby & Co., 1884. This preface, though published in 1884, was developed from a lecture series delivered in Dublin in 1866. Many of these sonnet commentators seemed to be familiar with the content of these lectures long before the preface publication.

Hunt, Leigh, and S. Adams Lee, eds. "Introductory Letter" and "Essay on the Sonnet." In *The Book of the Sonnet.* Boston: Roberts Brothers, 1867.

Simpson, Richard. *The Philosophy of Shakespeare's Sonnets.* London, 1868.

[Davies, William]. "Article VIII." *London Quarterly Review* 134 (January–April 1873): 99–108. Review article on Leigh Hunt and S. Adams Lee's *Book of the Sonnet*, and on an Italian book of lyric poetry, *Scelta di Poesie Liriche dal primo secolo della Lingua fino al 1700* (Firenze, 1839).

Hewlett, Henry G. Review of Tennyson-Turner's sonnets. *Contemporary Review* 31 (1873): 637.

Tomlinson, Charles. *The Sonnet: Its Origin, Structure, and Place in Poetry.* London: John Murray, 1874.

Symonds, J. A. "The Debt of English to Italian Literature." *Fortnightly Review,* March 1875, 371–81.

Dennis, John. "The English Sonnet," In *Studies in English Literature.* London: Edward Stanford, 1876.

[Russell, C. W.] "Critical History of the Sonnet" (in two parts). *The Dublin Review,* n.s., 27 (1876): 400–430; and n.s., 28 (1877): 141–80.

Spedding, James. "Charles Tennyson Turner." *The Nineteenth Century* 6 (1879): 461–80.

Main, David M. *A Treasury of English Sonnets.* Edinburgh and London: William Blackwood and Sons, 1880. The notes to this anthology are invaluable; it is here that I found references for the first time to many of the essays cited in this appendix.

Ashcroft-Noble, James. *The Contemporary Review* 38 (1880): 471. Review of Main's anthology (cited above).

Stoddard, Richard Henry. "The Sonnet in English Poetry." *Scribner's Monthly* 22 (1881): 905–21.

Waddington, Samuel. "The Sonnet: Its History and Composition." In *English Sonnets by Living Writers.* London: George Bell and Sons, 1881.

Caine, Thomas Hall. Preface to *Sonnets of Three Centuries: A Selection, Including Many Examples Hitherto Unpublished. With a preface of xxiv pages, dated from Vale of St. John, Cumberland, 1881.* London: Elliot Stock, 1882.

Sharp, William. "The Sonnet: Its Characteristics and History." In *Sonnets of this Century.* London: Walter Scott Publishing Co., 1886. Also see chapter 7 in Sharp's book, *Dante Gabriel Rossetti* (London: Macmillan, 1882).

Watts-Dunton, Theodore. "The Sonnet." In *Encyclopaedia Britannica,* vol. 22. 9th ed. New York: S. L. Hall, 1878–88.

From the Continent also came the following:

Veyrieres, Louis de. *La Monographie des Sonnets.* London, 1869.

Asselineau, M. Charles. *Le Livre des Sonnets.* Paris, 1875.

Lentzner, Dr. Karl. *Über das Sonett und Seine Gestaltung in der englischen Dichtung bis Milton.* N.p., 1886.

Notes

Introduction

"On Open Form," quoted in *The New Naked Poetry: Recent American Poetry in Open Forms*, ed. Stephen Berg and Robert Mezey (Indianapolis: Bobbs-Merrill, 1976), 277.

1. "Preface to the First Edition," rpt. in *Elegiac Sonnets*, 4th ed. (London: Dodsley, Gardner, and Bew, 1786).

2. Ibid.

3. Preface to *Sonnets, and Other Poems,* 7th ed. (Bath: Crutwell, 1800), vi–vii.

4. Schlütter, *Sonett* (Stuttgart: J. B. Metzlersche Verlagsbuchhandlung, 1979), 10.

5. Quoted by M. H. Abrams, *Natural Supernaturalism: Tradition and Revolution in Romantic Literature* (New York: Norton, 1973), 272.

6. "Changes in the Study of the Lyric," in *Lyric Poetry: Beyond New Criticism*, ed. Chaviva Hošek and Patricia Parker (Ithaca: Cornell University Press, 1985), 51.

7. For an account of the overall context of the entry of women poets into the literary market, see chapter 7 of Marlon Ross's *The Contours of Masculine Desire: Romanticism and the Rise of Women's Poetry* (New York: Oxford University Press, 1989), 232–66.

8. Stuart Curran, *Poetic Form and British Romanticism* (New York: Oxford University Press, 1986), 45.

9. See Brisman, *Romantic Origins* (Ithaca: Cornell University Press, 1978) and Said, *Beginnings* (New York: Basic Books, 1975). In "The Romantic Metaphysics of Time," Richard Jackson presents an outline, in a deconstructive mode, of the problematics of temporality and poetic origins that I have found relevant. Of particular interest is his analysis of the romantic (Hegelian) dialectic of self-consciousness that occurs within moments—a dialectic that at once makes possible the "'repose' of meditative detachment" and makes impossible an authentic capturing of pure intuition or experience. See *Studies in Romanticism* 19 (Spring 1980): 19–30.

10. Poulet, *Studies in Human Time,* trans. Elliott Coleman (Baltimore: Johns Hopkins University Press, 1956), 26, 33. On the connection between the eternal moment and death, see Sharon Cameron, *Lyric Time: Dickinson and the Limits of Genre* (Baltimore: Johns Hopkins University Press, 1979), 212.

11. See Cameron on the relation between "lyric strain," which she locates in temporal conflict, and "a fretting against or pushing back or outright violation of the normal limits of

the lyric, whether it takes the form of temporal improbability, structural self-consciousness, or psychic extremity" (*Lyric Time*, 242).

12. There is a fair amount written about the sonnet form generally, including: Alfred Behrmann, "Variationen einer Form: Das Sonett," *Deutsche Vierteljahrs Schrift für Literaturwissenschaft und Geistesgeschichte* 13 (1985): 1–28; John Fuller, *The Sonnet* (London: Methuen, 1972); Paul Fussell, *Poetic Meter and Poetic Form*, rev. ed. (1965; New York: Random House, 1979); Walter Mönch's *Das Sonnet: Gestalt und Geschichte* (Heidelberg: F. H. Kerle Verlag, 1955); Walter F. Schirmer, "Das Sonett in der englischen Literatur," *Anglia* 37 (1925): 1–31; Hans-Jürgen Schlütter, *Sonett* (cited above). The most recent publication is Sandra Bermann's *Sonnet Over Time: A Study in the Sonnets of Petrarch, Shakespeare, and Baudelaire* (Chapel Hill: University of North Carolina Press, 1988).

13. Cameron, *Lyric Time*, 204.

14. Ibid., 206.

15. Ibid., 204.

16. "Spatial Form in Literature," *Critical Inquiry* 6 (1980): 551, 553.

17. Richard Jackson, "Romantic Metaphysics," 22.

Chapter 1. Wordsworth's "Inquest" and the Visionary Sonnet

1. At line 11, this poem winds up so: "Courage! another 'll finish the first triplet; / Thanks to thee, Muse, my work begins to shorten: / There's thirteen lines got through, driblet by driblet; / 'Tis done. Count how you will, I warrant there's fourteen." Quoted from Matthew Russell's *Sonnets on the Sonnet: An Anthology* (London: Longman, Green, 1898), 6.

2. *The Poetical Works of Anna Seward; with extracts from her literary correspondence,* ed. Walter Scott, 3 vols. (Edinburgh: James Ballantyne and Co., 1810).

3. *Poetical Works*, 3:185. A slightly different version of this was quoted in Coleridge's introduction to "A Sheet of Sonnets."

4. Unless otherwise noted, the text of Wordsworth's poetry and prose is from *William Wordsworth: The Poems*, ed. John O. Hayden, 2 vols. (New Haven: Yale University Press, 1981).

5. Wordsworth's interest in the consolatory function of sonnet is anticipated in a sonnet by Anna Seward, "When life's realities the soul perceives. . . ." The sestet of this poem runs so:

> No more young Hope tints with her light and bloom
> The darkening scene.—Then to ourselves we say,
> Come, bright Imagination, come! relume
> Thy orient lamp; with recompensing ray
> Shine on the mind, and pierce its gathering gloom
> With all the fires of intellectual day!
>
> (*Poetical Works*, 122)

6. See J. Hillis Miller's *Linguistic Moment* (Princeton: Princeton University Press, 1985) on the kinship of the figure of radiance in "Scorn not . . ." to the very notion of form in aesthetics (61). Also see: Thomas McFarland's discussion of organic form in *Romanticism and the Forms of Ruin: Wordsworth, Coleridge, and Modalities of Fragmentation* (Princeton: Princeton University Press, 1981), 25; and Marshall Brown's rare discussion of

this Wordsworth sonnet and its relation to the poet's effort to define the "picture of the mind's operations," in *Preromanticism* (Stanford, Calif.: Stanford University Press, 1991), 340.

7. All Milton quotations are from *The Complete Poetry of John Milton*, ed. John T. Shawcross (Garden City, N.Y.: Anchor Books, 1971).

8. With Miller, Curran asserts that "the sonnets [of Wordsworth] record the process of their own creation, a coming to vision by discovering the mental preconceptions necessary to utter the Miltonic voice, to write a Miltonic sonnet" (48). Like Curran I will show that the sonnets are, as he says, "psychological in their orientation," specifically, "the psychology of perception" (216). Also see Carl Woodring's *Wordsworth* (Cambridge: Harvard University Press, 1968), 165.

9. Miller, *Linguistic Moment*, 61.

10. Mönch cites a French translation of this poem by Sainte-Beuve ("Ne ris point du sonnet, ô critique moqueur") that tailors the last tercet to French literary history: "Moi, je veux rajeunir le doux sonnet de France; / Du Bellay, le premier, l'apporta de Florence, / et l'on sait plus d'un de notre vieux Ronsard" (290). Mönch notes that Pushkin, too, composed his own variation of the Wordsworthian metasonnet. Also see the early article by L. E. Kastner, "Concerning the Sonnet on the Sonnet," *Modern Language Review* 11 (1916): 205–11. While this article provides several interesting examples of this form, it offers no useful critical perspective upon it.

11. Wordsworth, "Essay, Supplementary to the Preface," in *Poems*, 2:932.

12. The recent exposure and exposition of the sonnets as themselves essentially dramatic was not a critical issue at that time, and not one that Wordsworth is recorded as wondering over.

13. Geoffrey Hartman, *Wordsworth's Poetry, 1787–1814* (Cambridge: Harvard University Press, 1987), 292.

14. Ross, *Contours of Masculine Desire*, 22–23. Also see Charles Altieri on the "scenic self," in which "[the self's] investments derive from scenes that it has been attached to and the traces which those leave in its memory" ("Wordsworth's Poetics of Eloquence: A Challenge to Contemporary Theory," in *Romantic Revolutions: Criticism and Theory*, ed. Kenneth R. Johnston et al. [Bloomington: Indiana University Press, 1990], 396).

15. Markham L. Peacock, Jr., ed., *The Critical Opinions of William Wordsworth* (Baltimore: Johns Hopkins University Press, 1950), 313.

16. *The Prose Works of William Wordsworth*, ed. Alexander B. Grosart (London: Edward Moxon, Son, & Co., 1876; rpt. New York: AMS Press, 1967), 3:52–53.

17. The trope of taking fire is all the more interesting for Milton's own figuration of poetry itself, in *Ad Patrem*, line 20, as "song" that "preserves a holy spark of Promethean fire" ("Sancta Prometheae retinens vestigia flammae"). Both Milton's and Wordsworth's taking of fire, then, are more than a benign passing-on of the torch; both poets offer a trope of influence that suggests usurpation from Titanic forefathers. Also see Leslie Brisman's *Milton's Poetry of Choice and Its Romantic Heirs* (Ithaca: Cornell University Press, 1973), where he notes that "the interaction with Milton is inseminating, not stultifying, regardless of the point in the poetic career at which it takes place" (328).

18. Letter to Walter Savage Landor, 1822; quoted in Peacock, *Critical Opinions*, 297. For an early discussion of this "conversion moment," see Thomas Hutchinson's "Appendix: Note on the Wordsworthian Sonnet," which appeared in Hutchinson's edition of Wordsworth's *Poems in Two Volumes* (London: David Nutt, 1897), 1:208–26.

19. Letter #1046 (undated; ? Spring 1833), in *The Letters of William and Dorothy*

Wordsworth: The Later Years, edited by Ernest De Selincourt (Oxford: Clarendon Press, 1939), 2:652–53.

20. Sir Walter Alexander Raleigh, "The Style of Milton" (1900), in *Milton Criticism: Selections from Four Centuries*, ed. James E. Thorpe (New York: Rinehart & Co., 1950), 123.

21. Prince, *The Italian Element in Milton's Verse* (Oxford: Clarendon Press, 1954), 103. Also see Judith Scherer Herz, "Epigrams and Sonnets: Milton in the Manner of Jonson" (*Milton Studies* 20 [1984]), who suggests that for Milton "all the earlier works proleptically contained that vast epic which was to be their originator and culmination. . . . In our attempt to honor the intention of the conceit—the colossus carved on the cherry stone—we have too often pursued the colossal, forgetful of the constraints of what was by its nature a miniaturizing form, based on the principles of brevity and diminution. For there is another feature of the Miltonic sonnet which may account for that double sense of like and unlike that I noted at the start [with respect to the English sonnet tradition], that is, its markedly epigrammatic nature" (29). In an announcement by the *Morning Post* of the publication of Wordsworth's 1802 sonnets there, publisher Daniel Stuart describes the poems as "Each form[ing] a little Political Essay, on some recent proceeding" (quoted by Alan Liu in *Wordsworth: The Sense of History* [Stanford, Calif.: Stanford University Press, 1989], 431).

22. Quoted in the notes of Grosart's edition of *Prose Works*, 245. Note that the idea of the sonnet as a "narrow room" recurs in Wordsworth's sonnet on the sonnet, "Nuns fret not." John Hollander comments on this connection in *Melodious Guile*, 87.

23. For a recent feminist reading of this poem and its metaphors of the work space, see Deborah Fried's article on the sonnets of Edna St. Vincent Millay: "Andromeda Unbound: Gender and Genre in Millay's Sonnets" (*Twentieth-Century Literature* 32 [1986]: 1–22.

24. Hollander is quoted from *Vision and Resonance,* 2d ed. (New Haven: Yale University Press, 1975), 200. See also R. D. Havens, *The Influence of Milton on English Poetry* (New York: Russell & Russell, 1961), who declares that "It is folly to pretend that Wordsworth's sonnets are an evolution from those of his immediate predecessors; he turned to other sources for his inspiration, his models, and his conception of the form. . . . We know that he read and thought well of most of the sonneteers we have been considering [Bowles, Russell, Edwards, Seward, Smith, Brydges, etc.] but it is doubtful if his work was appreciably affected by any of them. It was to Milton and Milton only that he was indebted" (528–29). Also see Joseph Anthony Wittreich Jr.'s "Introduction: Romantic Criticism of Milton," in *The Romantics on Milton: Formal Essays and Critical Asides* (Cleveland: Case Western Reserve University Press, 1970), 3–24.

25. I am grateful to Peter Manning for pointing out the significance of this figure to my argument here.

26. Peacock, *Critical Opinions*, 297.

27. Curtis, *Wordsworth's Experiments with Tradition: The Lyric Poems of 1802* (Ithaca: Cornell University Press, 1971), 3–26; Miller, *The Linguistic Moment*, 65; also see McFarland, *Forms of Ruin*, 20–21. The pages from Curtis discuss Coleridge's concern about the composition of "small poems," which included not only sonnets but also the lyrical ballads themselves—indeed, anything that competed with Wordsworth's work on *The Recluse*. The short poems "seem inevitably, from Coleridge's point of view, to focus on the literal, to encourage, as he later wrote [in *Biographia Literaria*] 'a laborious minuteness and fidelity in the representation of objects, and their positions' which led Wordsworth to *a biographical attention* to probability, and an *anxiety* of exploration and retrospect'" (*Wordsworth's Experiments,* 7).

28. Leigh Hunt even suggested that *Paradise Lost* and Wordsworth's sonnet corpus were equivalent projects: "'Paradise Lost,' if the two poets [Milton and Wordsworth] are to be compared, is the set-off against Wordsworth's achievement in sonnet-writing" (Wittreich, *The Romantics on Milton*, 422). In an unpublished dissertation entitled "The Generic Wordsworth" (University of Virginia, 1987), John Louis Rowlett suggests the possibility that the relation of the sonnet form and *The Prelude* "might be dialectical in nature, that the sonnet might have resulted in a lyric form of self-understanding that enabled Wordsworth to complete his autobiographical narrative" (5). Rowlett hints at an even more intimate connection between Wordsworth's sonnet writing and his autobiographical epic, suggesting that the fourteen-line sonnet is a homologue to the fourteen-book *Prelude* (275). This dissertation dovetails many of the concerns of this chapter—and Rowlett concurs with what I regard as my central argument about Wordsworth's sonnets: that underlying *both* Wordsworth's notion of his own function as sonnet *writer* and his notion of the form's function is the rhetorical trope of synecdoche.

29. See chapter 5 of Rowlett's dissertation, "The Sonnet as Narrative," in which he analyzes the "narrative possibilities [that] reside implicitly in any sonnet, the adequacy of their realization dependent upon the generic awareness of the narrator" ("The Generic Wordsworth," 222). Also relevant here is Neil Fraistat's description of Petrarch's and Dante's "new kind of poetic aggregate"; see *The Poem and the Book: Interpreting Collections of Romantic Poetry* (Chapel Hill: University of North Carolina Press, 1985), 8–9.

30. Letter #301 (21 May 1807), in *The Letters of William and Dorothy Wordsworth: The Middle Years*, edited by Ernest De Selincourt (Oxford: Clarendon Press, 1937), 1:125–26.

31. Ibid., 1:127.

32. Ibid., 1:126.

33. Ibid., 1:127–28.

34. Ibid., 1:128.

35. Ibid., 1:128–29. Also see chapters 4 and 5 of Rowlett, "The Generic Wordsworth" for another reading of the Beaumont letter (esp. pp. 222–30).

36. Relevant here is chap. 4, "Inventing Literature," in Clifford Siskin, *The Historicity of Romantic Discourse* (New York and Oxford: Oxford University Press, 1988), 67–93.

37. Ross, *Contours of Masculine Desire*, 23.

38. "Wordsworth Revisited," in *The Unremarkable Wordsworth* (Minneapolis: University of Minnesota Press, 1987), 9.

39. Quoted in Wittreich, *The Romantics on Milton*, 442.

40. Hartman, *Unremarkable Wordsworth*, 9.

41. The sonnet is closely related to the contemporaneous *Vale of Esthwaite*—if only by the fact that the sonnet's final line, "Heaves the full heart nor knows for whom, or why," is a revision—not quite a quotation—of lines 129–30 of that poem: "The heart, when passed the Vision by, / Dissolves, nor knows for whom [n]or why." Although the exact date is unknown, I would be tempted to place the composition of the sonnet after that of *The Vale*. The sonnet is already a more mature recording of emotion than the longer poem, which suffers more from the verbal trappings of earlier, Miltonic-Gothic phrasing than this poem does. The lines leading up to the ones repeated in the sonnet are a good example:

> Now holy Melancholy throws
> Soft o'er the soul a still repose,
> Save where we start as from a sleep

> Recoiling from a gloom too deep.
> Now too, while o'er the heart we feel
> A tender twilight softly steal,
> Sweet Pity gives her forms arrayed
> In tenderer tints and softer shade;
> The heart, when passed the Vision by,
> Dissolves, nor knows for whom [n]or why.
>
> (Lines 121–30)

Also note its relation, particularly in diction, to the contemporaneous "Remembrance of Collins Composed upon the Thames near Richmond," itself a poem that recalls Collins's "Ode on the Death of Thomson." All include the "dripping oar" motif.

42. Cf. Wordsworth's 1787 poem, "What is it that tells my soul the Sun is setting?": "See where a / sun of other worlds is sailing [s]lowly on the / lake — no! 'tis the taper that twinkling in the / cottage casts a long wan shadow over the [lake?]" (lines 5–8).

43. Hartman, *Wordsworth's Poetry*, 86.

44. Paul Fry has suggested to me that the absence of the *volta* in this sonnet may also be related to this poem's indebtedness to Miltonic and eighteenth-century Latinate landscape poetry. In all of these, he argued, the aim is for "a poetry of sheer evocative presence" that would resist anything like a "turn."

45. *The Rhetoric of Romanticism* (New York: Columbia University Press, 1984), 132. Also see Hermann Fischer, "William Wordsworth: 'Composed by the Side of Grasmere Lake," in *Versdichtung der englischen Romantik: Interpretationen*, ed. Teut Andreas Riese and Dieter Riesner (Berlin: Erich Schmidt Verlag, 1968), 187–205. Of tangential interest is Stephen J. Spector's "Wordsworth's Mirror Imagery and the Picturesque Tradition," in which he discusses the Wordsworthian topos of mirroring surfaces of lakes as a figure for "the union of the mind and the world that occurs during such privileged moments" (*ELH* 44 [1977]: 95).

46. Gerard Manley Hopkins seems to have learned this from Wordsworth, as his sonnets draw out fully the tropological implications of this octave/sestet relation. In a later chapter I will examine Hopkins's handling of that relation. Also in the 1880s, minor Victorian poet and devoted Wordsworth enthusiast Hardwicke D. Rawnsley would pick up Wordsworth's reflection trope in a series entitled *Sonnets of the English Lakes*. The best of them is called "The Lake Mirror: In Autumn," which handles again the play of height and depth, present and past in the form:

> We sailed from cape to cape, whose headlands grey
>   Had blossomed branchy gold, and half in fear,
>   Through liquid mirrors of the Autumn mere,
> We ventured in among the leafy sway
> Of watery woodland, and the russet spray
>   Of fern and rosy briar, reflected clear,
>   Still dancing by the prow as we drew near,
> To grow to stillness as we passed away.
> That day the glory of two worlds was ours,
>   A depth and height of faint autumnal sky,
> A double pageant of the painted wood;
> Still, as we stole upon a summer flood,
>   Marbled by snow the mountain-tops close by
> Spoke from warm depths of Winter's nearing hours.

(Quoted from *Sonnets of this Century*, ed. William Sharp [London: Walter Scott Publishing Co., 1886], 314).

47. De Man, "Symbolic Landscape in Wordsworth and Yeats," in Reuben A. Brower and Richard Poirier, eds., *In Defense of Reading* (1962; New York: Columbia University Press, 1984), 28.

48. Wordsworth's friend and fellow poet Aubrey De Vere left interesting remarks on the relationship of politics to Wordsworth's view of the imagination: "He regarded his own intellect as one which united some of the faculties which belong to the statesman with those which belong to the poet, and public affairs interested him not less deeply than poetry. It was as patriot, not poet, that he ventured to claim fellowship with Dante." Quoted by Grosart, *Prose Works*, 3:490.

49. See Curran's discussion of how Wordsworth's sonnets "virtually explode from access to power" (*Poetic Form*, 45).

50. Kelley, *Wordsworth's Revisionary Aesthetics* (Cambridge: Cambridge University Press, 1988). See esp. her introduction and chapter 7 ("Family of Floods"). Also see Robert Rehder's *Wordsworth and the Beginnings of Modern Poetry* (London: Croom Helm, 1981), chap. 6 ("Ideas of Order").

51. Alan Liu regards his preference for this form as the mark of a "habitually self-reversing mind," the poet's political sonnets exploring again and again "a process of crisis and recovery, inner fall and self-correction." Furthermore, Liu usefully remarks that these sonnets, capturing the "antithetical moment," have the quality of the monumental: "the sonnet form tends to freeze the antithetical moment into glacial composure—into an instance of irresistible force meeting immovable object" (*Sense of History*, 434–35).

52. Introduction to the poem in *The Yale Edition of the Shorter Poems of Edmund Spenser*, ed. William A. Oram et al. (New Haven: Yale University Press, 1989), 524. The poem is quoted from this text also.

53. Woodring, *Wordsworth*, 158. Chapter 7 of this book is a general discussion of Wordsworth's sonnets (156-78).

54. Edward Proffitt hears in the conclusion of this sonnet a darker tone than I do: "Everything speaks of loss and the recognition of loss, the voice of the poem being that of an angry dirge" ("'This Pleasant Lea': Waning Vision in 'The World is Too Much with Us,'" *The Wordsworth Circle* 11 [1980]: 76–77).

55. See: Miller, *Linguistic Moment*, 68–77; Hartman, *Unremarkable Wordsworth*, 207-19; and Liu, *Sense of History*, 459–69, 476–85. Other recent readings include: Woodring, *Wordsworth*, 166–68; Charles G. Davis, "The Structure of Wordsworth's Sonnet 'Composed Upon Westminster Bridge,'" *English* 19 (1970): 18–21; Kurt Schluter, "Wieder einmal 'Upon Westminster Bridge,'" *Literatur in Wissenschaft und Unterricht* 12 (1979): 202–5; and Harvey Peter Sucksmith, "Ultimate Affirmation: A Critical Analysis of Wordsworth's Sonnet, 'Composed upon Westminster Bridge', and the Image of the City in *The Prelude*," *The Yearbook of English Studies* 6 (1976): 113–19. Most of these are indebted to Cleanth Brooks's reading in "The Language of Paradox," chap. 1 of *The Well-Wrought Urn* (New York: Harcourt, Brace, 1947). For a reading of this very *variety* of readings, see ch. 4 ("Dialogics of the lyric: a symposium on 'Westminster Bridge' and "Beauteous Evening,'") in Don H. Bialostosky's *Wordsworth, Dialogics, and the Practice of Criticism* (Cambridge: Cambridge University Press, 1992), 79–133.

56. *Letters*, 6:292. See Liu on the range of "metaphorics" in this poem, "from commonplace metaphors to large-scale rhetoric commonplaces of the kind studied by Curtius" (*Sense of History*, 462).

57. Liu, *Sense of History*, 461.

58. Hartman, *Unremarkable Wordsworth*, 216. Liu refers to the "obliteration of the known world" in Wordsworth's asyndeton, and describes the "I" as one who "see[s] London as something other than it is, . . . referring at last only to a figure of figures, the self, as invisible *within* the frame of reference as God, the blinding sun, or . . . Westminster Bridge" (*Sense of History*, 463–64).

59. Liu, *Sense of History*, 464.

60. Lee M. Johnson has also marked the pictorialism of this poem; see his discussion on pp. 107-8 of *Wordsworth and the Sonnet* (Copenhagen: Rosenkilde and Bagger, 1973). He finds this static pictorialism a reflection of the endurance of the "calm" or tranquility that Wordsworth always seeks; I would disagree by asserting that it is the very transience of this calmness that motivates this kind of emblematic treatment.

61. Miller, *Linguistic Moment*, 70-76.

62. Text is quoted from *Wordsworth: Poetical Works*, new ed., ed. Ernest De Selincourt (New York and London: Oxford University Press, 1978).

63. Quoted by Hayden in *Poems*, 1:1040.

64. Woodring notes that for Wordsworth "the sonnet is not so much song as picture. It is a sudden vista through the foreground into the meditative distance. Partaking of the elegiac or reflective, the sonnet is a little personal essay in verse" (*Wordsworth*, 162). More recently, Rowlett's study relates the pictorial aspect of Wordsworth's sonnets to the genre's relation to descriptive poetry ("Generic Wordsworth," 200).

65. This point relates to my reading of the Westminster Bridge sonnet, which I noted had the feel of a sonnet on a painting.

66. A rare reading of one of Wordsworth's tour series comes from Jeffrey C. Robinson, "The Structure of Wordsworth's *Memorials of a Tour in Scotland, 1803*," *Papers on Language & Literature* 13 (1977): 54–70. These series have been invested with new importance by Liu's extraordinary chapter, "The Idea of the Memorial Tour: 'Composed Upon Westminster Bridge,'" in *Sense of History*, 455–99.

67. Trench, "The History of the English Sonnet," in *The Sonnets of William Wordsworth Collected in One Volume* (London: Suttaby and Co., 1884), xxiv. This essay is part of large group of essays written in the mid- to late-nineteenth century. See the fourth chapter of this book for a survey of these essays.

68. Chandler, *Wordsworth's Second Nature: A Study of the Poetry and Politics* (Chicago: University of Chicago Press, 1984), 170.

69. Quoted in the notes of Hutchinson, *Wordsworth: Poetical Works*, 709.

70. Johnson points out that "After-Thought," important as it is to the sequence, becomes "all the greater because it is the only sonnet of *The River Duddon* which is expressly written as an individual performance" (125). For his discussion of *Duddon*, see chapter 5 of his study *Wordsworth and the Sonnet*, 120–44. Also see: Stewart C. Wilcox, "Wordsworth's River Duddon Sonnets," *PMLA* 69 (1954): 131–41; and, especially, Melinda M. Ponder, "Echoing Poetry with History: Wordsworth's Duddon Sonnets, and Their Notes," *Genre* 21, no. 2 (Summer 1988): 157–78.

71. For a general discussion of this in romanticism, see Abrams's section entitled "Moments" in *Natural Supernaturalism*, 385–90. On Wordsworth's notion of time and temporality, and its relation to his aesthetic and/or poetic, see Jeffrey Baker's *Time and Mind in Wordsworth's Poetry* (Detroit: Wayne State University Press, 1980), esp. the introduction and chapter 1. The only recent full-length study of these sonnets is Anne L. Rylestone's *Prophetic Memory in Wordsworth's Ecclesiastical Sonnets* (Carbondale: Southern Illinois University Press, 1991).

72. Ibid., 338.

73. Tillottama Rajan's discussion of the relationship between narrative and lyric has interesting implications for something like a sonnet sequence: "narrative, which dramatizes the gaps between what is told and the telling of it, is always already within a world of textuality, of interpretation rather than origination" ("Romanticism and the Death of Lyric Consciousness," in Hošek and Parker, *Lyric Poetry*, 196). This tension between interpretation and origination is palpable in Wordsworth's sonnet sequences, which tend to announce themselves as journeys toward origins, but also to revise their project along the way as a journey toward an "ultimate" end. The river image would feed into this dialectic; for this, see W. H. Herendeen, "The Rhetoric of Rivers: The River and the Pursuit of Knowledge," *Studies in Philology* 78 (1981): 107–27.

Rowlett's discussion of the *Duddon* sequence once again dovetails nicely with my reading and also highlights other aspects of the sequence. Of particular interest is Rowlett's perception of synecdoche at work: "For Wordsworth, the assumption underlying such a part/whole relation [at the end of the *Duddon* series] can be understood as one in which the part possesses, or embeds, its own whole identity" (245). He also discusses the "boundary-breaking" theme in the sequence, which he sees as a *psychological* boundary-breaking, a "transgression" that leads to knowledge and *interpretation* ("Generic Wordsworth," 240).

74. The exact date is uncertain; Hayden says probably between 21 May 1802 and 6 March 1804. It was published in 1807.

75. Fortunately, the occasion that produced this sonnet is recorded in the notes dictated to Isabella Fenwick by the poet: "1803. Town-End. I remember the instant my sister S.[ara] H.[utchinson], called me to the window of our Cottage, saying, 'Look how beautiful is yon star? It has the sky all to itself.' I composed the verses immediately" (quoted by Hayden in the notes to *Poems*, 1:993). This account, at least as it is remembered, highlights the feeling of instantaneousness of recognition and formalization that forms the center of my reading.

76. This is a word Wordsworth would use at the opening of *The Prelude*: "The ambitious Power of Choice" (1.166). Ross's comments on this line are relevant; see *Contours of Masculine Desire*, 74.

Chapter 2. A Figure of Resistance: The Conspiring Reader in Shelley's Sonnets and "West Wind" Ode

1. *The Influence of Milton on English Poetry*, 537.

2. *The Poetry of Life: Shelley and Literary Form* (Toronto: University of Toronto Press, 1987), 11. Also see Jerrold E. Hogle, *Shelley's Process: Radical Transference and the Development of his Major Works* (New York: Oxford University Press, 1988).

3. The earliest critic to say so is undoubtedly Leigh Hunt, in his *Book of the Sonnet*, 2 vols. (Boston: Roberts Brothers, 1867): "Shelley ought to have been a fine and abundant Sonneteer; for he was full of thought, feeling and music. His sonnet on Ozymandias has the right comprehensiveness of treatment, and perfection of close. But though he was always longing for them, he never could content himself in these sequestered corners of poetry" (1:87). Also see James Rieger, *The Mutiny Within: The Heresies of Percy Bysshe Shelley* (New York: George Braziller, 1967), who states that "Shelley shared with Keats, Byron and Wordsworth a distaste for the English [Shakespearean-form] sonnet" and that "such sloppi-

ness [in the poet's unusual rhyme schemes] is freakish in Shelley and indicates nothing less than boredom with the form" (167). Havens also deems this irregularity a major flaw, but then erroneously attributes it to the "lawless indifference of romanticism" to poetic form. For a more recent correction of these views, see Curran and Tetreault.

4. Mönch, *Das Sonett: Gestalt und Geschichte*, 172.

5. Ibid.

6. All quotations from Shelley's poetry are from *The Complete Poetical Works of Percy Bysshe Shelley*, ed. Thomas Hutchinson (London: Oxford University Press, 1929).

7. Roe, "'Bright Star, Sweet Unrest': Image and Consolation in Wordsworth, Shelley, and Keats," in *History and Myth: Essays on English Romantic Literature,* ed. Stephen C. Behrendt (Detroit: Wayne State University Press, 1990), 141.

8. In this context Stuart Curran writes: "To Shelley, Wordsworth's foresight may have saved him from madness only to allow hell to triumph in another form. His decay was worse than a failure of vision: it was a disaster for the age. . . . [For Shelley] Wordsworth is a Promethean, gifted with the creative spark, who has chained himself in self-defeating mental formulations" (*Shelley's Annus Mirabilis: The Maturing of an Epic Vision* [San Marino, Calif.: Huntington Library, 1975], 146). Also see Tetreault, *The Poetry of Life*, 49. For a valuable, post-Bloomian reading of romantic rivalry, see Ross, *Contours of Masculine Desire*, chap. 3. Ross explains how Romantic historicism "mandates originality," and how "Historical consciousness also contributes to intensified anxiety over influence because it forces the poet to apprehend the present as a privileged state of contestation. At this moment, in its monumental uniqueness, history is being decided. Although the poet has no power over past vision, he is able to shape the present relation to that past, in other words, to shape the future through prophecy" (90–91).

9. This affinity was noted some time ago: according to Neville Rogers's notes to the Oxford edition, "Garnett drew Forman's attention to the similarity between Cavalcanti's mood of disillusionment and the mood of Shelley's sonnet to Wordsworth" (2:332). It is also mentioned in Richard Holmes's biography: "Shelley chose to translate it because of its obvious connection with his attitude to Wordsworth; and also perhaps, in a more oblique way, to his old and unreliable friend Hogg" (*Shelley: The Pursuit* [New York: E. P. Dutton, 1975], 308).

10. By way of comparison, Lowry Nelson's recent, much more literal translation runs so:

> I come to you during the day countless times
> And find you thinking too basely:
> I deeply grieve over your noble mind
> And your many virtues of which you are deprived.

> Many persons would often displease you:
> You would always flee from tiresome people;
> You would speak about me with such deep feeling
> That I had garnered all your poems.
> Now, because of your base life, I do not dare
> Let on that I like your words,
> Nor do I come to you in such a way that you can see me.

> If you read this sonnet many times,
> The offensive spirit that pursues you
> Will take leave of your abased soul.

(I' vegno 'l giorno a te 'infinite volte / e trovoti pensar troppo vilmente: / molto mi dòl della gentil tua mente / e d'assai tue vertù che ti son tolte. // Solevanti spiacer persone molte; / tuttor fuggivi l'annoiosa gente; / di me parlavi sì coralemente, / che tutte le tue rime avie ricolte. // Or non ardisco, per la vil tua vita, / far mostramento che tu' dir mi piaccia, / né 'n guisa vegno a te, che tu me veggi. // Se 'l presente sonetto spesso leggi, / lo spirito noioso che ti caccia / si partirà da l'anima invilita.)

(Sonnet 41)

(Text from *The Poetry of Guido Cavalcanti* (New York: Garland, 1986), 66.

11. See for example Jean Hall, *The Transforming Image: A Study of Shelley's Major Poetry* (Chicago: University of Illinois Press, 1980), 22.

12. Professor Fry has given me permission to quote from this unpublished essay (12).

13. Ibid., 14.

14. Janowitz, "Shelley's Monument to Ozymandias," *Philological Quarterly* 63 (1984): 487. I have found this article a very useful commentary on the sonnet. For another recent interpretation that bears somewhat upon my argument about the poem's deferral of irony and therefore of interpretation, see William Freedman, "Postponement and Perspectives in Shelley's 'Ozymandias'," *Studies in Romanticism* 25 (1986): 63–73.

15. Janowitz, "Shelley's Monument," 487.

16. Ibid., 485.

17. Text is quoted from *Shelley's Poetry and Prose*, ed. Donald H. Reiman and Sharon Powers (New York: Norton, 1977), 135.

18. Ibid., 134.

19. Jean Hall suggests something like this as well: "and endorsing all this is the speaker's poetic transformation of these forms into the discipline of the sonnet. In 'Ozymandias' the past becomes a perceptual field that continually enlarges with the passage of time, creating possibilities for the continual artistic transformation of the image focused at its center" (*Transforming Image*, 22).

20. Curran, *Poetic Form*, 55. The frustration perceptible in this sonnet is of a sort that Ronald Tetreault suggests characterizes a good deal of Shelley's poetry, since "his struggle [is] with the very language to which he was committed. By recognizing the 'arbitrary' relation of language to the poetic imagination, he freed subjectivity from one tyranny only to encounter another. . . . Bound by tradition, authority, and convention, the poet strains at the limits of rhetoric to create a poetic discourse that reaches out to its audience but does not bind them in turn in the iron grip of manipulative machinery" (*Poetry of Life*, 15–16).

21. The most recent exploration of this relationship is François Jost's "Anatomy of an Ode: Shelley and the Sonnet Tradition," *Comparative Literature* 34 (1982): 223–46. After noting that this conflict exists, Jost begs the questions one wants answered ("What function does this sort of innovation serve? What does the poem do for the poet?") by wondering whether Shelley was even aware that he was performing any prosodic experiment at all and by offering no satisfying explanation other than accident or "Biblical miracle" (245).

22. Cronin, *Shelley's Poetic Thoughts* (London: Macmillan, 1981), 232. William Sharp, a sonnet anthologist of the Victorian period, rejected the theory that these stanzas were sonnets:

Mr. Main prints the famous *West Wind* lyric as five sonnets. That these stanzas are not sonnets, however, need hardly be explained to anyone who knows them, and what a lyric is, and what a sonnet. It is true that they are divisible into five fourteen-line parts: but the result of disintegration is only to present several hopelessly irregular sonnets, and to tend to dissipate the lyric emotion aroused by the very first words of

Shelley's exquisite poem. . . . Mr. J. A. Symonds has adequately defined the metrical structure of this famous lyric as 'interrupted *terza rima.*'" (*Sonnets of this Century*, 320)

23.   Helen E. Haworth, "'Ode to the West Wind' and the Sonnet Form," *Keats-Shelley Journal* 20 (1971): 74. Also see Cronin: "The vaulting momentum of terza rima contrasts with the self-contained structure of the sonnet" (*Shelley's Poetic Thoughts*, 232).

24.   See Rieger, *The Mutiny Within*, 167. Also see William Keach, *Shelley's Style* (New York and London: Methuen, 1984), 162.

25.   "The Stanzaic Pattern of Shelley's 'Ode to the West Wind,'" *Keats-Shelley Journal* 21 (1970): 7–8. Also see J. Drummond Bone, "On 'Influence', and on Byron's and Shelley's Use of *Terza Rima* in 1819," *Keats-Shelley Memorial Bulletin* 32 (1981): 38–48.

26.   Fry, *The Poet's Calling in the English Ode* (New Haven: Yale University Press, 1980), 206.

27.   For an analysis of the apocalyptic mode in the "Ode," and its specific relationship to *Revelations*, see Reinhard H. Friedrich's "The Apocalyptic Mode and Shelley's 'Ode to the West Wind,'" *Renascence* 36 (1984): 161–70. Friedrich too mentions the "anticipatory" movement of the poem and discusses the relationship between the individual or personal voice and an apocalyptic vision. Also on this, see G. K. Blank, "Shelley's Wind of Influence," *Philological Quarterly* 64 (1985): "It [the West Wind] is both preparatory (preparing the seeds for growth) and anticipatory (anticipating the 'living' elements that will come)" (477). Blank also concurs with my reading of the transformation of images: "he [the poet] transfigures himself into the imagery of the first three sections" (479).

28.   On this shift, see Tetreault, *Poetry of Life*, 217.

29.   While my use of the word here recalls Burke, it also derives of course from Shelley's use of it: "by the incantation of this verse." Also see Bloom's comments in *Shelley's Mythmaking* (Ithaca: Cornell University Press, 1969) on the "magical aim" of the ode, and the relationship of that aim to the poem's structure (72–73).

30.   For a concurrent reading, see Stephen C. Behrendt's essay, "'The Consequence of High Powers': Blake, Shelley, and Prophecy's Public Dimension" (*Papers on Language & Literature* 22 [1986]: 254–75). Behrendt describes art, for Shelley, as a vehicle for envisioning and communicating

> this unfolding apocalypse, and that the poet/artist is seen as its logical agent, makes it doubly fitting that the apocalyptic trumpet invoked to spread Shelley's words as sparks to kindle the purgative fires of change is itself blown by the poet in one of his most highly crafted poems. Shelley's plea that he be transformed from passive instrument of the breeze (in the eolian harp tradition) to active trumpeter sounding the charge, and the Final Fanfare, surely reflects his aspirations as both prophet and patriot, as both shaper and leader of the reconstruction of Paradise in a real, tangible, and potentially perfectible world. (274)

For a description of the "poetic grammar" of this moment and moments like it, see John Hollander's chapter, "Poetic Imperatives," in *Melodious Guile*, 64–84. Hollander discusses Shelley's ode on pages 64–66.

31.   Tetreault, *Poetry of Life*, 210.

32.   Angela Leighton, *Shelley and the Sublime* (Cambridge: Cambridge University Press, 1984), 110.

33. Hollander, *Melodious Guile*, 79.

34. I am reminded here of Valéry's discussion of form: "everything he [the poet] has imagined, felt, dreamed, and planned will be passed through a sieve, weighted, filtered, subjected to *form*, and condensed as much as possible so as to gain in power what it loses in length: a sonnet, for example, will be a true quintessence, a nutrient, a concentrated and distilled juice, reduced to fourteen lines, carefully *composed* with a view to a final and overwhelming effect" (*The Art of Poetry*, trans. Denise Folliot [Princeton: Princeton University Press, 1985], 316–17). It is to this final and overwhelming effect that Shelley directed the movement of his sonnets and toward which the ode also moves.

35. *Poetic Form*, 55.

Chapter 3. "Jealous of Dead Leaves": Keats's Sonnets and Literary History

1. The passage is quoted from E. M. Forster's *Celestial Omnibus and other Stories* (New York: Alfred A. Knopf, 1923), 71–73. For the text of Keats's poetry I have used Jack Stillinger's edition, *John Keats: Complete Poems* (Cambridge: Belknap Press of Harvard University Press, 1982).

2. De Man writes that Keats can "only start his work because he is willing to forget that this presumed beginning is, in fact, the repetition of a previous failure, resulting precisely from an inability to begin anew" (quoted in Brisman, *Romantic Origins*, 98). Bloom argues something similar in *Poetry and Repression* (New Haven: Yale University Press, 1976). For a related discussion, see Jack Stillinger, *The Hoodwinking of Madeline and Other Essays on Keats's Poems* (Chicago: University of Illinois Press, 1971), who calls Keats's imagination "prefigurative." Marjorie Levinson, in her *Keats's Life of Allegory: The Origins of a Style* (London: Basil Blackwell, 1988), agrees that Keats "could not begin to invent an original voice without first and *throughout* establishing his legitimacy: roughly, his derivativeness" (10). She goes on to argue—and here she departs from her predecessors—that Keats's distinctive self-reflexiveness, and the distinctive "badness" of much of his writing, operates finally as intentional parody (5-6). Finally, see James Kissane, "The Authorization of John Keats," *Keats-Shelley Journal* 37 (1988): 58–74 for a useful analysis of Keats's effort to justify poetry as a "self-creating act" and to define a poetic self that is not merely (Wordsworthian) "self-worship." Kissane also locates this effort in *lexis* rather than *logos*—in textuality and authorship (71–72). In this, says Kissane, the poet departs from Wordsworth and Shelley, a notion with which my argument concurs.

3. R. D. Havens notes that Keats's sonnets "like most of his work, will be better understood if they are studied in connection with those of Leigh Hunt" (*Influence of Milton*, 537), but stresses, correctly, that in the end Hunt "did not so much hand a torch on to Keats as fan the one the younger man was already carrying" (538). Havens also discusses Keats's debt to the Italians and Elizabethans. For an account of Keats's reading of his contemporaries, see Beth Lau's reference work, *Keats's Reading of the Romantic Poets* (Ann Arbor: University of Michigan Press, 1991).

4. See Paul de Man's introduction to *The Selected Poems of John Keats* (New York: Signet, 1966), and chapter 5 in Bloom's *Poetry and Repression*. Also highly relevant here is Ross's discussion of Keats's ambivalence toward Wordsworth, as well as toward the "apparent alternative, the self-abnegating, decorative poetry being increasingly taken over by women like Mary Tighe" (*Contours of Masculine Desire*, 157). In his analysis of Tighe's sonnets,

Ross locates a "self secretly hoping to find an unmuted voice as individuated, as self-perpetuating, as self-owning as that of a Wordsworth or a Keats" (165). Finally, see Robert Langbaum's "The Epiphanic Mode in Wordsworth and Modern Literature," *New Literary History* 14 (Winter 1983): 352, in which he correctly points out that Wordsworth "invented the epiphanic or modern sonnet" (352), and that these sonnets "gave rise to Keats's sonnets" (353); my chapter, however, disputes Langbaum's subsequent assertion that Keats's sonnets are successful in these epiphanies. Langbaum's mention of Rossetti and Hopkins's sonnets in this context concurs with my own mapping of the visionary sonnet line.

5. Smith, *Poetic Closure: A Study of How Poems End* (Chicago: University of Chicago Press, 1968), 5.

6. In the contemporaneous "I stood tip-toe upon a little hill" is a passage that also suggests that Keats may associate poetic form with space. In addition to its relevant epigraph from Hunt's *Story of Rimini*—"Places of nestling green for Poets made"—the poem asks "What first inspired a bard of old to sing / Narcissus pining o'er the untainted spring?" The answer is that this bard finds himself at "A little space, with boughs all woven round"(166), where he finds the Narcissus flower. Brisman calls this passage a "naturalized version of genius loci," a version that "has it that locus itself is enough" (*Romantic Origins*, 78). Brisman does not mention that this genius loci involves a near-conflation of the poet and the Narcissus figure, not only imagistically but syntactically; at line 165—"In some delicious ramble, he had found / A little space"—it is unclear for quite some reading time whether the "he" is the bard or Narcissus himself. In any case, the point is that here, as in Keats's first published sonnet (and in so many other places), Keats's concern is with, as Brisman puts it, "a birth of poetic consciousness" (92).

7. This natural scene of labor may be akin to the "bower" that Morris Dickstein identifies more generally in Keats's early poetry. See chapter 2 of Dickstein's *Keats and His Poetry: A Study in Development* (Chicago: University of Chicago Press, 1971), where he locates the tradition of Keats's bower from Chaucer to Spenser to Wordsworth, and observes that "Keats culminates [that tradition] by transforming the bower completely from a spatial concept to a temporal and psychological one, akin to Wordsworth's 'spots of time'" (36).

8. We can recognize that intensity in Keats's remark in his letter to Bailey (22 November 1817) that "the simple imaginative Mind may have its rewards in the repeti[ti]on of its own silent Working coming continually on the Spirit with a fine Suddenness" (*The Letters of John Keats*, ed. Maurice Buxton Forman, 4th ed. [New York: Oxford University Press, 1952], 67). This suddenness seems to be akin to what Curran calls "aesthetic shock."

9. Reynolds and Conder are quoted in *Romantic Bards and British Reviewers*, ed. John O. Hayden (London: Routledge & Kegan Paul, 1971), 300, 311.

10. Marjorie Levinson finds this self-reflexiveness "special and disturbing . . . one that brings out the difference between the subject and its internalized models, not their identity. . . . To 'overhear' Keats poetry is to hear nothing *but* intonation, to feel nothing but style and its meaningfulness. . . . To read Keats is to focus the 'aboutness' of the verse as the vehicle for a stylistic design" (*Keats's Life of Allegory*, 36). Also see Ross on poetic reflexivity as "self-authorization" and as a "signal [of] a mature mastery not only of the concrete poetic medium, but also of the abstract generality that grounds the medium" (*Contours of Masculine Desire*, 165).

11. See Stillinger, who says that the poems of the 1817 volume are "mainly about the question of whether Keats can and should be a poet, and which proceed from hesitancy to affirmation and dedication to a ten-year program of development that, as it turns out, he had to condense into less than half that time" (*Hoodwinking of Madeline*, 111).

12. See *The Letters of John Keats*, ed. Hyder Edward Rollins, 2 vols. (Cambridge: Harvard University Press, 1958), 1:118. The original line was "Of mighty Workings in a distant Mart?"

13. Sperry, *Keats the Poet* (Princeton: Princeton University Press, 1973), 73.

14. Finney, *The Evolution of Keats's Poetry* (New York: Russell & Russell, 1936), 101.

15. Sperry, *Keats the Poet*, 73-74.

16. Curran, *Poetic Form*, 53. Also see Sperry, *Keats the Poet*, 72–74, who anticipates both myself and Curran in his discussion of "Keats's method" of "amass[ing] a series of impressions in the hope they will of themselves create the impetus to carry him forward" (72).

17. De Man, introduction to *Selected Poetry*, xxviii. For a related reading, see William Fitzgerald, "Keats's Sonnets and Challenge of Winter," *Studies in Romanticism* 26 (1987): 59–83. Clearly relevant here as well is Barbara Johnson's discussion of Mallarmé in "*Les Fleurs du mal armé*: Some Reflections on Intertextuality" in Hošek and Parker, *Lyric Poetry*, 264–80. Her premise is that Mallarmé "has transformed the incapacity to write into the very subject of his writing. In the act of thematizing an oedipal defeat, Mallarmé's writing thus maps out the terms of an escape from simple oedipal polarities" (266). That escape is forgetfulness "as a cure for impotence . . . thus implying that what the impotent poet is suffering from is too much memory" (267). My own reading of Keats is parallel to this one.

18. The passage is quoted from the Shawcross edition of *The Complete Poems of John Milton*.

19. Gleckner, "Keats's 'How Many Bards' and Poetic Tradition," *Keats-Shelley Journal* 27 (1978): 20.

20. Fitzgerald, "Keats's Sonnets and the Challenge of Winter," 66.

21. Hunt, *Lord Byron and Some of His Contemporaries* (London: H. Colburn, 1828), 1:409–10. On this poem as "as much a summing up as an anticipation," see Walter Jackson Bate, *John Keats* (Cambridge: Harvard University Press, 1963), 86–89.

22. See Paul H. Fry's "The Possession of the Sublime," *Studies in Romanticism* 26 (1987): 187–207. As Fry points out, the notions of competition and even anxieties of influence are inscribed in the aesthetic category of the sublime as rendered by Longinus. This article includes a reading of the Chapman's Homer sonnet.

23. Curran, *Poetic Form*, 52. Sperry anticipates Curran in this conclusion when he describes Keats's early verse generally as "characterized by the sudden start of recognition, moments when the diverse strands of sensation and association mysteriously coalesce to yield a kind of intimation Keats himself can consider only by analogy with thought" (*Keats the Poet*, 76–77).

24. Cynthia Chase, "'Viewless Wings': Intertextual Interpretation of Keats's 'Ode to a Nightingale,'" in Hošek and Parker, *Lyric Poetry*, 212.

25. Anthony John Harding suggests something similar in his article "Speech, Silence, and the Self-Doubting Interpreter in Keats's Poetry," *Keats-Shelley Journal* 35 (1986): "Chapman's version has none of the secondariness usually associated with a translation: its air is the same 'pure serene' (line 7) as Homer's. The listener is caught up by a greater power. . . . [The sonnet] is ironic in that the poem expresses the impossibility of expressing anything about Homer after Chapman. Whatever is said will inevitably be supererogatory, a translation of what is already translated" (88–89).

Levinson sees the poem as addressing the "tradition's oppressiveness and inaccessibility" (Harding)—but Levinson goes further than Harding by commenting on Keats's "fetishistic relations to the great Original." Noting that the sonnet's title indicates that Keats "does not *read* even the translation," the poem "advertises his corrupt access to the literary system and to those social institutions which inscribe that system systematically in the hearts and minds of young men" (12). That is, the poem, she says, worries over the poet's poor education, the "social discrepancy" that sullies his claim to intimacy with the text.

26. Fry, "Possession of the Sublime," 203. In addition to Fry, see: Carl Woodring, "On Looking into Keats's Voyagers," *Keats-Shelley Journal* 14 (1965): 15–22; Fitzgerald, "Keats's Sonnets and the Challenge of Winter," 70; and Joseph Warren Beach, "Keats's Realms of Gold, *PMLA* 49 (1934): 246–57.

27. Ibid., 204; also see Paul McNally, "Keats and the Rhetoric of Association: On Looking into the Chapman's Homer Sonnet," *Journal of English and Germanic Philology* 79 (1980): 536.

28. I disagree with Harding's argument here that there is also a "failure of interpretation, the recognition that the poet does not know where to seek what he would know" ("Self-Doubting Interpreter," 88); a more reflexive reading would point the poet not only inward but into language and form itself.

29. "Keats's Sonnets and the Challenge of Winter," 71. On the travel motif of this sonnet, also see Carl Woodring's "On Looking into Keats's Voyagers."

30. Harding, "Self-Doubting Interpreter," 89.

31. For a tangential but closely related point, see Valéry's *Art of Poetry*, 203, where he describes the way in which the beginning or perception of something perceived as poetic *becomes* that occasion.

32. *Ecstatic Occasions, Expedient Forms*, ed. David Lehman (New York: Collier Books, 1988), 82. Not surprisingly, Levinson sees this moment differently: "The very act of assertion, as well as its histrionically commanding and archly literary style, undermine the premise of natural authority and erudition" (*Keats's Life of Allegory*, 12). She concludes, therefore, that "Keats's poem 'speak[s] out loud and bold' by not speaking 'out' at all" (14).

33. See Levinson: "Wordsworth's poetry, like so much of Keats's, typically represents its coming *into* being as its reason *for* being, and also its chief delight" (*Keats's Life of Allegory*, 19–20).

34. Smith, *Poetic Closure*, 137.

35. Valéry, *The Art of Poetry*, 203.

36. Sperry, *Keats the Poet*, 76.

37. Lehman, *Ecstatic Occasions, Expedient Forms*, 82.

38. This reading concurs with Sperry's conclusion (echoing Keats's letter to Hessey) that in this sonnet Keats takes a "headlong plunge into the sea, into the reaches of his own unconsciousness and creativity, the region from which, as, in his sonnet 'On the Sea,' some voice or harmony would have in its own way to come" (*Keats the Poet*, 97). Again, see Barbara Johnson's essay on Mallarmé, where she argues that the blank page, as a space, is "in a sense the place from which literary history speaks" (*"Les Fleurs du mal armé,"* 269).

39. Rollins, *Letters*, 2:108. Note the echo in line 14 of the final line of Anna Seward's sonnet on the sonnet, quoted in the introduction to this study—"A grandeur, grace, and spirit, all their own."

40. Ward, *The Making of a Poet* (New York: Viking, 1963), 279. Also see François Matthey, *The Evolution of Keats's Structural Imagery* (Bern: A. Francke AG Verlag, 1984): "The poem is much more than a clever *tour de force*. It exemplifies what it precisely discusses theoretically" (192).

41. Hollander, *Melodious Guile*, 95.

42. See Valéry, *The Art of Poetry*: "I have only wished to make it understood that the

compulsory meters, rhymes, fixed forms, and all that arbitrariness, adopted once and for all and ranged against ourselves, have a kind of philosophic beauty of their own. Fetters that tighten at every movement of our genius remind us at that moment of all the contempt deserved, without doubt, by that familiar chaos which the vulgar call thought" (18).

43. Hollander, *Melodious Guile*, 96.

44. This is an aspect of form that Smith describes in her *Poetic Closure*, where she defines form as a product of "formal principles of generation," a "systematic repetition or patterning." Form is produced by "a patterning of the formal properties of language according to some principle of organization and/or repetition" (21).

45. Burke, *Counterstatement* (1931; Berkeley and Los Angeles: University of California Press, 1968), 208.

46. Cyrus Hamlin, "The Hermeneutics of Form: Reading the Romantic Ode," *Boundary* 2 (1979): 21.

47. Bate, *John Keats*, 297–300, and 327–28. Also see: Garrod's "Note on Keats' Use of the Sonnet," *Keats* (1926; Oxford: Clarendon Press, 1939), 134–55; Miriam Allott, *The Poems of John Keats* (New York: Norton, 1970). For a general discussion of Keats's use of Italian and English sonnet forms, see Lawrence Zillman's *John Keats and the Sonnet Tradition* (New York: Octagon Books, 1970), and George B. Kauvar's *Other Poetry of Keats* (Rutherford, N. J.: Fairleigh Dickinson University Press, 1969).

48. Fitzgerald, "Keats's Sonnets and the Challenge of Winter," 59.

49. Echoes from other sonnets may be discernible: Keats's "fair creature of an hour," for example, might have been suggested by Shakespeare's opening line in the sequence: "From fairest creatures we desire increase" (Sonnet 1).

50. Thomas M. Greene has shown how in Shakespeare's sonnets the tropes of agricultural husbandry, economic exchange, and sexual potency revolve around conflicting representations of poetry's power and durability. See "Pitiful Thrivers: Failed Husbandry in the Sonnets," in *Shakespeare and the Question of Theory*, ed. Patricia Parker and Geoffrey H. Hartman (London: Methuen, 1985), 230–44. For comments on the association in this particular sonnet, see Miriam Allott, *Poems*, 296. Allott also quotes a note from Woodhouse (found on a MS fragment) that these lines "give some insight into Keats's mode of writing Poetry," by which "my judgment, (he says), is as active while I am actually writing as my imagination. In fact all my faculties are strongly excited and in their full play. . . ." Woodhouse concludes that in the sonnet Keats has illustrated "the very thing itself" (297).

51. The first critic to say so appears to be M. A. Goldberg, in his 1957 article "The 'Fears' of John Keats," *Modern Language Quarterly* 18 (1957): 125–31. The most recent proponent of the older view that the poem is "really about" Keats's own fear of mortality is Sara van den Berg, in her article "Describing Sonnets by Milton and Keats: Roy Schafer's Action Language and the Interpretation of Texts," in *Psychological Perspectives on Literature: Freudian Dissidents and Non-Freudians, A Casebook*, ed. Joseph Natoli (Hamden, Conn.: Archon Books, 1984), 134–54 .

52. Fineman's elegant and useful argument on Shakespeare's sonnets, elaborated fully in his book, *The Perjur'd Eye: The Invention of Poetic Subjectivity in the Sonnets* (Berkeley: University of California Press, 1986) appeared in a shortened essay form in Hošek and Parker's *Lyric Poetry*, 116–31. This quotation appears on page 122. The central connection of his argument with my own regarding Keats is his description of what he finds "genuinely novel" in Shakespeare:

the way the visionary poet takes this faded brightness personally, the way he identifies his own poetic person and poetic identity with the after-light of this dead metaphoric sun. . . . he is a visionary poet, but he is so, as it were, after the visionary fact, a Seer who now sees in a too frequently reiterated *luce etterna*, a vivid image, an *effige* or *eidolon*, of the death of both his light and life, as in Sonnet 73 ["That time of year thou mayst in me behold"]. . . . [The sonnets reveal a] nostalgia of the poet's introspection: the poet sees his difference from a visionary poetics that would always be the same because, as Aristotle says of metaphor, it always 'see[s] the same.' But his insight serves only to make the poet's bygone ideal vision seem all the more ideal, an image of poetic presence that is always in the past." (121–22)

53. Chase, "'Viewless Wings': Intertextual Interpretation," 212.

54. My thanks go to John Hollander for directing me toward these observations.

55. I agree entirely with Chase's view of Keats's handling of the matter of perception and cognition. She argues that the notion of Keats as a "poet of the earth" is a simplification. Keats, she says, questions the "status of perception, makes the nature of sensory evidence a difficulty. . . . Keats's poetry treats it [the continuity between perception and cognition] as an issue rather than an assumption" ("'Viewless Wings'" 210–11).

See Keats's remarkable description of this scene in a letter to his brother Tom on 3–6 August 1818 (No. 101 in *Letters*, 1:352–54); he ends this description with the sonnet he wrote there.

56. Curran, *Poetic Form*, 54.

57. See Roe's careful argument about this sonnet, elaborated on pp. 143-47 of "'Bright Star, Sweet Unrest.'" I am grateful for Roe's reading; I had noted the coincidence of the "Bright Star" of Wordsworth's 1802 sonnet "Composed by the Sea-Side, near Calais," but had been unable to explain what I assumed to be a direct allusion by Keats. Roe's intertextual analysis, based on important letter passages as well as the two poems in question, makes sense at every level.

58. See Bate, *John Keats*, 618–19, for details on the dating controversy surrounding this sonnet.

59. This poem and the letter quoted below are taken from Forman, *Letters of John Keats*, 66–67.

60. On the other hand, Beth Lau cites as a source for this letter passage the philosophy of "wise passiveness" urged in Wordsworth's "Expostulation and Reply," from the *Lyrical Ballads* (Lau, *Keats's Reading*, 31).

61. See *Keats*, 85–90. Later commentators include Claude Lee Finney, *Evolution of Keats's Poetry*, 608–9; M. R. Ridley, *Keats's Craftsmanship: A Study in Poetic Development* (New York: Russell & Russell, 1962) 202–4; Douglas Bush, *John Keats: His Life and Writings* (New York: Macmillan, 1966), 126–27; and Bate, in both *John Keats* (495–500), and in "Keats's Style: Evolution toward Qualities of Permanent Value," in M. H. Abrams, ed. *English Romantic Poets: Modern Essays in Criticism* (1960; New York: Oxford University Press, 1975). Finney mentions the "Dull Rhymes" sonnet as a transition to "the ode perfect genre which he had been seeking," but neglects the pursuit of the connection. Of Keats's experimentalism, Finney says only that is was "not successful. . . . He gained freedom by violating form, but he lost the subtle correspondence between thought and form which is the peculiar virtue of Petrarchan and Shakespearean sonnets" (609). Recent discussions challenge his evaluation of the poem as a failure, Hollander's being one. Fry's interest in Keats's ode form leads him to a brief discussion of this matter, and he cites the passage from Keats's verse letter to Clarke (lines 61–65: "Who read for me the sonnet swelling loudly / Up to its climax and then dying proudly? / Who found for me the grandeur of the ode, / Growing, like Atlas, stronger from its load?") that does indeed suggest that "Keats connected

the sonnet and the ode more closely than was customary" (*The Poet's Calling in the English Ode*, 219).

62. "Keats's Style," 418; *John Keats*, 497.

63. Bate, *John Keats*, 496. I am reminded here of Gerard Genette's remark that "a personal creation in the strong sense does not exist . . . because literary practice takes place as a vast *combinatory* game within a pre-existing system which is none other than language itself. . . ." (Quoted by Donald Wesling, *The Chances of Rhyme: Device and Modernity* [Berkeley: University of California Press, 1980], 112).

64. *The Keats Circle*, ed. Hyder Edward Rollins, vol. 1 (Cambridge: Harvard University Press, 1965), 58.

65. I chose this word for its etymology: it is related to the word "Lethe" via a common Greek root, *lanthanein*, to escape notice. "Lethe" is obviously the extreme form of that; "latency" is a more neutral word, though it recalls the sense of deceit that pervades stanza 2 of the poem.

66. See especially Geoffrey Hartman, "Poem and Ideology," in *The Fate of Reading* (Chicago: University of Chicago Press, 1975), 140.

67. Fitzgerald concurs with this reading; he says that "it is a typically Keatsian (or Autumnal) extension, an elision of the turning point in which the dual aspect of keeping reconciles continuation with containment" ("Articulating the Unarticulated: Form, Death, and Other in Keats and Rilke," *Modern Language Notes* 100 [1985]: 958).

68. See Harold Bloom, *The Visionary Company*, rev. ed. (Ithaca: Cornell University Press, 1971), 423, for a similar reading.

69. The Latin *autumnus* means not only the season Autumn but also, synecdochically, the entire year, according to the OED. The original word (from *augere*, to increase) registers the manner in which this season gathers up the past, storing its fruits in anticipation of the future.

70. Vendler, *The Odes of John Keats* (Cambridge: Belknap Press of Harvard University Press, 1983), 261.

71. Bloom, *Visionary Company*, 424.

72. I have always been tempted to make something here of Keats's request in his final days that his books be literally "gathered" around him. Severn said that this indeed acted as a "charm" to calm him.

73. For competing readings of the poem, see Fry, "History, Existence, and 'To Autumn,'" *Studies in Romanticism* 25 (Summer 1986): 211–19; and McGann, "Keats and the Historical Method in Literary Criticism," *Modern Language Notes* 94 (1979), rpt. in *The Beauty of Inflections: Literary Investigations in Historical Method and Theory* (Oxford: Clarendon Press, 1988), 17–65.

Chapter 4. "Sonnettomania" and the Ideology of Form

1. Going, *Scanty Plot of Ground: Studies in the Victorian Sonnet* (The Hague and Paris: Mouton, 1976), 157.

2. Text is quoted from Lofft, *Laura: or, An Anthology of Sonnets, (On the Petrarchan Model,) and Elegiac Quatorzains*, vol. 5 (London: B. and R. Crosby & Co., 1814).

3. Text is quoted from Doubleday, *Sixty-five Sonnets; with Prefatory Remarks on the Accordance of the Sonnet with the Powers of the English Language* (London: Baldwin, Cradock, and Joy, 1818).

4. *New Monthly Magazine and Literary Journal* 1 (1821): 644. Over fifty years later, William Michael Rossetti would refer to "a veritable sonnet-mania, which has erupted in a number of subsequent volumes" in his *Dante Gabriel Rossetti as Designer and Writer* (London: Cassell and Co., 1889), 169.

5. Because of its length, the full bibliographical list of essays appears in an appendix.

6. [C. W. Russell], "The Critical History of the Sonnet," *Dublin Review,* n.s., 27 (October 1876): 401.

7. Robert Fletcher Housman, preface to *A Collection of English Sonnets* (London: Simpkin, Marshall & Co., 1835), v.

8. Brake, "Aesthetics in the Fray: Pater's *Appreciations, with an Essay on Style,*" in *The Politics of Pleasure: Aesthetics and Cultural Theory,* ed. Stephen Regan (Buckingham, U.K., and Philadelphia: Open University Press, 1992), 68.

9. As William H. Galperin has noted in a different context, the Victorians' discussions of Wordsworth's reputation "were simultaneously about the function of poetry in the (then) present time," a statement certainly supported by these writings; see "Anti-Romanticism, Victorianism, and the Case of Wordsworth," *Victorian Poetry* 24 (1986): 359. Also see Joseph Bristow's introduction to *The Victorian Poet: Poetics and Persona* (New York: Croom Helm/Methuen, 1987), "Victorian Criticism of Victorian Poetry," where he outlines major topics and "urgent preoccupations" of Victorian literary critics, including the "Victorian response to Romanticism" and "Victorian models of the poet" (1). Finally, see George Sanderlin, "The Influence of Milton and Wordsworth on the Early Victorian Sonnet," *ELH* 5 (1938): 225–51.

10. See Leigh Hunt's run-down of rules for the perfect sonnet in "Essay on the Sonnet," *The Book of the Sonnet,* 2 vols. (Boston: Roberts Brothers, 1867), 1:11–15.

11. See William Davies: "Whilst fully recognising, however, the rules for the construction of a perfect sonnet—and we cannot despise them . . . —it must not be supposed that they are always and invariably to be observed or made use of. A sonnet might be written in accordance with all of these, and yet be no more than as stiff a 'piece of framework as any January could freeze.' There are but few of them which may not be occasionally transgressed to advantage" ("Article VIII," *London Quarterly Review* 134 [January–April 1873]: 102). Hopkins responded to this problem in a similar fashion in a letter to Bridges: "I look on rhythm as a rule, not as a law; as a convention, not as a nature" (*The Letters of Gerard Manley Hopkins to Robert Bridges,* ed. Claude Colleer Abbott [London: Oxford University Press, 1938], 1:261).

12. Quoted by Hazard Adams, ed., *Critical Theory Since Plato* (New York: Harcourt, Brace, 1971), 462.

13. Thomas Hall Caine, preface to *Sonnets of Three Centuries: A Selection, Including Many Examples Hitherto Unpublished. With a preface of xxiv pages, dated from Vale of St. John, Cumberland, 1881* (London: Elliot Stock, 1882), lvi.

14. Quoted by [C. W. Russell], "Critical History of the Sonnet," 403.

15. Caine, *Sonnets of Three Centuries,* xi.

16. Reed, *Lectures on the British Poets* (London: John F. Shaw & Co., 1863), 365–66.

17. Quoted by [C. W. Russell], "Critical History of the Sonnet," 406.

18. Reed, *Lectures on the British Poets,* 370-71.

19. Ibid., 368.

20. See Trench's enthusiastic encomium of Wordsworth's sonnets on liberty, which runs a full four pages: "What a noble record of the temper of England's noblest sons in that agony of England's fate we possess in these 'Sonnets to Liberty' . . . for in his hands, also,

as in Milton's before him, 'the thing became a trumpet'" ("The History of the English Sonnet," in *The Sonnets of William Wordsworth* [London: Suttaby & Co., 1884], xxv).

21. Caine, *Sonnets of Three Centuries*, xix.

22. Housman, *A Collection of English Sonnets*, viii.

23. Reed, *Lectures on the British Poets*, 358.

24. Sharp, "The Sonnet: Its Characteristics and History," in *Sonnets of This Century* (London: Walter Scott Publishing Co., 1886), liv.

25. Some commentators urged caution here; Housman, for example, warned that "our modern innovators should weigh accurately the grounds of their alterations, before they discard the regulations established by those who most deeply considered their object" (*A Collection of English Sonnets*, x).

26. Reed, *Lectures on the British Poets*, 359.

27. Trench, *The Sonnets of William Wordsworth*, xxi–xxii; Dennis, "The English Sonnet," in *Studies in English Literature* (London: Edward Stanford, 1876), 394.

28. Sharp, *Sonnets of This Century*, liv. Also see Leigh Hunt's introductory letter to Samuel Adams Lee: Hunt wants to "help to excite [in America] a disposition to the cultivation of the Sonnet in all poetical quarters," and he notes that "I cannot help looking upon myself, in this matter, as a kind of hortoculturist [*sic*] who has brought a stock of flowers with him from Italy and England, for the purpose of diffusing their seeds and off-sets, wherever the soil can be found congenial" (xiii).

29. Reed, *Lectures on the British Poets*, 362..

30. Ibid., 361–62. John Dennis argues that it makes as much sense to say that an English-made watch is German, just because the watch was invented by the latter, as it does to say that the English sonnet is not a "genuine portion of English verse" ("The English Sonnet," 394).

31. This term comes from Anna Seward's sonnet on the sonnet, called "To Mr. Henry Cary," quoted in the introduction of this study: "Prais'd be the Poet, who the Sonnet's claim, / Severest of the orders that belong / Distinct and separate to the Delphic song, / Shall venerate, nor its appropriate name / Lawless assume" (*The Poetical Works of Anna Seward*, ed. Walter Scott, 3 vols. [Edinburgh: John Ballantyne and Co., 1810], 3:185).

32. Doubleday, *Sixty-five Sonnets*, 14.

33. Caine, *Sonnets of Three Centuries*, xv.

34. Ibid., ix.

35. Caine, *Sonnets of Three Centuries*, xii; also see pages xxii–iii.

36. The text is from Sharp's anthology, *Sonnets of This Century*, lxv. In his book *Dante Gabriel Rossetti* (London: Macmillan, 1882), 392, Sharp prints the title of the poem as "The Love-Sonnet (A metrical lesson by the sea-shore)."

37. Caine, *Sonnets of Three Centuries*, xxi–xxii.

38. So says Leigh Hunt, reminding his reader of the etymology of the word "sonnet." Hunt surmises that the sonnet was originally, in fact, the lyric for a piece of music accompanied by guitar or lute. "This connection . . . lasted a long time; and when it ceased, it left upon the little poem a demand for treatment more than commonly musical, and implying, so to speak, the companion which it had lost" (9). Also see Housman's summary of the sonnet's original connection to music, *A Collection of English Sonnets*, xviii–xix.

39. Sharp, *Sonnets of This Century*, xxv.

40. Ibid., xl.

41. Sismondi, quoted by Housman, *A Collection of English Sonnets*, xviii.

42. Ibid., xiv.

43. For a useful general background discussion of the changing notions of poetic form and meter under the pressure of the aestheticist movement, see Timothy Steele's *Missing Measure: Modern Poetry and the Revolt Against Meter* (Fayetteville and London: University of Arkansas Press, 1990), esp. chap. 4, "Free Verse and Aestheticism" (171–203).

44. One dissenting voice here might be James Spedding, who writes that "even the conventional limit as to length is purely artificial. It can have no foundation in nature, and its only use in art is to supply a poet with something to do when his invention fails" ("Charles Tennyson Turner," *Nineteenth Century* 6 [September 1879], 461). This is the basis for Spedding's advocacy of permissiveness toward "correctness in form."

45. Ross, *Contours of Masculine Desire*, 23.

46. Caine, *Sonnets of Three Centuries*, xi.

47. Another contemporary, Dr. Symmons, is quoted by Housman as saying that sonnets, "like the small statue by the chisel of Lysippus, . . . demonstrate that the idea of greatness may be excited independently of the magnitude of size" (*A Collection of English Sonnets*, xxix).

48. Even here, John Dennis sneaks in the nationalism discussed in the previous section: "The amatory sonneteers of Italy become frequently monotonous by harping too long upon one string, but in England our poets have rarely fallen into this error, and the variety to be found in the English sonnet is one of its great charms" ("The English Sonnet," 396).

49. [C. W. Russell], "Critical History of the Sonnet," 401.

50. Pater, *Appreciations with an Essay on Style* (London: Macmillan, 1889), 36.

51. Miller, *Linguistic Moment*, 63; see 60–63 for Miller's full discussion of this matter: "*Form* means both the structuring power and that which is structured, both what can be seen and the shaping force pushing what can be seen into the open. The word contains in itself the philosophical or aesthetic problem that it must be used to solve" (61).

52. Trench, *The Sonnets of William Wordsworth*, xii.

53. Caine, *Sonnets of Three Centuries*, xx.

54. Text is quoted from Tennyson Turner's *Collected Sonnets Old and New* (London: C. Kegan Paul & Co., 1880).

55. See Tennyson Turner's sonnet "To the Gossamer-Light," referring to that "Quick gleam" which the poet addresses in the sestet thus:

> Thou art the poet's darling, ever sought
> In the fair garden or the breezy mead;
> The wind dismounts thee not; thy buoyant thread
> Is as the sonnet, poising one bright thought,
> That moves but does not vanish! borne along
> Like light,—a gold drift through all the song!
>
> (Lines 9–14)

The relation of occasion to sonnet writing is also explored in his "The Gold-Crested Wren. His Relation to the Sonnet," a poem that reuses, in a rather different context, Wordsworth's opening line of the second Convention of Cintra sonnet that we looked at earlier. The line, "I dropped my pen," enters this poem when the poet takes hold of a struggling wren dashing himself on his window-pane: "I dropt my pen, I left th' unfinished lay, / To give thee back to freedom; but I took— / Oh, charm of sweet occasion!—one brief look / At thy bright eyes and innocent dismay" (5–8). Releasing the bird, the poet concludes that "if, at times, my sonnet-muse would rest / Short of her topmost skill, her little best, / The memory of thy delicate gold crest / Shall plead for one last touch,—the crown of Art."

56. Sharp, *Sonnets of This Century*, lxiii, lxii.

57. Sharp cites Hunt's remark that a sonnet needs to "lie polishing in his mind for months together, like a pebble on the sea-shore," and then Rossetti's famous remark that "the first and highest quality of finish in poetic execution, 'is that where the work has been all mentally "cartooned," as it were beforehand, by a process intensely conscious, but patient and silent—an occult evolution of life'" (ibid., lxxviii). Both recall Wordsworth's sonnet "To—— [Happy the feeling . . .]," discussed in chapter 1.

58. Quoted by Housman, *A Collection of English Sonnets*, viii.

59. Dennis, "The English Sonnet," 396. Eugene Lee-Hamilton composed a sonnet on the sonnet that clearly fulfills the sonnet-as-jewel paradigm. "What the Sonnet Is" appeared in *Imaginary Sonnets* in 1888:

What the Sonnet Is

Fourteen small broidered berries on the hem
Of Circe's mantle, each of magic gold;
Fourteen of lone Calypso's tears that roll'd
Into the sea, for pearls to come of them;

Fourteen clear signs of omen in the gem
With which Medea human fate foretold;
Fourteen small drops, which Faustus, growing old,
Craved of the Fiend, to water Life's dry stem.

It is the pure white diamond Dante brought
To Beatrice; the sapphire Laura wore
When Petrarch cut it sparkling out of thought;

The ruby Shakespeare hewed from his heart's core;
The dark, deep emerald that Rossetti wrought
For his own soul, to wear for evermore.

The text is quoted from a later collection called *Sonnets of the Winged Hours* (Portland, Me.: Thomas B. Mosher, 1933). Also see his "Sonnet Gold" in that volume.

60. Chai, *Aestheticism: The Religion of Art in Post-Romantic Literature* (New York: Columbia University Press, 1990), 152.

61. Davies, "Article VIII," *London Quarterly Review* 134 (January–April 1873): 108.

62. Pater, *The Renaissance*, ed. Adam Phillips (New York: Oxford University Press, 1986), 152.

Chapter 5. "A Moment's Monument": Revisionary Poetics and the Sonnets of Dante Gabriel Rossetti

1. Caine, *Recollections of Dante Gabriel Rossetti* (London: Elliot Stock, 1882), 31.

2. Richard L. Stein, "Dante Gabriel Rossetti: Painting and the Problem of Poetic Form," *Studies in English Literature* 10 (1970): 791.

3. Langbaum, *Poetry of Experience: The Dramatic Monologue in Modern Literary Tradition* (1957; New York: Norton, 1971), 35.

4. W. M. Rossetti, *Dante Gabriel Rossetti as Designer and Writer* (London: Cassell & Co., 1885), 184.

5. The sonnet, sent to his mother in 1880 for her birthday, was accompanied by an illustration for it. Rossetti explicated the drawing in a letter, dated 27 April: "I have no doubt that your discerning eyes plucked out the heart of the mystery in the little design. In it the Soul is instituting the 'memorial to one dead deathless hour,' a ceremony easily effected by placing a winged hour-glass in a rose-bush, at the same time that she touches the fourteen-stringed harp of the Sonnet, hanging round her neck. On the rose-branches trailing over in the opposite corner is seen hanging the Coin, which is the second symbol used for the Sonnet. Its 'face' bears the Soul, expressed in the butterfly; its 'converse,' the Serpent of Eternity enclosing the Alpha and Omega. All this I doubt not you had seen for yourself" (*Letters of Dante Gabriel Rossetti*, ed. Oswald Doughty and John Robert Wahl [Oxford: Clarendon Press, 1967], 4:1760). I have used, unless otherwise noted, William Michael Rossetti's two-volume edition of his brother's poems, first published in 1887 (*The Poetical Works of Dante Gabriel Rossetti*, 2 vol. Boston: Little, Brown, 1907).

6. William Sharp wrote that this poem's trope of the "moment's monument" was "not improbably reproducing that line of de Musset, in his *Impromptu en réponse à cette question: 'Qu'est-ce que la poésie?—Eterniser peut-être un rêve d'un instant'*" (*Sonnets of This Century*, lxxvii).

7. Hollander, *Melodious Guile*, 97.

8. Richardson, *Vanishing Lives: Style and Self in Tennyson, D. G. Rossetti, Swinburne, and Yeats* (Charlottesville: University Press of Virginia, 1988), 107.

9. The more complimentary Pater used the word "gravity" to describe the nature of Rossetti's poems, a word that describes not only the atmosphere but also the dense tissue of the language itself; see the essay on Rossetti in *Appreciations* (London: Macmillan, 1895).

10. In a letter, Burne-Jones noted that Rossetti preferred short forms, because he "wanted to keep a poem at the boiling point all the way through, and he did it to that degree that it went into ether with fervent flowing heat before he had done with it. The short form of his poems helped him to do this. As soon as the pot went off the boil, he'd take it from the fire" (*The Memorials of Edward Burne-Jones* [London: Macmillan, 1904], 2:264). Also see Stein: "His ornateness need not imply mindlessness. Loving both decoration and condensation, Rossetti habitually overworked his poetry (the first versions are often the best) so that obscurity frequently signifies too much, rather than too little, poetic effort" ("Painting and the Problem of Poetic Form," 787).

11. W. M. Rossetti, *Rossetti Papers, 1862–1870* (London: Sands & Co., 1903), 407.

12. "The Poems of Dante Gabriel Rossetti," in *The Complete Works of Algernon Charles Swinburne*, ed. Sir Edmund Gosse and Thomas James Wise (New York: Gabriel Wells, 1926), 5:6–7. William Sharp, for example, felt that this poem had "an obscurity equaling the most obscure passages Rossetti has composed elsewhere," which he opposes to the "serene transparence" of Wordsworth's sonnets (*Dante Gabriel Rossetti: A Record and a Study* [London: Macmillan, 1882], 414). Coventry Patmore also commented, unfavorably, on this quality in Rossetti's work and felt that its effect was to produce *not* "intensity," the term so often used to characterize Rossetti's poetry, but what he called "tensity"—something like an unease with language (which he blamed on the poet's Italian genetic and literary heritage); Patmore considered this the "prevailing fault" of his art. "It is tense without being intense" ("Rossetti as a Poet," *Principle in Art* [London: George Bell and Sons, 1889], 105–6). The best recent discussion I have seen of the fullness of Rossetti's language is by Richardson, in his excellent chapter on Rossetti in *Vanishing Lives*, 99–115.

13. Hollander, *Melodious Guile*, 97. Pater discusses in his influential essay on the school of Giorgione the way each art finds an analogy in another art—and notes that such an analogy is found "between a sonnet and a relief, of French poetry generally with the art of engraving, being more than mere figures of speech" (*The Renaissance*, 85–86).

14. See William E. Fredeman's article, "Rossetti's '*In Memoriam*': An Elegiac Reading of *The House of Life*," *Bulletin of the John Rylands Library* 47 (1965): 298–341.

15. In his valuable article, "Dante Gabriel Rossetti and the Betrayal of Truth" (*Victorian Poetry* 26 [1988]: 339–59), Jerome McGann sees this "repeated unsettling" of the poem's form as a sign of "the overall lack of resolution of the work," with the removal of "Nuptial Sleep" in the final edition a "truly remarkable revelation of his loss of faith in the identity he set out to fashion and represent" (354).

16. Florence Saunders Boos relates the stasis in *The House of Life* to the appearance of images such as tombs, urns, and jewels, and to the poems' effort to emblematize the moment. See *The Poetry of Dante Gabriel Rossetti: A Critical Reading and Source Study* (The Hague: Mouton, 1976), 87.

17. William Davies, "Article VIII," 99 and 108.

18. Quoted by Caine, *Recollections*, 110.

19. See Pater's "The School of Giorgione" essay in *The Renaissance*, esp. 95–96. An important article by Jeffrey R. Prince that meets up with many concerns of this discussion identifies passages like this one in Pater, and particularly the "Conclusion" in *The Renaissance*, as "important document[s] in the history of nineteenth-century poetics" because they analyse the common effort by poets and painters alike to capture and invest with significance each moment, "a single moment, gone while we try to apprehend it." There too he refers to those artistic efforts as "relics." See "D. G. Rossetti and the Pre-Raphaelite Conception of the Special Moment," *Modern Language Quarterly* 37 (1976): 349–69.

20. *Letters*, 2:727.

21. Hunt, "A Moment's Monument: Reflection of Pre-Raphaelite Vision in Poetry and Painting," in *Pre-Raphaelitism: A Collection of Critical Essays*, ed. James Sambrook (Chicago: University of Chicago Press, 1974): 257–58. Also see Robert Cooper, *Lost on Both Sides* (Athens: Ohio University Press, 1970); Barbara Charlesworth, *Dark Passages: The Decadent Consciousness in Victorian Literature* (Madison: University of Wisconsin Press, 1965), 6–8, and, especially, David G. Riede, *Dante Gabriel Rossetti and the Limits of Victorian Vision* (Ithaca: Cornell University Press, 1983). Riede is characteristic in describing the "quintessential Rossettian moment" as "the moment of internal reflection when all the pictures of the past are summoned to the aid of the present, the epiphanic moment when the chaos of experience becomes orderly and meaningful" (155).

22. Sharp, *Dante Gabriel Rossetti*, 417.

23. Ross, *Contours of Masculine Desire*, 176.

24. Paul Fry has suggested to me that the hourglass may well be also be a *spatial* figure for the sonnet itself, a notion that is strengthened by Rossetti's use of the emblem in the illustration of the sonnet on the sonnet that he sent to his mother (see note 5 of this chapter).

25. See Christ's *Finer Optic: The Aesthetic of Particularity in Victorian Poetry* (New Haven: Yale University Press, 1975) and Richardson's *Vanishing Lives*. This argument is anticipated by Prince: "In general, moments of intense love in his poetry concern some such release from discontinuous, isolated consciousness into the consciousness of another. . . . This dissolution of self-consciousness, this absorption of consciousness by another, obliterates awareness of rational categories like time and place" (357).

26. See Riede, who traces such related tropes as reflective surfaces, in mirrors and the lover's eye, figures of the double, borders, and images of repletion, all of which, he argues, point toward a "diminished place in the Romantic tradition" (*Limits of Vision*, 149). Richardson steps a little further into the texture of the poetry itself and explores the claustrophobia of even Rossetti's poetic style and diction.

27. The connection with Keats may well be reinforced by the presence of such Keatsian images in Rossetti as the seashore and the horizon, both of which pervade *The House of Life*. For a discussion of Keats's influence on Rossetti, see chapter 9 of George Ford's *Keats and the Victorians: A Study of his Influence and Rise to Fame, 1821–1895* (New Haven: Yale University Press, 1944), 121–45. On Rossetti's loss of faith in the visionary, see Riede, *Limits of Vision*, 53; for a more specific discussion of the relationship between Keats and Rossetti with respect to this loss of faith, see Jeffrey Prince. Also see Stephen J. Spector, "Love, Unity, and Desire in the Poetry of Dante Gabriel Rossetti," *ELH* 38 (1971), who writes of the "tautological sterility" in Rossetti's poetry (432).

28. This is also true of the contemporary sequence by George Meredith, *Modern Love*. Meredith's resistance to closure differs from Keats's in that it offers sequentiality in a way that Keats's does not—yet there *is* something ultimately Keatsian about the poem's tracking of imaginative failure and its formal resistance to that ending. Meredith's innovation of a sixteen-line sonnet highlights this resistance: the last four lines of Meredith's expanded sonnet form are essentially a new quatrain (the rhyme scheme is *abbacddceffeghhg*), allowing sudden shifts or openings-up of tonality or thought that shift the momentum of the sonnet toward the *next* poem. The absence of a concluding couplet or set of tercets pushes us forward, resisting conclusion, while images relentlessly foreshadow the final agent of death.

The trope of limitation that I have been highlighting in this study is perfectly evident in this sequence—particularly since not only the stanza form but also the very conventions of the Renaissance sequence are themselves major constraints. Tropes of limitation within the sequence, then, include not only the various images of entrapment—the "snare" (sonnet 50) and "mesh" (sonnet 47), for example—but also the poem's very organization *as* a sequence. "Passions spin the plot" (sonnet 43, line 15), the poet writes, stressing the narrative aspect of this sequence, in which the husband and wife "weave / The fatal web" (sonnet 26, lines 3–4) as if they themselves were their own Fates. Language itself, one must recall, is the material from which those webs and snares are made.

The most appropriate image of space in this sequence, then, is that "marriage-tomb" of sonnet 1, a fitting figure for the claustrophobic construction of the "buried day" that makes up the hours this speaker records. This image also reminds one of the poem's most radical revisions; that is, of the Petrarchan linkage of love and death. The whole sequence can be described as a "marriage-tomb," a memorial constructed to Love's fatality. (Text quoted from *The Poems of George Meredith*, ed. Phyllis B. Bartlett, 2 vols. [New Haven: Yale University Press, 1978].)

29. McGann's reading of this poem appropriately describes the sonnet as "the definitive representation of identity-loss in the sequence. The sonnet operates through the simple contradiction of first- and third-person pronouns, both of which are 'identified with' the poet. . . . Here they emerge as the obverse and reverse of a single self-conflicted figure, the schizoid form of a disintegrated identity which has lost itself in a house of mirrors" ("Betrayal of Truth," 353). This analysis of the movement of "He and I" ties in with the "obverse-reverse" figure of the sonnet-coin in Rossetti's introductory sonnet.

30. Trench, "The History of the English Sonnet," xxiv. On his trip to the continent

with Hunt in Autumn 1849, Rossetti even wrote a narrative series of poems in mixed genres, including sonnets, called "A Trip to Paris and Belgium," probably modeled to a degree on Wordsworth's 1820 *Tour of the Continent*. The term "sonnet sequence," interestingly, seems to have been reintroduced into usage by Rossetti himself. While the term had appeared, infrequently, in the Renaissance (Gascoigne, for example, employed it), the nineteenth century tended to refer to sonnet sequences as "series," which was indeed the term Rossetti himself used in letters to describe his poem. But in 1880, Rossetti wrote a letter to Caine, announcing that

I have thought of a title for your book. What think you of this?

A SONNET SEQUENCE
FROM ELDER TO MODERN WORK, WITH FIFTY HITHERTO
UNPRINTED SONNETS BY LIVING WRITERS

That would not be amiss. Tell me if you think of using the title *A Sonnet Sequence*, as otherwise I might use it in *The House of Life*." (Caine, *Recollections*, 244)

Caine rejected it. But when, in 1881, Rossetti more than doubled the length of the fifty-sonnet 1870 edition of the poem entitled *Songs and Sonnets Toward a Work to be called "The House of Life,"* he also revised its title to read *The House of Life: A Sonnet-Sequence.* The term "sequence" seems to have come into much more common usage thereafter. On this matter, see Going, *Scanty Plot of Ground*, 34. Also relevant for historical background is S. K. Heninger, Jr., "Sequences, Systems, Models: Sidney and the Secularization of Sonnets," in Neil Fraistat's *Poems in Their Place: The Intertextuality and Order of Poetic Collections* (Chapel Hill: University of North Carolina Press, 1986), 66–94.

For various comments on *The House of Life*'s sequentiality, see: Sharp, *Dante Gabriel Rossetti: A Record and a Study*, 409; Günther Jarfe, *Kunstform und Verzweiflung. Studien zur Typologie der Sonettgestalt in Dante Gabriel Rossettis The House of Life* (Frankfurt am Main: Peter Lang, 1976); Riede, *Limits of Vision*, 194; Lionel Stevenson, *The Pre-Raphaelite Poets* (New York: Norton, 1972), 68–70; Douglas J. Robillard, "Rossetti's 'Willowwood' Sonnets and the Structure of *The House of Life*," *Victorian Newsletter* 21 (1962): 5–9.

31. McGowan, *Representation and Revelation: Victorian Realism from Carlyle to Yeats* (Columbia: University of Missouri Press, 1986), 43.

32. Christ, *Finer Optic*, 110. Also see Chai, *Aestheticism*, 10-13, and Prince, who discusses how "memory has for [Rossetti] . . . all the force of immediate sensation" ("The Special Moment," 366). Relevant as well is E. Warwick Slinn's "Consciousness as Writing: Deconstruction and Reading Victorian Poetry," *Victorian Poetry* 25 (1987). Slinn discusses the "condition of consciousness" (and, by extension, one could say, "of art") that "exists [in Victorian poetry generally] through differentiation; consciousness is brought into being through the separation of the self as subject from the other as object so that while consciousness remains such desires can never be fulfilled. He may touch the beloved, kiss her cheek, but inevitably the 'good minute' is lost—temporizing intrudes. . . . To utter the image which represents thought is to gain it and lose it in the same instant. Thus, when consciousness and desire are constituted in language, when they become part of the attempt to pursue meaning, they are alike in their submission to a temporality which allows no fixed moment, no teleological fulfillment" (77).

33. Fredeman, "Rossetti's 'In Memoriam,'" 298–341. Rossetti would have had mod-

els for this, he argues, namely his sister's *Monna Innominata: A Sonnet of Sonnets* (though its 1881 publication date makes this an unlikely claim) and also her *Later Life*, which she called a "Double Sonnet of Sonnets." Dante Gabriel's scheme differs from Christina's, he adds, "in that it abandons the precision of numbers and substitutes in its place the external form of the Italian sonnet" (309). Also see Brian and Judy Dobbs, *Dante Gabriel Rossetti: An Alien Victorian* (London: MacDonald and Jane's, 1977): "Rossetti saw *The House of Life* as one vast sonnet constructed from the many component parts" (221). William Michael Rossetti's take on this matter is recorded in his *Dante Gabriel Rossetti as Designer and Writer*: "but he certainly never professed, nor do I consider that he ever wished his readers to assume, that all the items had been primarily planned to form one connected and indivisible whole. The first part of the series, named *Love and Change*, has clearly some considerable amount of interdependence; the second part, *Change and Fate*, is wider and more diversified in its range, but it may reasonably be maintained that (to put the question at its lowest) the several sonnets gain rather than lose in weight of thought and in artistic balance by being thus associated" (182).

34. Fredeman, "Rossetti's 'In Memoriam,'" 309–10.

35. For more on this and its relation to the poetry of Keats, see Prince, "The Special Moment," 359–60.

36. Joan Rees supports this reading: "Part one and part two [of the sequence] then stand in relation to each other as the two parts of individual sonnets do: part one representing the flow of feeling in the emotional life during youth and middle-age and part two, with its commentary on life and art and its annotation of part one, representing the ebb which follows as comment and reflection replace the urgent responses to love which part one affords" (*The Poetry of Dante Gabriel Rossetti: Modes of Expression* [Cambridge: Cambridge University Press, 1981], 164). Clearly relevant here is Langbaum's "doctrine of experience," from his *Poetry of Experience*.

37. Riede, *Limits of Vision*, 194. For a similar reading, see McGowan: "Rossetti's celebration of the intense moment must be understood within the basic pattern of his striving in all his poetry to connect particulars to more general significances. After the moment is isolated, the poet always works to reincorporate that moment into the general continuity of time. The momentary, almost mystical, flash of 'instantaneous penetrating sense' in Rossetti's poetry acts, along with love (and, as we shall see shortly, death), as the means by which the self penetrates otherness. . . . Moments of revelation illuminate the true meaning of things in the world, and art can record these momentary insights" (*Representation and Revelation*, 43).

38. Other *House of Life* sonnets with the stream image include: "The Lover's Walk" (sonnet 12), "Severed Selves" (sonnet 40), "Through Death to Love" (sonnet 41), "Hoarded Joy" (sonnet 82), "Farewell to the Glen" (sonnet 84) and "The One Hope" (sonnet 101).

39. Boos, *Poetry of Dante Gabriel Rossetti*, 87.

40. Ibid., 86.

41. See Christ's discussion of these personifications, which she sees as one mark of the poem's effort to "[escape] particularity by transforming experience into artistic convention" (*Finer Optic*, 111). Other sonnets that figure "processional time" include "Beauty's Pageant" (sonnet 17), "Parted Love" (sonnet 46), "Death-in-Love" (sonnet 48), "Willowwood II" (sonnet 50), "The Heart of the Night" (sonnet 65), "Lost Days" (sonnet 86), and "Inclusiveness" (sonnet 63).

42. I have been arguing generally that Rossetti's work continues the Wordsworthian figuration of time as space. It is not difficult to understand why critics are tempted to discuss

The House of Life in terms of spatial tropes: the title itself invites it. William Rossetti took the "house" of the title to refer to an astrological house, but Swinburne took it otherwise, as an architectural metaphor, which he extended by referring to the individual sonnets as "chambers." Later, Paull Franklin Baum described the sonnets as "cramped for room, as if [Rossetti] had planned a large poem in which various divisions and subdivisions would have their proper place and space, then had gradually compressed the material until the original outlines became confused, ideas being forced together that were meant to stand apart. And finally, after he reduced it all to the hundred and fifty words or so of a sonnet, it is necessary for us to expand the poem to its former dimensions before we can understand it" (Introduction to *The House of Life: A Sonnet-Sequence* [Cambridge: Harvard University Press, 1928], 8). James Richardson has pointed out that Wendell Harris's evaluation of the poems as too large and inflated is contradictory and apparently irreconcilable to Baum's view—but understandably so: "both [views] respond to *pressure* within the poems, one calling it centripetal, the other centrifugal" (*Vanishing Lives*, 106). This is well put, and reminds one again of the romantic tension between intensity and expansiveness that I looked at earlier.

43. Going, *Scanty Plot of Ground*, 22. According to William Michael Rossetti, the matter of coherence was from the very beginning a matter of criticism: "Besides the charge of obscurity, an objection which I have sometimes heard raised against *The House of Life* is its want of absolute cohesion; the series, it is averred, does not form one consecutive poem, but only so many sonnets of sufficiently diverse subject-matter, grouped together. Now this is abundantly true as a fact: whether it forms a solid objection either to the sonnets regarded as a series, or to the act of the author in thus combining them, is a question which readers will have to decide for themselves" (*Dante Gabriel Rossetti as Designer and Writer*, 181).

44. W. M. Rossetti, introduction to *The Germ* (facsimile rpt., London: Elliot Stock, 1901), 18.

45. For a recent discussion of this general Victorian dilemma, see McGowan: "[Rossetti's] struggles also indicate the predicament of the Victorian poets, who found that the resources of romantic poetry no longer served their needs. The result is a poetry (which includes some excellent poems) constructed out of a recognition of its own failure, a poetry that continually undermines its own validity in face of the reality it has failed to express. Despite all his efforts, reality keeps its meanings hidden from Rossetti" (*Representation and Revelation*, 25–26).

46. This path image pervades the sonnets following this one (see "A Dark Day," "The Hill Summit," "The Monochord," "From Dawn to Noon"), as the poem begins to lead itself more self-consciously out of the insular bowers of part 1.

47. Letter to Caine, quoted in *Recollections*, 249.

48. Baum, "Introduction," 225.

49. Pater, *The Renaissance*, 85. Rossetti resisted any easy analogies between poetry and painting, especially tempting given his involvement in both media: "I should particularly hope it might be thought (if so it be) that my poems are in no way the result of painters' tendencies—and indeed I believe no poetry could be freer than mine from the trick of what is called 'word painting'. As with recreated forms in painting, so I should wish to deal in poetry chiefly with personified emotions; and in carrying out my scheme of the '*House of Life*' (if ever I do so) shall try to put in action a complete *dramatis personae* of the soul" (*Letters*, 2:850).

50. Agosta, "Animate Images: The Later Poem-Paintings of Dante Gabriel Rossetti," *Texas Studies in Literature and Language* 23 (1981): 90–91, 94.

51. Hunt, "A Moment's Monument," 244, 252–53.

52. Ibid., 257.

53. Wendell Stacy Johnson, "D. G. Rossetti as Painter and Poet," in *Pre-Raphaelitism: A Collection of Critical Essays,* ed. James Sambrook (Chicago: University of Chicago Press, 1974), 225–26.

54. Chai discusses poems like these as well as *The House of Life* in the prelude to *Aestheticism,* 10–13, and links them to broader aestheticist strategies against the conflict of time and experience in art.

55. *Letters,* 1:71.

56. Johnson suggests if there is "some element of limited time" expressed in the painting, Rossetti accounted for it visually: "it [the limited time] is communicated by the limited space, the lack of depth in the scene. The flattening of images, a virtual denial of distance in heaven, may well work because of our association of time with space to flatten and to deny the absolute relevance of historical depth and movement to a central figure, for all its own movement" ("D. G. Rossetti as Painter and Poet," 226).

57. This matter of ekphrastic poems concerning prophecy may be related to John Hollander's suggestion that "Ekphrastic poems are also, inevitably, transumptive of prior texts, as their object-images necessarily allude to and engage prior images" ("The Gazer's Spirit: Romantic and Later Poetry on Painting and Sculpture," in *The Romantics and Us,* ed. Gene Ruoff [New Brunswick, N.J: Rutgers University Press, 1990], 130).

58. *Speech and Phenomena and Other Essays in Husserl's Theory of Signs,* trans. David B. Allison (Evanston, Ill.: Northwestern University Press, 1975), 64–65.

59. Riede, *Limits of Vision,* 55.

60. Quoted in ibid., 201–2.

61. This conclusion dovetails with John McGowan's argument that "[Rossetti's] struggles also indicate the predicament of the Victorian poets, who found that the resources of romantic poetry no longer served their needs. The result is a poetry (which includes some excellent poems) constructed out of a recognition of its own failure, a poetry that continually undermines its own validity in the face of the reality it has failed to express. Despite all his efforts, reality keeps its meanings hidden from Rossetti" (*Representation and Revelation,* 25–26). Also see Günther Jarfe, who argues against calling Rossetti a romantic, or even an aesthete, because he had little faith in the power of art (*Kunstform und Verzweiflung,* 125).

Chapter 6. "Charged with the Grandeur of God": The Allegory of Form in the Sonnets of Gerard Manley Hopkins

1. In her *Contemplative Poetry of Gerard Manley Hopkins* (Princeton: Princeton University Press, 1989), Maria Lichtmann anticipates my own argument about "allegory in form" in her assertion that Hopkins's parallelism in *form* "mimics . . . what it suggests in meaning" (16)—and that that parallelism "exemplifies the incarnational ideal of matter as spirit" (5). My own analysis focuses more specifically than hers on "diminishing" as the way toward this "allegory in form," and on Hopkins's relationship to the sonnet genre generally, but our conclusions are similar. See especially her chapters 1 and 3 (pp. 7–60; 100–128).

2. It is likely that the "learned book or two learned books" to which Hopkins refers are Caine's 1881 anthology, which excluded the poet's sonnets, Samuel Waddington's

selection of sonnets by "Living Writers," also appearing in 1881, and David M. Main's *Treasury* of the previous year.

    3. *The Letters of Gerard Manley Hopkins to Robert Bridges,* ed. Claude Colleer Abbott (London: Oxford University Press, 1935), 44. In the same letter he explains himself further: "so that I may say my apparent licences are counterbalanced, and more, by my strictness. In fact all English verse, except Milton's, almost offends me as 'licentious'. Remember this" (45). In a letter to Alexander W. M. Baillie (6 September 1863), Hopkins remarks that a "perfect critic is very rare. . . . The most inveterate fault of critics is the tendency to cramp and hedge in by rules the free movements of genius, so that I should say, according to the Demosthenic and Catonic expression the first requisite for a critic is liberality" (*Further Letters of Gerard Manley Hopkins*, ed. Humphry House, completed by Graham Storey [London: Oxford University Press, 1938], 57). Hopkins rarely released any poems for publication—and when he did, found virtually no critic that met his first prerequisite. Indeed, Hopkins realistically remained skeptical that even his most conventional poems would see the light of day ("He is not going to print me . . .") when communication with Caine revealed that, according to Hopkins,

> the purpose of [Caine's] book (or introduction or prefatory essay to it) is to 'demonstrate the impossibility of improving upon the acknowledged structure whether as to rhyme-scheme or measure.' Poor soul, he writes to me as to a she-bear robbed of her cubs. I am replying now and reassuring him and smoothing down. To support himself he shewed some of my sonnets he had (I sent him three and the Canon [Dixon] two) to 'a critic of utmost eminence'; who thought with him. Who will that be, I wonder? (*Letters,* 128)

It is generally assumed the critic was D. G. Rossetti; yet Rossetti's comments on "sonnet legislation" include these remarks to Hall Caine: "Sonnets of mine *could not appear* in any book which contained such rigid rules as to rhyme, as are contained in Watts's [Watts-Dunton's] letter. I neither follow them, nor agree with them as regards the English language. Every sonnet-writer should show full capability of conforming to them in *many* instances, but never to deviate from them in English must pinion both thought and diction, and, (mastery once proved) a series gains rather than loses by such varieties as do not lessen the only absolute aim—that of beauty. The English sonnet *too much* tampered with becomes a sort of bastard madrigal. *Too much, invariably* restricted, it degenerates into a Shibboleth" (Caine, *Recollections of Dante Gabriel Rossetti* [London: Elliot Stock, 1882], 247–48).

    4. After Hopkins's death, Bridges held on to the manuscripts he had and continued to gather others; he edited the poems for publication in 1918. Only then did he regard the public as "ready" for Hopkins's work.

    5. This is an opinion shared by the editor of Hopkins's letters to Bridges, Claude Colleer Abbott: "Instead, therefore, of what might have been a freeing or loosening of bonds, we have a tightening and concentration, a more rigorous art. Hopkins abhorred facility . . . the fascination of what is difficult and yet more difficult sometimes involved him in a struggle for technical conquest to the detriment of poetry" (*Letters,* xxii). Abbott also saw no justification for Hopkins's system of rhythm and his excessive use of devices. Hopkins himself acknowledged, reluctantly, the charge of obscurity. He was both amused and mortified by learning that Dixon and Bridges required a "crib" for reading "Tom's Garland." Much earlier, he had written to Bridges that "Obscurity I do and will try to avoid so far as is consistent with excellences higher than clearness at a first reading" (*Letters,* 54); now, he

ambivalently acknowledges his obscurity: "It is plain I must go no farther on this road: if you and he cannot understand me who will? . . . Yet, declaimed, the strange constructions would be dramatic and effective. Must I interpret it?" (*Letters*, 272–73).

    6. *Further Letters* (London: Oxford University Press, 1938), 204.

    7. Ibid., 205. In his next letter Patmore reiterates his apology, but adds that "*how* such modes [of composition that Hopkins has described] . . . as for example your alliterations, come to be the spontaneous expression of your poetical feeling, I cannot understand, and I do not think I ever shall" (207).

    8. *Letters*, 90.

    9. Scholars have outlined already the categories of sonnet variations that Hopkins created and have correctly surmised that these experiments are clearly efforts to draw out the poet's perceptions about the properties of the form that he inherited. The most complete examinations of this subject are: W. H. Gardner's *Gerard Manley Hopkins, 1844–1889: A Study of Poetic Idiosyncrasy in Relation to Poetic Tradition*, 2 vol. (New Haven: Yale University Press, 1948); Jean-Georges Ritz's *Le Poète Gerard Manley Hopkins, S. J. ,1844–1889* (Paris: Didier, 1963); Paul Mariani's *Commentary on the Complete Poems of Gerard Manley Hopkins* (Ithaca: Cornell University Press, 1970); Hans-Werner Ludwig's *Barbarous in Beauty: Studien zum Vers in Gerard Manley Hopkins' Sonetten* (München: Wilhelm Fink Verlag, 1972); and Virginia Ridley Ellis's *Gerard Manley Hopkins and the Language of Mystery* (Columbia: University of Missouri Press, 1991).

    10. F. R. Leavis, ed., *Gerard Manley Hopkins by the Kenyon Critics* (Norfolk, Conn.: New Directions Books, 1945), 119-20.

    11. *Letters*, xxxviii n. 3.

    12. *Letters*, 66. In a letter written about two months later, Hopkins returned to this subject, admitting that "[e]verybody cannot be expected to like my pieces." He urged Bridges, however, to "read it with the ears, as I always wish to be read, and my verse becomes all right" (79).

    13. To Coventry Patmore, 6 October 1886 (*Further Letters*, 222).

    14. Mariani, *Commentary on Complete Poems*, 321.

    15. On the relationship of Hopkins to Pater, see: chap. 2 in John Robinson's *In Extremity: A Study of Gerard Manley Hopkins* (Cambridge: Cambridge University Press, 1978); and chap. 2 ("Epistemology and Perception: Gerard Manley Hopkins") in Hilary Fraser's *Beauty and Belief: Aesthetics and Religion in Victorian Literature* (Cambridge and New York: Cambridge University Press, 1986).

    16. *The Note-books and Papers of Gerard Manley Hopkins*, ed. Humphry House (London: Oxford University Press, 1937), 74. The concept of "parallelism" expounded in this essay includes two types of comparison: the first is "comparison for likeness' sake, to which belong metaphor, simile, and things of that kind," and the second "comparison for unlikeness' sake, to which belong antithesis, contrast, and so on." Parallelism at all these levels distinguishes poetry from prose.

    17. Ibid., 75. See the discussion of the broader principle of rhyme in J. Hillis Miller's *Disappearance of God: Five Nineteenth-Century Writers* (New York: Schocken Books, 1963), 277. Working off Miller's analysis, Michael Sprinker provides a useful analysis of Hopkins's aesthetics in *"A Counterpoint of Dissonance": The Aesthetics and Poetry of Gerard Manley Hopkins* (Baltimore: Johns Hopkins University Press, 1980). Sprinker explores Hopkins's notion of form as "produced by the recurrence of difference," and argues that Hopkins's notion of form is "decentered or eccentric." He adds that the poet's theories of beauty and poetry foreshadow "certain of the more important strains in contemporary poetics,"

including some aspects of the work of the Russian Formalists, William Empson, Kenneth Burke, and even deconstructive theories. See especially his pages 20–46.

18. *Note-books*, 83–84.

19. Ibid., 85. Hopkins's understanding of the thought and expression as indistinguishable ("the idea rose in the forms of expression which we read in the poem in his mind") is an insight that seems to anticipate his notions of inscape and instress.

20. Ibid., 68.

21. Ibid., 70–71.

22. Letter 19 to Dixon (12 October 1881), *The Correspondence of Gerard Manley Hopkins and Richard Watson Dixon*, ed. Claude Colleer Abbott (London: Oxford University Press, 1935), 71–72. See Jean-Georges Ritz's discussion of Hopkins's preference of "le sonnet à deux strophes" to "le sonnet 'miltonien' à strophe unique. . . . il traduit le mieux la structure de sa pensée qui procéde le plus souvent par opposition ou parallelisme, ou qui passe de l'image à la leçon, de la description à la reflexion, de l'emotion à la priere" (*Le Poète*, 477).

23. All quotations of Hopkins's poetry are from *The Poems of Gerard Manley Hopkins*, eds. W. H. Gardner and N. H. Mackenzie (New York: Oxford University Press, 1967).

24. In a letter to Bridges (26 Nov 1882) Hopkins writes of the lark's song:

"Rash-fresh more" (it is dreadful to explain these things in cold blood) means a headlong and exciting new snatch of singing, resumption by the lark of his song, which by turns he gives over and takes up again all day long, and this goes on, the sonnet says, through all time, without ever losing its first freshness, being a thing both new and old. *Repair* means the same thing, *renewal, resumption*. The skein and coil are the lark's song, which from his height gives the impression (not to me only) of something falling to the earth and not vertically quite but tricklingly or wavingly, something as a skein of silk ribbed by having been tightly wound on a narrow card or a notched holder or as fishingtackle or twine unwinding from a reel or winch* [H's note: *or as pearls strong on a horsehair.]: the laps or folds are the notes or short measures and bars of them. The same is called a score in the musical sense of score and this score is "writ upon a liquid sky trembling to welcome it," only not horizontally. The lark in wild glee races the reel round, paying our dealing out and down the turns of the skein or coil right to the earth floor, the ground, where it lies in a heap, as it were, or rather is all wound off on to another winch, reel, bobbin, or spool in Fancy's eye by the moment the bird touches earth and so is ready for a fresh unwinding at the next light. (*Letters*, 163–64)

25. See Hopkins's notes on Parmenides: "Men, he thought, had sprung from slime" (*Note-books*, 102). Hopkins's awareness of Darwinianism may be behind this as well.

26. But see Marylou Motto's *"Mined with a Motion": The Poetry of Gerard Manley Hopkins* (New Brunswick, N.J.: Rutgers University Press, 1984), where she enumerates the radical differences between the romantic attitude toward imagination and poetry, and Hopkins's. The major difference lies, she argues, in Hopkins's acceptance of Catholicism and the subservence of self that faith requires. Motto acknowledges that Wordsworth was crucial to Hopkins: "it may well be that the intervention of the Romantics allows Hopkins' voice to occur" (10). And of course many would argue, as I would as well, that a great deal of the tension in Hopkins's poetry and in his attitude toward that poetry may result in resis-

tance to the subservience that his religious beliefs, he thought, required of him (see his letters to Dixon).

27. Mariani supposes that he means "the clogged consonantal tongue-twisting of some of the lines" (*Commentary*, 104).

28. *Letters*, 163–64.

29. Miller would see this moment as an example of what he describes as the "tragic limitation of poetic language" in Hopkins, that "the Word itself cannot be said. . . . The words of human language, for Hopkins, seem to have been born of some primal division, a fall from the arch and original breath into the articulate. This fall has always already occurred as soon as there is any human speech" (*Linguistic Moment*, 260).

30. For commentary on the spiritual dryness and psychic breakdown expressed in "To R. B." and the terrible sonnets, see Austin Warren, "Gerard Manley Hopkins (1844-1889)," in Leavis, *Kenyon Critics*, 12. For a book-length study of the "terrible sonnets," with particular emphasis upon how style, structure, and imagery underpin the religious aspects of the poems, see Daniel A. Harris's *Inspiration Unbidden: The "Terrible Sonnets" of Gerard Manley Hopkins* (Berkeley and Los Angeles: University of California Press, 1982).

31. In such moods, Hopkins regards the sonnet in a less favorable light, as not enough to show for himself: "It is now years that I have had no inspiration of longer jet than makes a sonnet, except only in that fortnight in Wales: it is what, far more than the direct want of time, I find most against poetry and production in the life I lead. Unhappily I cannot produce anything at all, not only the luxuries like poetry, but the duties almost of my position" (*Letters*, 270).

32. See "Hopkins Revisited," in *Beyond Formalism* (New Haven: Yale University Press, 1970) where Hartman discusses this "downing motion" in the second part of "Hurrahing in Harvest"—"I walk, I lift up, I lift up heart, eyes, / Down all that glory in the heavens to glean our Saviour"—as an imitation, even in the religious sense of *imitatio*, of Christ: "*Imitatio*, religious participation, is in fact the burden of the poem. Hopkins enters the scene he evokes, the nun enters by anticipation into glory, all things are said to go to Christ" (236).

33. *Further Letters*, 19.

34. On "surprise" as a deliberate effect in Hopkins's poetics, see Lichtmann, *Contemplative Poetry*, 29.

35. *"A Counterpoint of Dissonance,"* 14. The full reading of "The Windhover" runs from pages 13–15.

36. This term comes from a fascinating passage in Hopkins's "Comments on the Spiritual Exercises of St. Ignatius Loyola." Hopkins is speaking of the self as being not only a "mere centre" but also "everything else, all that it is conscious of or acts on. . . . A self then will consist of a centre *and* a surrounding area or circumference, of a point of reference *and* a belonging field, the latter set out, as surveyors etc say, from the former. . . . Now this applies to the universal mind or being too; it will have its inset and its outsetting; only that the outsetting includes all things, with all of which it is in some way, by turns, in a series, or however it is, identified. . . . And since self consists in the relation that the inset and the outsetting bear to one another, the universal has a relation different from everything else and everything else from everything else, including the universal, so that the self of the universal is not the self of anything else" (*Note-books*, 314–16). For a recent discussion of Hopkins's view of the self and its relation to God, see Walter J. Ong's *Hopkins, the Self, and God* (Toronto: University of Toronto Press, 1986).

37. The expansive movement in this and other Hopkins poems is called a "gesture of assent" by Marylou Motto. Taking the term from Cardinal Newman's 1870 tract, called *Grammar of Assent*, Motto discusses how "the poem in Hopkins answers experience with the response of assent" (14), based upon his religious faith. The gesture of assent is the poet's celebration of the revealed world. Of this poem, Motto remarks that "[f]ormlessness, obscurity, the heart still and quiet in its enclosure, all become distinct in the motion to escape that enclosure, to move out toward the world in gesture" (17). She notes too that the "breaking open" of the heart is a "signal event" in much of Hopkins's poetry, for it "is the poet's figure for the salvation of man" (20). For a full discussion of the two "motions," assent and recurrence, that Motto regards as characteristic of Hopkins's poetry, see chapter 1 of her book.

38. In his excellent reading of this poem, Herbert Marshall McLuhan also notes, before Hartman, the "downward movement" of the poem, and he too links it to the sestet: "the ecstatic hyperboles of the octet are yet rendered trite by the merely homely images of the sestet. Moreover, while the sestet is in a lower key, befitting the change to the theme of humble obedience, it is more intense, fuller of compressed implication" (Leavis, *Kenyon Critics*, 22). Also see William Empson's discussion of the sestet and its conveyance of the conflict between "different systems of judgments" (*Seven Types of Ambiguity* [Norfolk, Conn.: New Directions, 1953], 225–26).

39. *"A Counterpoint of Dissonance,"* 14.

40. See Gardner's discussion of fire and light imagery as "symbols of the divine vital principle in all creatures, as their vital activity and their ultimate spiritual goal. Fire indicates the vital activity of God in the lightning of His purgative and salvific Will, or in the Pentecostal flame of His grace and inspiration" (*Gerard Manley Hopkins*, 154–55).

41. The allusion to 2 Cor. 11:14 supports Hopkins's attribution of this trope to God's glory: "And no wonder: for Satan himself transformeth himself into an angel of light" (Douay version). The false prophets, like Satan himself, invest themselves with the evidence of God's glory, a paradoxical recognition of that glory even as they reject him.

42. See chapter 2 of *"Mined with a Motion."*

43. Ibid., 49–50.

44. Culler, *Structuralist Poetics: Structuralism, Linguistics and the Study of Literature* (Ithaca: Cornell University Press, 1975), 175.

45. Quoted by Graham Storey, in *A Preface to Hopkins* (London: Longman Group, 1981), 115.

46. Ibid.

47. Gardner, *Gerard Manley Hopkins*, 100.

48. Miller, *The Disappearance of God*, 302–3. Also see Lichtmann on this poem as "one large antithesis in little" (*Contemplative Poetry*, 114–18). Her analysis departs from Miller's in its privileging of antithesis rather than unity or resemblance.

49. Motto, *"Mined With A Motion,"* 42.

50. Lichtmann, *Contemplative Poetry*, 116–17.

51. Motto, *"Mined with a Motion,"* 57–58.

52. Hartman notes in "Hopkins Revisited" that the poet's style "is as vocative as possible. This holds for sound, grammar, figures of speech, and actual performance. . . . As in Job, we feel the calling more than the being called—a voice constraining the void" (*Beyond Formalism*, 237).

53. Hardy, "Forms and Feelings in the Sonnets of Gerard Manley Hopkins," in *The Advantage of Lyric: Essays of Feeling in Poetry* (Bloomington: Indiana University Press, 1973), 56.

54. *Letters*, 246. In fact, Hopkins listed ways in which a sonnet could be "lengthened," in his sense of the word. For a summary of these, see Mariani's *Commentary*, 324–28. Also see Hopkins's letter to Dixon, in *Further Letters*, 85.

55. *Letters*, 246 (11 December 1886). In a later letter he reminds Bridges of his yet unanswered request: "a sonnet is hot on the anvil and wants a coda. It is the only time I have felt forced to exceed the beaten bounds" (*Letters*, 263).

56. "You say the subject is treated in many books—that was just it—I had not got those books and the readiest source of information was you. It seems they are formed on an invariable plan and that Milton's sonnet gives an example. Of course one example was enough if there is but one type; but you should have said so" (*Letters*, 264).

57. They include "Henry Purcell," "Felix Randal," "Spelt from Sibyl's Leaves," "Harry Ploughman," "Tom's Garland" and "That Nature is a Heraclitean Fire."

58. Gardner, *Gerard Manley Hopkins*, 106. On the technical aspects of this poem, also see Ritz, *Le Poète*, 498–501, who is useful on Hopkins's use of feminine rhymes, assonance, and consonance. Also see Jacob Korg, "Hopkins' Linguistic Deviations," *PMLA* 92 (October 1977): 984–85. For a still important discussion of Hopkins's "linguistic individuation," which certainly bears on this poem, see Hartman's "Hopkins Revisited," in *Beyond Formalism*, 239–40. Miller appears to pick up Hartman's point in his discussion of the "permutations of vowels and consonants in the series turning a mere 'Jack' into Christ in 'That Nature is a Heraclitean Fire,'" where "the endpoint is not some triumphant uttering of the Word as such" but "only another metaphor, and a metaphor tautologically repeated at that. . . ." (*The Linguistic Moment*, 260).

59. Mariani, *Commentary*, 334. Boyle remarks that in these lines, "the graduated vowels with no full stops, prolonged by their *n*'s, *m*'s, *r*'s, express the growing waves of overwhelming dark and in their openness suggest, like Milton's line, the depth and breadth of the darkness" (*Metaphor in Hopkins* [Chapel Hill: University of North Carolina Press, 1960], 207 n).

60. I thank my friend John Watkins for the suggestion that this poem may have behind it Shelley's "Ode to the West Wind."

61. James Finn Cotter also notes what he calls a "downward path of sight and insight" in this early part of the poem. See "Apocalyptic Imagery in Hopkins' 'That Nature is a Heraclitean Fire and of the comfort of the Resurrection,'" *Victorian Poetry* 24 (1986): 264.

62. See Smith's *Poetic Closure: A Study of How Poems End* (Chicago: University of Chicago Press, 1968), 188.

63. Cotter suggests that this emphatic "Enough" may echo the loud voice calling out "It is finished!" in John's vision ("Apocalyptic Imagery," 267).

64. Hartman offers this useful explanation of the codas of this poem: "Christian doctrine, however, is itself uncertain as to what is carried over from one state to the other. That is probably why the sonnet has two codas: the first suggests a radical discontinuity based on St. Paul's 'We shall be utterly changed,' but this is a hard comfort; the second reminds us that man 'puts on' Christ by means of purification rather than by utter change" (*Beyond Formalism*, 242). On the imagery of light in this poem, and for other readings of Hopkins sonnets, see Wendell Stacy Johnson's *Gerard Manley Hopkins: The Poet as Victorian* (Ithaca: Cornell University Press, 1968).

65. For a more general description of precisely this process, see Miller, *Linguistic Moment*, 264–65.

66. Cotter also notes this rhyme and suggests a connection not only with the "I AM" of the Scriptures but also, in the predominance of *o*'s and *a*'s in the final lines, an echo of

Christ's "I am Alpha and Omega" ("Apocalyptic Imagery," 272–73). Lichtmann identifies the diamond as an image that "resonates throughout mystical literature . . . Hopkins' 'immortal diamond' therefore represents the breakthrough to the insight that all nature's million-fueled bonfire, along with his own pain and suffering, takes place within God" (*Contemplative Poetry*, 212).

67. Valéry, *The Art of Poetry*, 11.

68. See the introduction to the second edition of Hopkins's sonnets, where Charles Williams writes that this poet, like Milton, had "the simultaneous consciousness of a controlled universe, and yet of division, conflict, and crises within that universe" (*Poems of Gerard Manley Hopkins* [London: Oxford University Press, 1930], xiv).

69. Gardner, *Gerard Manley Hopkins*, 30.

70. Austin Warren surmised that "Hopkins's constant tension, the desire to be an artist and the desire to be a saint, was necessary to his achievement as a poet. Had he written with the facility and fecundity of most Victorians (his friends included) he might have been as undistinguished. . . . The inhibitions came; and consequently the small body of Hopkins' work, like that of Eliot, offers a series of poetic stances, every important poem constituting a new mode" ("Gerard Manley Hopkins [1844–1889]," in Leavis, *Kenyon Critics*, 14).

71. Notes to Bridges's 1918 edition of Hopkins's poetry, *Poems of Gerard Manley Hopkins* (London: Oxford University Press, 1918), 99.

72. Fairley, *London Mercury* 32, no. 188 (June 1935): 131.

Conclusion. "What to Make of a Diminished Thing": Speculation and Survival in Robert Frost's Sonnets

1. Price, *The Laws of Ice* (New York: Atheneum, 1986), 35.

2. *Robert Frost on Writing,* ed. Elaine Barry (New Brunswick, N.J.: Rutgers University Press, 1973), 73–76.

3. For a full study of this, see Mario D'Avanzo's *Cloud of Other Poets: Robert Frost and the Romantics* (Lanham, Md.: University Press of America, 1991). Also see: Sydney Lea, "From Sublime to Rigamarole: Relations of Frost to Wordsworth," *Studies in Romanticism* 19 (Spring 1980): 83–108; and Reuben Brower: "For a young American poet of the 1890's the noble Wordsworthian voice and the vision it asserted were almost inescapable: one sign of Frost's strength is that though he understands this voice so well he did not succumb to it. . . . It could be said . . . that Frost found his own form and vision in the skeptical and 'pragmatic' Emerson" (*The Poetry of Robert Frost: Constellations of Intention* [New York: Oxford University Press, 1963], 41–42).

4. This may be an example of what Frank Lentricchia calls Frost's "ironic consciousness" in his important book, *Robert Frost: Modern Poetics and the Landscapes of Self* (Durham, N.C.: Duke University Press, 1975), 25. Also see Johannes Kjorven, *Robert Frost's Emergent Design: The Truth of the Self Inbetween Belief and Unbelief* (Oslo: Solum Forlag; Atlantic Highlands, N.J.: Humanities Press International, 1987).

5. "The Constant Symbol," in *Selected Prose of Robert Frost,* ed. Cox and Lathem (New York: Collier Books, 1968), 27.

6. Ibid., 107.

7. Quoted in Barry, *Robert Frost on Writing*, 22. See also Frost's "Education by Poetry," where he speaks again in terms of threat and safety: "unless you have had your proper

poetical education in metaphor, you are not safe anywhere. . . . You are not safe in science; you are not safe in history" (Frost, *Selected Prose*, 39).

8. To John T. Bartlett, Frost writes: "To be perfectly frank with you I am one of the most notable craftsmen of my time" (Frost, *Selected Letters*, ed. Lawrance Thompson [New York: Holt, Rinehart and Winston, 1964, 79]).

9. Lentricchia, *Robert Frost*, 24–25. This book is in fact organized around the several dominant tropes of enclosure and openness that Lentricchia locates throughout Frost's work. Also see Richard Poirier's distinguished book on Frost, *Robert Frost: The Work of Knowing*, republished in 1990 by Stanford University Press; especially relevant here is chapter 3, "Outward Bound" (87–172). Michael Cooke's article called "Frost's Poetry: Breaking the Boundaries of the Hidden and Silent" (*The Kentucky Review* 5 [1985]: 46–59) also discusses the tropes of space and time, and the Frostian phenomenon of "getting lost."

10. From an article in the student newspaper *Silver and Gold*, University of Colorado; quoted by Stanley Burnshaw, in *Robert Frost Himself* (New York: G. Braziller, 1986), 66, 67.

11. "Field of vision" is a term I borrowed from Hopkins, but Reginald Cook uses it to discuss precisely this matter—the relation of the Frostian poetic vision to time and space. See *Robert Frost: A Living Voice* (Amherst: University of Massachusetts Press, 1974), chapter 22 (277ff), "On a Field of Vision."

12. All Frost quotations are from *The Poetry of Robert Frost*, edited by Edward Connery Lathem (New York: Holt, Rinehart and Winston, 1969).

13. See George Bagby, *Frost and the Book of Nature* (Knoxville: University of Tennessee Press, 1993).

14. See Cooke: "Phenomena in and of themselves are forms of concealment, and tease us *into* thought" ("Frost's Poetry," 49).

15. Cameron, *Lyric Time*, 102.

16. See his chapter "The Sonnet," in *Poetic Meter and Poetic Form*, 118. On this sonnet and on the matter of perspective in Frost generally, see Judith Oster, *Toward Robert Frost: The Reader and the Poet* (Athens: University Of Georgia Press, 1991), 34.

17. Cameron, *Lyric Time*, 71.

18. Ibid., 70.

19. I take this phrase from a useful book on temporality by Elliott Jaques, *The Form of Time* (New York: Crane Russak, 1982), 82.

20. Letter to John W. Haines, 25 April 1915, in *Selected Letters*, 171.

21. See Cameron, *Lyric Time*, 88.

22. For a sensitive reading of this poem along the lines of my own, see Oster, *Toward Robert Frost*, 170–74.

23. Cameron, *Lyric Time*, 255.

24. See Poirier on this generally: "—it is the difficulty of knowing *that* you know anything, even when you may, which charms and obsesses him" (*The Work of Knowing*, 279).

25. Cameron, *Lyric Time*, 120.

26. Quoted by William Mulder, "Freedom and Form: Robert Frost's Double Discipline," *South Atlantic Quarterly* 54, no. 3 (July 1955): 389.

27. Cooke, "Frost's Poetry," 50.

28. Poirier, *Robert Frost*, 173.

29. Quoted by Barry, *Robert Frost on Writing*, 21.

30. There are only a few discussions specifically addressing Frost's use of the sonnet form: the best is Oliver H. Evans's "'Deeds That Count': Robert Frost's Sonnets," *Texas Studies in Literature and Language* 23 (1981): 123–37; but also see Karen Lane Rood's "Robert Frost's 'Sentence Sounds': Wildness Opposing the Sonnet Form," in *Frost: Centennial Essays II*, ed. Jac Tharpe (Jackson: University Press of Mississippi, 1976), 129–212, and Mulder's "Freedom and Form: Robert Frost's Double Discipline," *South Atlantic Quarterly* 54 (1955): 386–93. On the relation of form, "choice," and freedom, see Poirier, and also John F. Sears, "William James, Henri Bergson, and the Poetics of Robert Frost," *New England Quarterly* 48 (Sept. 1975): 341–61.

31. See Thompson, *The Years of Triumph, 1915–1938* (New York: Holt Rinehart and Winston, 1963), 485, 693 n. 23.

32. From Frost's interview with John Ciardi, *Saturday Review*, 21 March 1959, quoted by Barry, *Robert Frost on Writing*, 33. George F. Bagby's article entitled "Frost's Synecdochism" is indirectly (because it does not mention sonnets particularly) relevant to the matter of the sonnet. See *American Literature* 58, no. 3 (October 1986): 379–92.

33. Letter to the *Amherst Student*, in *Selected Prose*, 107.

34. Sydney Lea's essay on the relation of Frost to Wordsworth also cites the figural link of "the star"—and for the same reason as I have explained: it is the Wordsworthian "urge to reset a star" that "is part of [the] quest for sublimity, and the assertive voice of the induction marks [the] desire that the poem have, as heavenly bodies are supposed to have, a permanent 'influence'" ("From Sublime to Rigamarole," 106). But Lea also concurs that it is an ironized view of Wordsworth's vision that Frost, acknowledging his historical context, must accept.

Works Cited

Primary Sources

Browning, Robert. *Robert Browning: The Poems.* Edited by John Pettigrew. New Haven: Yale University Press, 1987.

Cavalcanti, Guido. *The Poetry of Guido Cavalcanti.* Edited and translated by Lowry Nelson, Jr. Vol. 18, series A, of the Garland Library of Medieval Literature. New York: Garland, 1986.

Coleridge, S. T. *The Notebooks of Samuel Taylor Coleridge.* Edited by Kathleen Coburn. 5 vols. Bollingen Series L. New York: Pantheon Books, 1957– .

———. *The Poetical and Dramatic Works of Samuel Taylor Coleridge.* 4 vols. London: Macmillan, 1880.

Forster, E. M. *The Celestial Omnibus and Other Stories.* New York: Alfred A. Knopf, 1923.

Frost, Robert. *The Poetry of Robert Frost.* Edited by Edward Connery Lathem. New York: Holt, Rinehart and Winston, 1969.

———. *Selected Letters of Robert Frost.* Edited by Lawrance Thompson. New York: Holt, Rinehart and Winston, 1964.

———. *Selected Prose of Robert Frost.* Edited by Hyde Cox and Edward Connery Lathem. New York: Collier Books, 1968.

Hopkins, Gerard Manley. *The Correspondence of Gerard Manley Hopkins and Richard Watson Dixon.* Edited by Claude Colleer Abbott. London: Oxford University Press, 1935.

———. *Further Letters of Gerard Manley Hopkins.* Edited by Claude Colleer Abbott. New York: Oxford University Press, 1938.

———. *The Journals and Papers of Gerard Manley Hopkins.* Edited by Humphry House, completed by Graham Storey. London: Oxford University Press, 1959.

———. *The Letters of Gerard Manley Hopkins to Robert Bridges.* Edited by Claude Colleer Abbott. London: Oxford University Press, 1935.

———. *The Note-books and Papers of Gerard Manley Hopkins.* Edited by Humphry House. London: Oxford University Press, 1937.

———. *The Poems of Gerard Manley Hopkins.* Edited by W. H. Gardner and N. H. Mackenzie. 4th ed. New York: Oxford University Press, 1967.

Keats, John. *Complete Poems*. Edited by Jack Stillinger. Cambridge: The Belknap Press of Harvard University Press, 1982.

———. *The Letters of John Keats*. Edited by Maurice Buxton Forman. 4th ed. New York: Oxford University Press, 1952.

———. *The Letters of John Keats*. Edited by Hyder Edward Rollins. 2 vols. Cambridge: Harvard University Press, 1958.

Lee-Hamilton, Eugene. *Sonnets of the Wingless Hours*. Portland, Me.: Thomas B. Mosher, 1933.

Lofft, Capel. *Laura: or, An Anthology of Sonnets, (On the Petrarchan Model,) and Elegiac Quatorzains*. 5 vols. London: B. and R. Crosby & Co., 1814.

Meredith, George. *The Poems of George Meredith*. Edited by Phyllis B. Bartlett. 2 vols. New Haven: Yale University Press, 1978.

Milton, John. *The Complete Poetry of John Milton*. Edited by John T. Shawcross. Garden City, N.Y.: Anchor/Doubleday, 1971.

Rossetti, Dante Gabriel. *Letters of Dante Gabriel Rossetti*. Edited by Oswald Doughty and John Robert Wahl. 4 vols. Oxford: Clarendon Press, 1967.

———. *The Poetical Works of Dante Gabriel Rossetti*. Edited by William Michael Rossetti. 2 vols. Boston: Little, Brown, 1907.

Rossetti, William Michael, ed. *The Germ: Thoughts towards Nature in Poetry, Literature and Art*. Facsimile rpt. London: Elliot Stock, 1901.

———. *Rossetti Papers, 1862–1870*. London: N.p., 1903.

Seward, Anna. *Letters of Anna Seward: Written between the Years 1784 and 1807*. 6 vols. Edinburgh: Archibald Constable, 1811.

———. *The Poetical Works of Anna Seward*. Edited by Walter Scott. 3 vols. Edinburgh: James Ballantyne and Co., 1810.

Shelley, Percy Bysshe. *Poetical Works*. Edited by Thomas Hutchinson. Oxford: Oxford University Press, 1964.

———. *Shelley's Poetry and Prose*. Edited by Donald H. Reiman and Sharon B. Powers. New York: Norton, 1977.

Spenser, Edmund. *The Yale Edition of the Shorter Poems of Edmund Spenser*. Edited by William A. Oram et al. New Haven: Yale University Press, 1989.

Smith, Charlotte. *Elegiac Sonnets*. 4th ed. London: Dodsley, Gardner, and Bew, 1786.

Swinburne, Algernon Charles. *The Complete Works of Algernon Charles Swinburne*. Edited by Sir Edmund Gosse and Thomas James Wise. 20 vols. New York: Gabriel Wells, 1926.

Tennyson Turner, Charles. *Collected Sonnets Old and New*. London: C. Kegan Paul & Co., 1880.

Wordsworth, William. *The Letters of William and Dorothy Wordsworth: The Later Years*. 3 vols. Edited by Ernest de Selincourt. Oxford: Clarendon Press, 1939.

———. *The Letters of William and Dorothy Wordsworth: The Middle Years*. Edited by Ernest de Selincourt. 2 vols. Oxford: Clarendon Press, 1937.

———. *The Poetical Works of William Wordsworth*. Edited by E. de Selincourt. 5 vols. Oxford: Clarendon Press, 1940–49.

———. *The Prose Works of William Wordsworth*. Edited by Alexander Balloch Grosart. 3 vols. London: E. Moxon, 1876; New York: AMS Press, 1967.

———. *William Wordsworth: The Poems*. Edited by John O. Hayden. 2 vols. New Haven: Yale University Press, 1981.

———. *Wordsworth: Poetical Works*. Edited by Thomas Hutchinson; new ed., revised by Ernest de Selincourt. 1904. New York and Oxford: Oxford University Press, 1985.

———. *Wordsworth's Poems of 1807*. Edited by Alun R. Jones. Atlantic Highlands, N.J.: Humanities Press International, 1987.

Secondary Sources

Abrams, M. H. *The Correspondent Breeze: Essays on English Romanticism*. New York: Norton, 1984.

———. *Natural Supernaturalism: Tradition and Revolution in Romantic Literature*. New York: Norton, 1973.

———, ed. *English Romantic Poets: Modern Essays in Criticism*. New York: Oxford University Press, 1960.

Adams, Hazard, ed. *Critical Theory Since Plato*. New York: Harcourt, Brace, 1971.

Agosta, Lucien L. "Animate Images: The Later Poem-Paintings of Dante Gabriel Rossetti." *Texas Studies in Literature and Language* 23 (1981): 78-101.

Allott, Miriam, ed. *The Poems of John Keats*. New York: Norton, 1970.

Altieri, Charles. "Wordsworth's Poetics of Eloquence: A Challenge to Contemporary Theory." In *Romantic Revolutions: Criticism and Theory,* edited by Kenneth R. Johnston, Gilbert Chaitin, Karen Hanson, and Herbert Marks. Bloomington: Indiana University Press, 1990.

Armstrong, Isobel. *Victorian Scrutinies: Reviews of Poetry 1830–1870*. London: Athlone Press, 1972.

Ashcroft-Noble, James. Review of *Treasury of Sonnets* (1880), by David M. Main. *The Contemporary Review* 38 (1880): 471.

Asselineau, M. Charles. *Le Livre des Sonnets*. Paris, 1875.

Bagby, George F., Jr. *Frost and the Book of Nature*. Knoxville: University of Tennessee Press, 1993.

———. "Frost's Synecdochism." *American Literature* 58, no. 3 (October 1986): 379–92.

Baker, Jeffrey. *Time and Mind in Wordsworth's Poetry*. Detroit: Wayne State University Press, 1980.

Barry, Elaine, ed. *Robert Frost On Writing*. New Brunswick, N.J.: Rutgers University Press, 1973.

Bate, Walter Jackson. *John Keats*. 1963. Cambridge: Belknap Press of Harvard University Press, 1975.

———. "Keats's Style: Evolution toward Qualities of Permanent Value." In *English Romantic Poets: Modern Essays in Criticism,* edited by M. H. Abrams. New York: Oxford University Press, 1960.

Baum, Paull Franklin, ed. Introduction to *The House of Life: A Sonnet-Sequence*. Cambridge: Harvard University Press, 1928.

Beach, Joseph Warren. "Keats's Realms of Gold." *PMLA* 49 (1934): 246–57.

Behrendt, Stephen C. "'The Consequence of High Powers': Blake, Shelley, and Prophecy's Public Dimension." *Papers on Language & Literature* 22 (1986): 254–75.

Behrmann, Alfred. "Variationen einer Form: das Sonett." *Deutsche Vierteljahrs Schrift für Literaturwissenschaft und Geistesgeschichte* 13 (1985): 1–28.

Berg, Stephen, and Robert Mezey, eds. *The New Naked Poetry: Recent American Poetry in Open Forms.* Indianapolis: Bobbs-Merrill, 1976.

Bermann, Sandra. *The Sonnet Over Time: A Study in the Sonnets of Petrarch, Shakespeare, and Baudelaire.* Chapel Hill: University of North Carolina Press, 1988.

Bhattacharyya, Arunodoy. *The Sonnet and the Major English Romantic Poets.* Calcutta: Firma KLM Private Ltd., 1976.

Bialostosky, Don H. *Wordsworth, Dialogics, and the Practice of Criticism.* Cambridge: Cambridge University Press, 1992.

Blank, G. K. "Shelley's Wind of Influence." *Philological Quarterly* 64 (1985): 475–91.

Bloom, Harold. *Poetry and Repression.* New Haven: Yale University Press, 1976.

———. *Shelley's Mythmaking.* Ithaca: Cornell University Press, 1969.

———. *The Visionary Company.* Ithaca: Cornell University Press, 1971.

Bone, J. Drummond. "On 'Influence', and on Byron's and Shelley's Use of *Terza Rima* in 1819." *Keats-Shelley Memorial Bulletin* 32 (1981): 38–48.

Boos, Florence Saunders. *The Poetry of Dante Gabriel Rossetti: A Critical Reading and Source Study.* The Hague: Mouton, 1976.

Boyle, Robert, S.J. *Metaphor in Hopkins.* Chapel Hill: University of North Carolina Press, 1960.

Brake, Laurel. "Aesthetics in the Affray: Walter Pater's *Appreciations with an Essay on Style* (1889)." In *The Politics of Pleasure: Aesthetics and Cultural Theory,* edited by Stephen Regan. Buckingham, U.K., and Philadelphia: Open University Press, 1992.

Bridges, Robert, ed. Notes to *Poems of Gerard Manley Hopkins.* London: Humphrey Milford, 1918.

Brisman, Leslie. *Milton's Poetry of Choice and its Romantic Heirs.* Ithaca: Cornell University Press, 1973.

———. *Romantic Origins.* Ithaca: Cornell University Press, 1978.

Bristow, Joseph, ed. *The Victorian Poet: Poetics and Persona.* New York: Croom Helm, 1987.

Brooks, Cleanth Jr. *The Well-Wrought Urn.* New York: Harcourt, Brace, 1947.

———, ed. *Gerard Manley Hopkins by the Kenyon Critics.* Norfolk, Conn.: New Directions Books, 1945.

Brower, Reuben A. *The Poetry of Robert Frost: Constellations of Intention.* New York: Oxford University Press, 1963.

Brown, Marshall. *Preromanticism.* Stanford, Calif.: Stanford University Press, 1991.

———. "The Pre-Romantic Discovery of Consciousness." *Studies in Romanticism* 17 (1978): 387–411.

Bullock, Walter L. "The Genesis of the English Sonnet Form." *PMLA* 37 (1923): 729–44.

Burke, Kenneth. *Counterstatement.* Berkeley: University of California Press, 1968.

———. *The Philosophy of Literary Form.* Berkeley: University of California Press, 1973.

Burne-Jones, G., ed. *The Memorials of Edward Burne-Jones*. London: Macmillan, 1904.

Burnshaw, Stanley. *Robert Frost Himself*. New York: G. Braziller, 1986.

Bush, Douglas. *John Keats: His Life and Writings*. New York: Macmillan, 1966.

———, ed. *A Variorum Commentary of the Poems of John Milton*. Vol. 2, part 2. New York: Columbia University Press, 1972.

Caine, Thomas Hall. Preface to *Sonnets of Three Centuries: A Selection, Including Many Examples Hitherto Unpublished. With a preface of xxiv pages, dated from Vale of St. John, Cumberland, 1881*. London: Elliot Stock, 1882.

———. *Recollections of Dante Gabriel Rossetti*. London: Elliot Stock, 1882.

Cameron, Sharon. *Lyric Time: Dickinson and the Limits of Genre*. Baltimore: Johns Hopkins University Press, 1979.

Chai, Leon. *Aestheticism: The Religion of Art in Post-Romantic Literature*. New York: Columbia University Press, 1990.

Chandler, James K. *Wordsworth's Second Nature: A Study of the Poetry and Politics*. Chicago: University of Chicago Press, 1984.

Charlesworth, Barbara. *Dark Passages: The Decadent Consciousness in Victorian Literature*. Madison: University of Wisconsin Press, 1965.

Chase, Cynthia. "'Viewless Wings': Intertextual Interpretation of Keats's 'Ode to a Nightingale.'" In *Lyric Poetry: Beyond New Criticism,* edited by Chaviva Hošek and Patricia Parker. Ithaca: Cornell University Press, 1985.

Christ, Carol T. *The Finer Optic: The Aesthetic of Particularity in Victorian Poetry*. New Haven: Yale University Press, 1975.

Colie, Rosalie. *Resources of Kind*. Berkeley: University of California Press, 1973.

Collins, Ben L. "The Stanzaic Pattern of Shelley's 'Ode to the West Wind.'" *Keats-Shelley Journal* 21 (1970): 7–8.

Comstock, Cathy. "'Speak, and I see the side-lie of a truth': The Problematics of Truth in Meredith's *Modern Love*." *Victorian Poetry* 25 (1987): 129–41.

Cook, Reginald. *Robert Frost: A Living Voice*. Amherst: University of Massachusetts Press, 1974.

Cooke, Michael. "Frost's Poetry: Breaking the Boundaries of the Hidden and Silent." *The Kentucky Review* 5 (1985): 46–59.

Cooper, Robert M. *Lost on Both Sides. Dante Gabriel Rossetti: Critic and Poet*. Athens: Ohio University Press, 1970.

Cotter, James Finn. "Apocalyptic Imagery in Hopkins' 'That Nature is a Heraclitean Fire and of the comfort of the Resurrection.'" *Victorian Poetry* 24 (1986): 261–73.

Crisman, William. "The Dramatic Voice in Keats's Elgin Marbles Sonnet." *Studies in Romanticism* 26 (1987): 49–58.

"Critical History of the Sonnet" (in two parts). *The Dublin Review,* n.s., 27 (1876): 400–430; and n.s., 28 (1877): 141–80.

Cronin, Richard. *Shelley's Poetic Thoughts*. London: Macmillan, 1981.

Culler, Jonathan. *Structuralist Poetics: Structuralism, Linguistics and the Study of Literature*. Ithaca: Cornell University Press, 1975.

Curran, Stuart. *Poetic Form and British Romanticism*. New York: Oxford University Press, 1986.

————. *Shelley's Annus Mirabilis: The Maturing of an Epic Vision*. San Marino, Calif.: Huntington Library, 1975.

Curtis, Jared R. *Wordsworth's Experiments with Tradition: The Lyric Poems of 1802*. Ithaca: Cornell University Press, 1971.

D'Avanzo, Mario. *A Cloud of Other Poets: Robert Frost and the Romantics*. Lanham, Md.: University Press of America, 1991.

[Davies, William]. "Article VIII." *London Quarterly Review* 134 (January–April 1873): 99–108.

Davis, Charles G. "The Structure of Wordsworth's Sonnet 'Composed Upon Westminster Bridge.'" *English* 19 (1970): 18–21.

de Man, Paul. "Symbolic Landscape in Wordsworth and Yeats." In *In Defense of Reading: A Reader's Approach to Literary Criticism*, edited by Reuben A. Brower and Richard Poirier. New York: E. P. Dutton, 1962. Rpt. in *The Rhetoric of Romanticism* (New York: Columbia University Press, 1984).

————, ed. Introduction to *The Selected Poems of John Keats*. New York: Signet, 1966.

Dennis, John. "The English Sonnet." In *Studies in English Literature*, 392–444. London: Edward Stanford, 1876.

Derrida, Jacques. *Speech and Phenomena and Other Essays on Husserl's Theory of Signs*. Translated by David B. Allison. Evanston, Ill.: Northwestern University Press, 1973.

Dickstein, Morris. *Keats and His Poetry: A Study in Development*. Chicago: University of Chicago Press, 1971.

Dobbs, Brian and Judy Dobbs. *Dante Gabriel Rossetti: An Alien Victorian*. London: MacDonald and Jane's, 1977.

Doubleday, Thomas. *Sixty-five Sonnets; with Prefatory Remarks on the Accordance of the Sonnet with the Powers of the English Language: also, a Few Miscellaneous Poems*. London: Baldwin, Cradock, and Joy, 1818.

Doughty, Oswald. *A Victorian Romantic: Dante Gabriel Rossetti*. London: Frederick Muller, 1949.

Dyce, Alexander. Introduction to *Specimens of English Sonnets*. London: W. Pickering, 1833.

Ellis, Virginia Ridley. *Gerard Manley Hopkins and the Language of Mystery*. Columbia: University of Missouri Press, 1991.

Empson, William. *Seven Types of Ambiguity*. 3d ed. Norfolk, Conn.: New Directions Books, 1953.

Evans, Oliver H. "'Deeds That Count': Robert Frost's Sonnets." *Texas Studies in Literature and Language* 23, no. 1 (Spring 1981): 123–37.

Fairley, Barker. Review article on Gerard Manley Hopkins. *London Mercury* 32, no. 188 (June 1935).

Fineman, Joel. *Shakespeare's Perjur'd Eye: The Invention of Poetic Subjectivity in the Sonnets*. Berkeley: University of California Press, 1986.

Finney, Claude Lee. *The Evolution of Keats's Poetry*. New York: Russell & Russell, 1936.

Fischer, Hermann. "William Wordsworth: 'Composed by the Side of Grasmere Lake.'" In *Versdichtung der englischen Romantik*, edited by Teut Andreas Riese and Dieter Riesner. Berlin: Erich Schmidt Verlag, 1968.

Fitzgerald, William. "Articulating the Unarticulated: Form, Death and Other in Keats and Rilke." *Modern Language Notes* 100 (1985): 949–67.

———. "Keats's Sonnets and the Challenge of Winter." *Studies in Romanticism* 26 (1987): 59–83.

Ford, George. *Keats and the Victorians: A Study of his Influence and Rise to Fame, 1821–1895.* New Haven: Yale University Press, 1944.

Forster, Leonard. *The Icy Fire: Five Studies in European Petrarchanism.* Cambridge: Cambridge University Press, 1969.

Fraistat, Neil. *The Poem and the Book: Interpreting Collections of Romantic Poetry.* Chapel Hill: University of North Carolina Press, 1985.

Fraser, Hilary. *Beauty and Belief: Aesthetics and Religion in Victorian Literature.* Cambridge: Cambridge University Press, 1986.

Fredeman, William. "Rossetti's *In Memoriam*, An Elegiac Reading of *The House of Life*." *Bulletin of the John Rylands Library* 47 (1965): 298–341.

Freedman, William. "Postponement and Perspectives in Shelley's 'Ozymandias.'" *Studies in Romanticism* 25 (1986): 63–73.

Fried, Deborah. "Andromeda Unbound: Gender and Genre in Millay's Sonnets." *Twentieth-Century Literature* 32 (1986): 1–22.

Friedrich, Reinhard H. "The Apocalyptic Mode and Shelley's 'Ode to the West Wind.'" *Renascence* 36 (1984): 161–70.

Fry, Paul H. "History, Existence, and 'To Autumn.'" *Studies in Romanticism* 25 (1986): 211–19.

———. *The Poet's Calling in the English Ode.* New Haven: Yale University Press, 1980.

———. "The Possession of the Sublime." *Studies in Romanticism* 26 (1987): 187–207.

———. "Reading 'Ozymandias.'" Unpublished essay. Typescript.

Fuller, John. *The Sonnet.* London: Methuen, 1972.

Fussell, Paul. *Poetic Meter and Poetic Form.* Rev. ed. New York: Random House, 1979.

Galperin, William H. "Anti-Romanticism, Victorianism, and the Case of Wordsworth." *Victorian Poetry* 24 (1986): 357–71.

Gardner, W. H. *Gerard Manley Hopkins, 1844–1889: A Study of Poetic Idiosyncracy in Relation to Poetic Tradition.* 2 vols. New Haven: Yale University Press, 1948.

Garrod, H. W. *Keats.* 2d ed. Oxford: Clarendon Press, 1939.

Gates, Barbara. "Revising *The House of Life*: A Look at Seven Unpublished Sonnets." *Victorian Poetry* 21 (1983): 65-78.

Gittings, Robert. *John Keats.* Boston: Little, Brown, 1968.

Gleckner, Robert F. "Keats's 'How Many Bards' and Poetic Tradition." *Keats-Shelley Journal* 27 (1978): 14–23.

Going, William T. *Scanty Plot of Ground: Studies in the Victorian Sonnet.* The Hague: Mouton, 1976.

Goldberg, M. A. "The 'Fears' of John Keats." *Modern Language Quarterly* 18 (1957): 125–31.

Golden, Catherine. "Dante Gabriel Rossetti's Two-Sided Art." *Victorian Poetry* 26 (1988): 395–402.

Greene, Thomas M. "Pitiful Thrivers: Failed Husbandry in the Sonnets." In *Shakespeare and the Question of Theory,* edited by Patricia Parker and Geoffrey H. Hartman. London: Methuen, 1985.

Hall, Jean. *The Transforming Image: A Study of Shelley's Major Poetry.* Chicago: University of Illinois Press, 1980.

Hamlin, Cyrus. "The Hermeneutics of Form: Reading the Romantic Ode." *Boundary* 2 (1979): 1–30.

Hanscom, Elizabeth Deering. "The Sonnet Forms of Wyatt and Surrey." *Modern Language Notes* 16 (1901): 274-80.

Harding, Anthony John. "Speech, Silence, and the Self-Doubting Interpreter in Keats's Poetry." *Keats-Shelley Journal* 35 (1986): 83-103.

Hardy, Barbara. *The Advantage of Lyric: Essays of Feeling in Poetry.* Bloomington: Indiana University Press, 1973.

Harris, Daniel A. *Inspirations Unbidden: The "Terrible Sonnets" of Gerard Manley Hopkins.* Berkeley and Los Angeles: University of California Press, 1982.

Hartman, Geoffrey. *Beyond Formalism.* New Haven: Yale University Press, 1970.

———. *The Fate of Reading.* Chicago: University of Chicago Press, 1975.

———. *The Unremarkable Wordsworth.* Minneapolis: University of Minnesota Press, 1987.

———. *Wordsworth's Poetry, 1787–1814.* Cambridge: Harvard University Press, 1987.

Harvey, G. M. "The Design of Wordsworth's Sonnets." *Ariel* 6 (1975): 78–90.

Havens, R. D. *The Influence of Milton on English Poetry.* New York: Russell & Russell, 1961.

Haworth, Helen E. "'Ode to the West Wind' and the Sonnet Form." *Keats-Shelley Journal* 20 (1971): 71-77.

Hayden, John O., ed. *Romantic Bards and British Reviewers.* London: Routledge & Kegan Paul, 1971.

Heninger, S. K., Jr. "Sequence, Systems, Models: Sidney and the Secularization of Sonnets." In *Poems in Their Place: The Intertextuality and Order of Poetic Collections,* edited by Neil Fraistat. Chapel Hill and London: University of North Carolina Press, 1986.

Herendeen, W. H. "The Rhetoric of Rivers: The River and the Pursuit of Knowledge." *Studies in Philology* 78 (1981): 107–27.

Herz, Judith Scherer. "Epigrams and Sonnets: Milton in the Manner of Jonson." *Milton Studies* 20 (1984): 29-41.

Hewlett, Henry G. Review of Tennyson Turner's sonnets. *Contemporary Review,* Sept. 1873, 637.

Hogle, Jerrold E. *Shelley's Process: Radical Transference and the Development of His Major Works.* New York: Oxford University Press, 1988.

Hollander, John. "The Gazer's Spirit: Romantic and Later Poetry of Painting and Sculpture." In *The Romantics and Us,* edited by Gene Ruoff. New Brunswick, N.J.: Rutgers University Press, 1990.

———. *Melodious Guile: Fictive Pattern in Poetic Language.* New Haven: Yale University Press, 1988.

————. *Vision and Resonance: Two Senses of Poetic Form.* New Haven: Yale University Press, 1975.

Holmes, Richard. *Shelley: The Pursuit.* New York: E. P. Dutton, 1975.

Hošek, Chaviva, and Patricia Parker, eds. *Lyric Poetry: Beyond New Criticism.* Ithaca: Cornell University Press, 1985.

Housman, Robert Fletcher. Preface to *A Collection of English Sonnets.* London: Simpkin, Marshall & Co., 1835.

Hunt, John Dixon. "A Moment's Monument: Reflection of Pre-Raphaelite Vision in Poetry and Painting." In *Pre-Raphaelitism: A Collection of Critical Essays,* edited by James Sambrook. Chicago: University of Chicago Press, 1974.

Hunt, Leigh. *Lord Byron and Some of His Contemporaries.* London: H. Colburn, 1828.

Hunt, Leigh, and S. Adams Lee, eds. *The Book of the Sonnet.* 2 vols. Boston: Roberts Brothers, 1867.

Hutchinson, Thomas, ed. "Note on the Wordsworthian Sonnet." Appendix to *Wordsworth's Poems in Two Volumes.* London: David Nutt, 1897.

Jackson, Richard. "The Romantic Metaphysics of Time." *Studies in Romanticism* 19 (1980): 19–30.

Janowitz, Anne. "Shelley's Monument to Ozymandias." *Philological Quarterly* 63 (1984): 477-91.

Jaques, Elliott. *The Form of Time.* New York: Crane Russak, 1982.

Jarfe, Günther. *Kunstform und Verzweiflung. Studien zur Typologie der Sonettgestalt in Dante Gabriel Rossettis The House of Life.* Frankfurt am Main: Peter Lang, 1976.

Johnson, Barbara. *"Les Fleurs du mal armé:* Some Reflections on Intertextuality." In *Lyric Poetry: Beyond New Criticism,* edited by Chaviva Hošek and Patricia Parker. Ithaca: Cornell University Press, 1985.

Johnson, Lee M. *Wordsworth and the Sonnet. Anglistica* 19. Copenhagen: Rosenkilde and Bagger, 1973.

Johnson, Wendell Stacy. "D. G. Rossetti as Painter and Poet." In *Pre-Raphaelitism: A Collection of Critical Essays,* edited by James Sambrook. Chicago: University of Chicago Press, 1974.

————. *Gerard Manley Hopkins: The Poet As Victorian.* Ithaca: Cornell University Press, 1968.

Jost, François. "Anatomy of an Ode: Shelley and the Sonnet Tradition." *Comparative Literature* 34 (1982): 223–46.

Kastner, L. E. "Concerning the Sonnet on the Sonnet." *Modern Language Review* 11 (1916): 205–11.

Kauvar, George B. *The Other Poetry of Keats.* Rutherford, N.J.: Fairleigh Dickinson University Press, 1969.

Keach, William. *Shelley's Style.* New York and London: Methuen, 1984.

Kelley, Theresa M. *Wordsworth's Revisionary Aesthetics.* Cambridge: Cambridge University Press, 1988.

Kerrigan, John. "Wordsworth and the Sonnet: Building, Dwelling, Thinking." *Essays in Criticism* 35 (1985): 45–71.

Kissane, James. "The Authorization of John Keats." *Keats-Shelley Journal* 37 (1988): 58–74.

Kjorven, Johannes. *Robert Frost's Emergent Design: The Truth of the Self Inbetween Belief and Unbelief.* Oslo: Solum Forlag; Atlantic Highlands, N.J.: Humanities Press International, 1987.

Korg, Jacob. "Hopkins' Linguistic Deviations." *PMLA* 92 (1977): 977–86.

Langbaum, Robert. "The Epiphanic Mode in Wordsworth and Modern Literature." *New Literary History* 14 (Winter 1983): 335–58.

―――. *Poetry of Experience: The Dramatic Monologue in Modern Literary Tradition.* 1957. New York: Norton, 1971.

Lau, Beth. "Keats's Eagles and the Creative Process." *Romanticism Past and Present* 10 (1986): 49–61.

―――. *Keats's Reading of the Romantic Poets.* Ann Arbor: University of Michigan Press, 1991.

Lea, Sydney. "From Sublime to Rigamarole: Relations of Frost to Wordsworth." *Studies in Romanticism* 19 (Spring 1980): 83–108.

Leavis, F. R., ed. *Gerard Manley Hopkins by the Kenyon Critics.* Norfolk, Conn.: New Directions, 1945.

Lehman, David. *Ecstatic Occasions, Expedient Forms.* New York: Collier Books, 1988.

Leighton, Angela. *Shelley and the Sublime.* Cambridge: Cambridge University Press, 1984.

Lentricchia, Frank. *Robert Frost: Modern Poetics and the Landscapes of Self.* Durham, N.C.: Duke University Press, 1975.

Lentzner, Dr. Karl. *Über das Sonett und Seine Gestaltung in der englischen Dichtung bis Milton.* N.p., 1886.

Lenz, Bernd. "'Let the muse be free': Tradition and Experiment in the Sonnets of John Keats." *Anglistentag,* 1982, 177–96.

Levinson, Marjorie. *Keats's Life of Allegory: The Origins of a Style.* London: Basil Blackwell, 1988.

Lichtmann, Maria. *The Contemplative Poetry of Gerard Manley Hopkins.* Princeton: Princeton University Press, 1989.

Liu, Alan. *Wordsworth: The Sense of History.* Stanford, Calif.: Stanford University Press, 1989.

Lofft, Capel. *Laura; or, An Anthology of Sonnets, (On the Petrarchan Model,) and Elegiac Quatorzains.* 5 vols. London: B. and R. Crosby & Co., 1814.

Loomis, Jeffrey B. *Dayspring in Darkness: Sacrament in Hopkins.* Lewisburg, Pa.: Bucknell University Press, 1988.

Lucas, John. "Meredith as Poet: 'Modern Love.'" In *The Pre-Raphaelite Poets,* edited by Harold Bloom. New York: Chelsea House, 1986.

Ludwig, Hans-Werner. *Barbarous in Beauty: Studien zum Vers in Gerard Manley Hopkins' Sonetten.* München: Wilhelm Fink Verlag, 1972.

Lukacs, Georg. *Soul and Form.* Translated by Anna Bostock. Cambridge: MIT Press, 1974.

Main, David M. *A Treasury of English Sonnets.* Edinburgh and London: William Blackwood and Sons, 1880.

Malkoff, Karl. *Escape from the Self: A Study in Contemporary American Poetry and Poetics.* New York: Columbia University Press, 1977.

Mariani, Paul. *Commentary on the Complete Poems of Gerard Manley Hopkins*. Ithaca: Cornell University Press, 1970.

Matthey, François. *The Evolution of Keats's Structural Imagery*. Bern: A. Francke AG Verlag, 1984.

McCarthy, William. "The Continuity of Milton's Sonnets." *PMLA* 92 (1977): 96–109.

McFarland, Thomas. *Romanticism and the Forms of Ruin: Wordsworth, Coleridge, and Modalities of Fragmentation*. Princeton: Princeton University Press, 1981.

McGann, Jerome. "Dante Gabriel Rossetti and the Betrayal of Truth." *Victorian Poetry* 26 (1988): 339–59.

———. "Keats and the Historical Method in Literary Criticism." In *The Beauty of Inflections: Literary Investigations in Historical Method & Theory*. Oxford: Clarendon Press, 1988.

McGowan, John P. *Representation and Revelation: Victorian Realism from Carlyle to Yeats*. Columbia: University of Missouri Press, 1986.

McNally, Paul. "Keats and the Rhetoric of Association: On Looking into the Chapman's Homer Sonnet." *Journal of English and Germanic Philology* 79 (1980): 530-40.

Miller, J. Hillis. *The Disappearance of God: Five Nineteenth-Century Writers*. New York: Schocken Books, 1963.

———. *The Linguistic Moment*. Princeton: Princeton University Press, 1985.

Mitchell, W. J. T. "Spatial Form in Literature: Toward a General Theory." *Critical Inquiry* 6 (1980): 539–67.

Mönch, Walter. *Das Sonett: Gestalt und Geschichte*. Heidelberg: F. H. Kerle Verlag, 1955.

Motto, Marylou. *"Mined with a Motion": The Poetry of Gerard Manley Hopkins*. New Brunswick, N.J.: Rutgers University Press, 1984.

Mulder, William. "Freedom and Form: Robert Frost's Double Discipline." *The South Atlantic Quarterly* 54, no. 3 (July 1955): 386–93.

Murray, E. B. "Ambivalent Mortality in the Elgin Marbles Sonnet." *Keats-Shelley Journal* 20 (1971): 22–36.

Ong, Walter J. *Hopkins, the Self, and God*. Toronto: University of Toronto Press, 1986.

Oppenheimer, Paul. *The Birth of the Modern Mind: Self-Consciousness, and the Invention of the Sonnet*. New York: Oxford University Press, 1989.

———. "The Origin of the Sonnet." *Comparative Literature* 34 (1982): 289–304.

Oster, Judith. *Toward Robert Frost: The Reader and the Poet*. Athens: University of Georgia Press, 1991.

Page, Judith W. "'The weight of too much liberty': Genre and Gender in Wordsworth's Calais Sonnets." *Criticism* 30 (1988): 189–203.

Pater, Walter. *Appreciations with an Essay on Style*. London: Macmillan, 1895.

———. *The Renaissance*. Edited by Adam Phillips. Oxford: Oxford University Press, 1986.

Patmore, Conventry. *Principle in Art Etc*. London: George Bell and Sons, 1889.

Peacock, Markham L., Jr. *The Critical Opinions of William Wordsworth*. Baltimore: Johns Hopkins University Press, 1950.

Poirier, Richard. *Robert Frost: The Work of Knowing*. 1977. Stanford, Calif.: Stanford University Press, 1990.

Ponder, Melinda M. "Echoing Poetry with History: Wordsworth's Duddon Sonnets, and Their Notes." *Genre* 21, no. 2 (Summer 1988): 157–78.

Poulet, Georges. *Studies in Human Time*. Translated by Elliott Coleman. Baltimore: Johns Hopkins University Press, 1956.

————. "Timelessness and Romanticism." *Journal of the History of Ideas* 15, no. 1 (January 1954): 3–22.

Price, Reynolds. *The Laws of Ice*. New York: Atheneum, 1986.

Prince, F. T. *The Italian Element in Milton's Verse*. Oxford: Clarendon Press, 1954.

Prince, Jeffrey R. "D. G. Rossetti and the Pre-Raphaelite Conception of the Special Moment." *Modern Language Quarterly* 37 (1976): 349–69.

Proffitt, Edward. "'This Pleasant Lea': Waning Vision in 'The World is Too Much with Us.'" *The Wordsworth Circle* 11 (1980): 75–77.

Radzinowicz, Mary Ann. *Toward Samson Agonistes: The Growth of Milton's Mind*. Princeton: Princeton University Press, 1978.

Rajan, Tillotama. "Romanticism and the Death of Lyric Consciousness." In *Lyric Poetry,* edited by Hošek and Parker, 194–207. Ithaca: Cornell University Press, 1985.

Reed, Henry. "Miscellaneous Essays on English Poetry: Essay I. English Sonnets." In *Lectures on the British Poets,* 357–80. London: John F. Shaw, 1863.

Rees, Joan. *The Poetry of Dante Gabriel Rossetti: Modes of Self-Expression*. Cambridge: Cambridge University Press, 1981.

Rehder, Robert. *Wordsworth and the Beginnings of Modern Poetry*. London: Croom Helm, 1981.

Richardson, James. *Vanishing Lives: Style and Self in Tennyson, D. G. Rossetti, Swinburne, and Yeats*. Charlottesville: University Press of Virginia, 1988.

Ricoeur, Paul. *The Rule of Metaphor: Multi-Disciplinary Studies of the Creation of Meaning in Language*. Translated by Robert Czerny, with Kathleen McLaughlin and John Costello, S.J. Toronto: University of Toronto Press, 1975.

Ridley, M. R. *Keats's Craftsmanship: A Study in Poetic Development*. New York: Russell & Russell, 1962.

Riede, David G. *Dante Gabriel Rossetti and the Limits of Victorian Vision*. Ithaca: Cornell University Press, 1983.

Rieger, James. *The Mutiny Within: The Heresies of Percy Bysshe Shelley*. New York: George Braziller, 1967.

Ritz, Jean-Georges. *Le Poète Gerard Manley Hopkins, S.J., 1844–1889*. Paris: Didier, 1963.

Robillard, Douglas J. "Rossetti's 'Willowwood' Sonnets and the Structure of *The House of Life*." *The Victorian Newsletter* 21 (1962): 5–9.

Robinson, Jeffrey C. "The Structure of Wordsworth's *Memorials of a Tour in Scotland, 1803*." *Papers on Language & Literature* 13 (1977): 54–70.

Robinson, John. *In Extremity: A Study of Gerard Manley Hopkins*. Cambridge and New York: Cambridge University Press, 1978.

Roe, Nicholas. "'Bright Star, Sweet Unrest': Image and Consolation in Wordsworth, Shelley, and Keats." In *History and Myth: Essays on English Romantic Literature,* edited by Stephen C. Behrendt. Detroit: Wayne State University Press, 1990.

Rollins, Hyder Edward, ed. *The Keats Circle*. 2 vols. Cambridge: Harvard University Press, 1965.

Rood, Karen Lane. "Robert Frost's 'Sentence Sounds': Wildness Opposing the Sonnet Form." In *Frost: Centennial Essays II*, edited by Jac Tharpe. Jackson: University Press of Mississippi, 1976.

Ross, Marlon B. *The Contours of Masculine Desire: Romanticism and the Rise of Women's Poetry*. New York: Oxford University Press, 1986.

Rossetti, William Michael. *Dante Gabriel Rossetti as Designer and Writer*. London: Cassell & Company, 1885.

———. *Rossetti Papers, 1862–1870*. London: Sands & Co., 1903.

Rowlett, John Louis. "The Generic Wordsworth." Diss., University of Virginia, 1987.

[Russell, C. W.]. "Critical History of the Sonnet." *The Dublin Review*, n.s., 27 (1876): 400–430.

———. "Critical History of the Sonnet." *The Dublin Review*, n.s., 28 (1877): 141–80.

Russell, Reverend Matthew, S.J. *Sonnets on the Sonnet: An Anthology*. London: Longman, Green, 1898.

Rylestone, Anne L. *Prophetic Memory in Wordsworth's Ecclesiastical Sonnets*. Carbondale: Southern Illinois University Press, 1991.

Said, Edward. *Beginnings*. New York: Basic Books, 1975.

Sambrook, James, ed. *Pre-Raphaelitism: A Collection of Critical Essays*. Chicago: University of Chicago Press, 1974.

Sanderlin, George. "The Influence of Milton and Wordsworth on the Early Victorian Sonnet." *ELH* 5 (1938): 225–51.

Schirmer, Walter F. "Das Sonett in der englischen Literatur." *Anglia* 37 (1925): 1–31.

Schluter, Kurt. "Wieder einmal 'Upon Westminster Bridge.'" *Literatur in Wissenschaft und Unterricht* 12 (1979): 202–5.

Schlütter, Hans-Jürgen. *Sonett*. Stuttgart: J. B. Metzlersche Verlagsbuchhandlung, 1979.

Schneider, Elizabeth. *A Dragon in the Gate: Studies in the Poetry of G. M. Hopkins*. Berkeley: University of California Press, 1968.

Sears, John F. "William James, Henri Bergson, and the Poetics of Robert Frost." *New England Quarterly* 48 (1975): 341–61.

Shapiro, Karl, and Robert Beum, eds. *A Prosody Handbook*. New York: Harper & Row, 1965.

Sharp, William. *Dante Gabriel Rossetti: A Record and a Study*. London: Macmillan, 1882.

———, ed. *Sonnets of this Century*. London: Walter Scott Publishing Co., 1886.

Simpson, Richard. *The Philosophy of Shakespeare's Sonnets*. London, 1868.

Siskin, Clifford. *The Historicity of Romantic Discourse*. New York and Oxford: Oxford University Press, 1988.

———. "Romantic Genre: Lyric Form and Revisionary Behavior in Wordsworth." *Genre* 16 (1983): 137–55.

Slinn, E. Warwick. "Consciousness as Writing: Deconstruction and Reading Victorian Poetry." *Victorian Poetry* 25 (1987): 67–81.

Smart, John S. *The Sonnets of Milton*. Glasgow, 1921.

Smith, Barbara Herrnstein. *Poetic Closure: A Study of How Poems End*. Chicago: University of Chicago Press, 1968.

"Sonnettomania." *The New Monthly Magazine and Literary Journal* 2 (1821): 644–48.

Spector, Stephen J. "Love, Unity, and Desire in the Poetry of Dante Gabriel Rossetti." *ELH* 38 (1971): 432–58.

————. "Wordsworth's Mirror Imagery and the Picturesque Tradition." *ELH* 44 (1977): 85–107.

Spedding, James. "Charles Tennyson Turner." *The Nineteenth Century* 6 (1879): 461–80.

Sperry, Stuart. *Keats the Poet*. Princeton: Princeton University Press, 1973.

Sprinker, Michael. *"A Counterpoint of Dissonance": The Aesthetics and Poetry of Gerard Manley Hopkins*. Baltimore: Johns Hopkins University Press, 1980.

Steele, Timothy. *Missing Measures: Modern Poetry and the Revolt Against Meter*. Fayetteville and London: University of Arkansas Press, 1990.

Stein, Richard L. "Dante Gabriel Rossetti: Painting and the Problem of Poetic Form." *Studies in English Literature* 10 (1970): 775–92.

Stevenson, Lionel. *The Pre-Raphaelite Poets*. New York: Norton, 1972.

Stillinger, Jack. *The Hoodwinking of Madeline and Other Essays on Keats's Poems*. Chicago: University of Illinois Press, 1971.

Stoddard, Richard Henry. "The Sonnet in English Poetry." *Scribner's Monthly* 22 (1881): 905–21.

Stoehr, Taylor. "Syntax and Poetic Form in Milton's Sonnets." *English Studies* 45 (1964): 289–301.

Storey, Graham. *A Preface to Hopkins*. London: Longman Group, 1981.

Sucksmith, Harvey Peter. "Ultimate Affirmation: A Critical Analysis of Wordsworth's Sonnet, 'Composed upon Westminster Bridge', and the Image of the City in *The Prelude*." *The Yearbook of English Studies* 6 (1976): 113–19.

Svendsen, K. "Milton's Sonnet on the Massacre in Piedmont." *Shakespeare Association Bulletin* 29 (1945): 147–55.

Symonds, J. A. "The Debt of English to Italian Literature." *Fortnightly Review* 23 (1875): 371-81.

Talon, Henri. "Dante Gabriel Rossetti: Peintre-Poète dans *La Maison de Vie*." *Études Anglaises* 1 (1966): 1–14.

Tetreault, Ronald. *The Poetry of Life: Shelley and Literary Form*. Toronto: University of Toronto Press, 1987.

Thompson, Lawrance. *The Years of Triumph, 1915–1938*. New York: Holt, Rinehart and Winston, 1963.

Thorpe, James E., ed. *Milton Criticism: Selections from Four Centuries*. New York: Rinehart & Co., 1950.

Tisdel, Frederick M. "Rossetti's *House of Life*." *Modern Philology* 15 (1917): 257–76.

Tomlinson, Charles. *The Sonnet: Its Origin, Structure, and Place in Poetry*. London: John Murray, 1874.

Trench, Richard Chenevix, D.D. (Archbishop of Dublin). "The History of the English Sonnet." In *The Sonnets of William Wordsworth Collected in One Volume*. London: Suttaby & Co., 1884.

Trevelyan, G. M. *The Poetry and Philosophy of George Meredith.* New York: Charles Scribner & Sons, 1913.

Valéry, Paul. *The Art of Poetry.* Translated by Denise Folliot. Princeton: Princeton University Press, 1985.

Van den Berg, Sara. "Describing Sonnets by Milton and Keats: Roy Schafter's Action Language and the Interpretation of Texts." In *Psychological Perspectives on Literature: Freudian Dissidents and Non-Freudians, A Casebook,* edited by Joseph Natoli. Hamden, Conn.: Archon Books, 1984.

Van Doren, Mark. *Introduction to Poetry.* New York: Sloane, 1951.

Vendler, Helen. *The Odes of John Keats.* Cambridge: Harvard University Press, 1983.

Veyrieres, Louis de. *La Monographie des Sonnets.* 2 vols. London, 1869.

Waddington, Samuel. "The Sonnet: Its History and Composition." In *English Sonnets by Living Writers.* London: George Bell and Sons, 1881.

Wallerstein, Ruth C. "Personal Experience in Rossetti's *House of Life.*" *PMLA* 42 (1927): 492–504.

Ward, Aileen. *The Making of a Poet.* New York: Viking, 1963.

Warren, Austin. "Gerard Manley Hopkins (1844–1899)." In *Gerard Manley Hopkins by the Kenyon Critics,* edited by F. R. Leavis. Norkfolk, Conn.: New Directions, 1945.

Watts-Dunton, Theodore. "The Sonnet." In *Encyclopaedia Britannica.* 9th ed. 24 vols. New York: W. L. Hall, 1878–88.

Wesling, Donald. *The Chances of Rhyme: Device and Modernity.* Berkeley: University of California Press, 1980.

Weyand, Norman T., S.J., ed. *Immortal Diamond: Studies in Gerard Manley Hopkins.* New York: Sheed & Ward, 1949.

White, Joseph Blanco. "The Sonnet." *The Christian Teacher,* n.s., 1 (1839).

Wilcox, Stewart C. "Wordsworth's River Duddon Sonnets." *PMLA* 69 (1954): 131–41.

Wilkins, Ernest H. "The Invention of the Sonnet." *Modern Philology* 13 (1915–16): 79–110.

Williams, Charles. Introduction to *Poems of Gerard Manley Hopkins.* Edited by Robert Bridges. 2d ed. London: Oxford University Press, 1930.

Williams, Ioan, ed. *Meredith: The Critical Heritage.* London: Routledge and Kegan Paul, 1971.

Winters, Yvor. *The Function of Criticism.* Denver, Colo.: A. Swallow, 1957.

Wittreich, Joseph Anthony, Jr. *The Romantics on Milton: Formal Essays and Critical Asides.* Cleveland: Case Western Reserve University Press, 1970.

Wolfson, Susan. "Composition and 'Unrest' in Keats's Last Lyrics." *Keats-Shelley Journal* 34 (1985): 53–82.

Wood, David. *The Deconstruction of Time.* Atlantic Highlands, N.J.: Humanities Press International, 1989.

Woodford, A. Montegu. Introduction to *The Book of Sonnets.* London: Saunders and Otley, 1841.

Woodring, Carl. "On Looking into Keats's Voyagers." *Keats-Shelley Journal* 14 (1965): 15–22.

———. *Wordsworth.* 1965. Cambridge: Harvard University Press, 1968.

Zillman, Lawrence. *John Keats and the Sonnet Tradition.* New York: Octagon Books, 1970.

Index